Corporate Society

Class, Property, and
Contemporary Capitalism

Interventions • Theory and Contemporary Politics
Stephen Eric Bronner, Series Editor

Corporate Society: Class, Property, and Contemporary Capitalism, John McDermott

Television and the Crisis of Democracy, Douglas Kellner

FORTHCOMING

Crises and Transitions: A Critique of the International Economic Order, David Ruccio, Stephen Resnick, and Richard D. Wolff

Social Regulation and the State, Charles Noble

Corporate Society

Class, Property, and Contemporary Capitalism

John McDermott

HD
60
.M376
1991
West

Westview Press

Boulder • San Francisco • Oxford

Interventions: Theory and Contemporary Politics

Copyright © 1991 by Westview Press, Inc.

Published in 1991 in the United States of America by Westview Press, Inc., 5500 Central Avenue, Boulder, Colorado 80301, and in the United Kingdom by Westview Press, 36 Lonsdale Road, Summertown, Oxford OX2 7EW

Library of Congress Cataloging-in-Publication Data
McDermott, John, professor.
    Corporate society : class, property, and contemporary capitalism / John McDermott.
        p.   cm. — (Interventions—theory and contemporary politics)
    Includes bibliographical references and index.
    ISBN 0-8133-0707-4 — ISBN 0-8133-0708-2 (if published as a pbk.)
    1. Industry—Social aspects—History.   2. Industrial organization—History.   3. Corporations—History.   4. Social classes—History.
5. Property—History.   6. Bureaucracy—History.   7. Capitalism—History.   I. Title.   II. Series.
HD60.M376   1991
306.3'6—dc20   90-48540
                                                                                                            CIP

Printed and bound in the United States of America

The paper used in this publication meets the requirements
of the American National Standard for Permanence of Paper
for Printed Library Materials Z39.48-1984.

10   9   8   7   6   5   4   3   2   1

To the memory of
Peggy Duff and *Bill Fitzgibbon*,
friends, guides, comrades;
like Joe Hill, "alive as you and me"

Contents

Preface   xiii

Acknowledgments   xv

Introduction: Renewing the Discussion   1

The Modern Corporation, 4
Class and Property, 5
Altering the Social Categories, 10
"Post-Society Industry," 12
Erasing Liberal Society, 13
Political Tendencies, 14
Historical Perspectives, 15
The Dictatorship of the Clever, 16
Bibliographical Essay, 18

1 Corporate Form: Organizing the Production of a New Physical World   21

The Corporation as a Social Structure of
    Production, 21
Alfred P. Sloan and General Motors: Managing
    the Managers . . . , 23
. . . Who Manage the Workers: Taylor, Taylorism,
    and Schmidt, 31
Corporate Form: The Corporation as a Technical
    Productive Structure, 39
Bibliographical Essay, 43

2 The Evolution of Corporate Form   47

Evolutions I: Upper Management, 47
Evolutions II: The Middle Managerial, Technical,
    and Professional Group, 51
Evolutions III: The Collective Worker, 55

A Social and Historical View of the Corporation, 57
Origins I: A Second and Greater Industrial
    Revolution, 58
Origins II: Dreadnoughts, Gunboats, and Other
    White Fleets, 61
Origins III: The Specter of Social Democracy, 64
Society Re-Created, 69
Bibliographical Essay, 69

3   Private and Corporate Property   73

Property as Private Property, 73
Collective Property and Corporate Form, 77
Who Owns the Corporation? 86
Bibliographical Essay, 93

4   The Ruling Class in Corporate Society   97

A Ruling Class, 101
"Public" and "Private," 108
Corporate Society: The Fabrication of the
    Social World, 118
Bibliographical Essay, 121

5   The Modern Middle Class   125

In the Middle? 125
The Professions and Professionalism, 129
The High Costs of the Middle Class: A Digression
    on Economic Class Conflict, 134
An International Class, 139
Bibliographical Essay, 142

6   Managing the Collective Worker   145

"Bureaucracy" and Class Domination, 145
Social and Political Taylorism, 150
Socially Compulsory Consumption, 157
Whose Trade Unions? 162
Sociological and Historical Methods, 167
Bibliographical Essay, 168

7   Neither Artisans nor Proletarians   173

Proletarians and After, 173

Corporation and Worker: A Symbiotic History, 175
What Is Class Consciousness? 186
Highly Cultivated Donkeys, 193
Bibliographical Essay, 196

*Epilogue: Alberich and Prometheus—The Modern
Corporation as a Social Institution*   199

About the Book and Author   203
Index   205

Preface

Corporate Society could be called "An Introduction to the Corporation as a Social Institution." It is a broad study of the mutual impact of the modern business corporation and modern society. I have tried to write the book in a style that students and others new to questions of social analysis will find interesting and readily understandable.

With those readers in mind, I begin the presentation with very basic material about the internal organization of corporations and how it has evolved to the present. Today's corporation is quite different from the creature its founders first shaped. Its evolution from a monopolistic trust to today's diversified firm is linked to the way the corporation has solved certain *internal* problems, and this has altered its relations to the *external* world. This tale of interaction rescues the subject, I believe, from similarity to dry-as-dust business administration texts or to some of the sterile "theory of the firm" found in economics. It is also the only material that can serve as a reliable basis for the wider discussions about the corporation and society that follow.

The chapter outline is straightforward. The first chapter examines the corporation as a productive organization of a certain type. Drawing particularly on the work of two important figures from U.S. business history, Alfred Sloan of General Motors and the fabled "scientific manager," Frederick W. Taylor, the chapter gives a first approximation for the concept—which is central to this whole study—of corporate form. The expression "corporate form" refers to the characteristic relationship or pattern found between and among the three fundamental corporate classes. The second chapter deals with changes in those classes, particularly from the standpoint of the roles of the classes within the process of production itself. Then there is a brief review of the broader historical impulses from which the corporation emerged at the turn of the century and that continue to influence its evolution. Essentially, these two chapters undertake the burden of characterizing the new physical and physical-social world made possible only by the development of the modern corporation.

Chapters 3 and 4, which are also paired, go beyond to look directly at the new social structures and the new social world created by the modern corporation. They make the transition from the corporation per se to corporate society. Chapter 3 takes up the all-important problem of modern property forms and argues that the system of private property has been superseded by a newer and very different corporate-property system. Chapter 4 develops this point by examining the dominant propertied class of the corporate system. Some of the distinctive characteristics of corporate society are brought out, in particular how modern property and productive structures have fabricated—and continue to refabricate—not merely the tools and gadgets of our society but society itself.

In the next three chapters, the growing and quite radical class stratification of corporate society, already hinted at earlier, is further examined and assessed. Chapter 5 is devoted to a description and analysis of the middle managerial, professional, and technical class. Its pair, Chapter 6, examines the relationship between this middle group and the working class. Of particular interest in this chapter is the rejection of Max Weber's famous analysis of "bureaucracy." In a closely related vein, this sixth chapter also touches on the rise of social Taylorism. The expression refers to the spread from factory to wider society of Taylorite ideas about controlling workers.

Chapter 7 completes the introduction to corporate society by examining the modern working class both in terms of its own development and in relation to the two dominant corporate classes. Insofar as it examines the least privileged class and the class least integrated into corporate society, this chapter, more than the others, looks a little more to the future. It tries to assess the role of the working class as a possible agent for social change. Of particular interest is the contrast between earlier and present-day forms of the working class.

John McDermott
Bristol and Warren, Rhode Island

Acknowledgments

Although a book's author bears sole responsibility for its errors of commission and omission, any worthwhile book bears the imprint of many contributors. John Annette's trenchant criticism of an earlier paper on the corporate class system, given at a humanities graduate seminar at Middlesex Polytech in London in 1984, contributed much to the development of the views argued here. Parts of this present study have been taken, with permission, from my "Corporate Form: A Unitary Theory of Technology, Property and Social Class," which appeared in *The Review of Radical Political Economics* 20:1. I was fortunate to have an extremely demanding and perceptive review panel; whatever is positive in the present study owes much to David Houston of the University of Pittsburgh (now managing editor of the *Review*), Heidi Gottfried of Purdue University, David Fasenfest of the Urban Studies Center in Louisville, Kentucky, Cyrus Bina of Providence College, and Kathleen Stanley and Dean Braa at the University of Kansas.

Professors Stephen Eric Bronner of Rutgers University, who doubles as series editor, and Charles Noble of California State College, Long Beach, read an earlier draft of *Corporate Society* with unusual care, made voluminous thoughtful criticisms, and proposed many fruitful alterations.

Others who contributed to the development of the present study include Lennie Goodings, Jonathan Ree of Middlesex Polytech, Thomas Germano of Cornell University's Institute for Industrial and Labor Relations, State University of New York, Holly Maguigan, Amy Gladstein, Edward Greer, Anthony Econom, and Nancy Krieger, as well as Rosalyn Baxandall, Francis Mark, and my labor studies students at the State University of New York, College of Old Westbury. A sabbatical leave the college granted in 1984 was extremely helpful, as was the generous assistance of the staffs of the Library of the College of Old Westbury and of the Reading Room at the British Museum.

I am grateful for the help, and also the friendly encouragement, that I consistently found at Westview Press: Miriam Gilbert helped to frame the concept of the book as a whole; Spencer Carr proposed changes that strengthened almost every phase of the argument; Mary Kay Scott and

Martha Leggett ably guided the project through its various stages; and Alice Colwell copyedited the manuscript—her sustained opposition to grammatical anarchy and obscure turns of phrase made for a much more readable and better book.

Many, many years ago, an essay of mine ("Technology: The Opiate of the Intellectuals," *New York Review of Books*, August 31, 1969), kindred to the present work, was to have been turned into a book-length study. The urging and very practical assistance of Robert Silvers of the *Review*, of John Simon, then of Random House, and of New York's Rabinowitz Foundation could not overcome my own inability to carry the erratic insights of that essay into a more systematic and penetrating view of modern social structure. I hope the present volume, so long delayed, makes up in part for that previous failure.

J. M.

Introduction:
Renewing the Discussion

One of the difficulties in writing about the corporation and society is that for so many readers the subject appears hopelessly dull, about as exciting as Latin irregular verbs. I have to admit that there is some truth to that perception—now. Many years ago, the place of the corporation in modern society was bitterly and dramatically fought out in this and some other industrial countries. Then, even academic and professional debates on the subject were as lively and important as those on the picket lines and in Congress and the courts. But the subject has fallen upon hard times of late. The main positions have become stereotyped and, in my view, neither especially interesting nor useful. With some simplification, ordinary citizens, academics, legislators, and editors tend to choose one of the following three positions:

Probably the most familiar is the populist conception. It's a simple view; basically, the populists see the corporations as overrich, overaggressive, and over everything and everybody, including the law. Antitrust and prolabor legislation, finance market and bank regulation, and some other restrictions on business came out of this populist idea. Nowadays, the populist conception remains exceptionally strong among ordinary citizens but has virtually no standing among academics, legislators, even lawyers. These latter types see it as an unsophisticated relic of an early age that still appeals to unsophisticated people. I don't like that snobbery, but I don't like the populist conception either.

Perhaps at the other pole is the view commonly adopted by businesspeople and the business press. Its greatest champions are to be found among some of the economics fraternity. It has several familiar names—ultra-free-market economics; right-wing libertarianism; Manchester liberalism—but it might as well be called the "horse blinders" approach to the subject of the corporation. That sounds strong, but it isn't really unfair. These people seem to have a religious-like faith in "the market." So long as that market is okay, that is, free of government interference, everything else is likely to be okay too. One of its popularizers, the economist Milton Friedman, has argued that "the market" is really much more democratic than democracy itself. Each dollar, as he puts it, is a vote and thus gives the "voter" much more real choice than his or her single vote at the polls. His view—widely shared by his colleagues—is that this sort of dollar democracy should replace the other kind to the greatest extent possible. Within the narrow scope of these blinkers, even the largest international corporation is just another business organization pure and simple: no different, really, than the little newsdealer down the street. Both are subject to "the laws of the market" and will work best if not interfered with. Consequently, corporations should be left absolutely free of government meddling. I haven't oversimplified this view; in fact, one of the attractions of the ultra-free-market position is its utter simplicity. It doesn't have to be an elaborate and elegant position. The business leaders who support it are extremely powerful. In a sense, their power (certainly not their disinterestedness) places them "above the fray."

And there is the third view. Its champions see themselves as the judicious center between these two wild and thoughtless extremes. They currently make up the vast bulk of educated and professional opinion in the West. Their stand is stronger than ever because—they believe—it is the position currently being adopted by the reform and democratic movements of Eastern Europe and by some of the socialist movements of Western Europe. As we'll be looking much more closely at their arguments later, a crude statement of their position isn't out of order here. First of all, we should name them. Historically, they've called themselves "pluralists," "moderates," sometimes "liberals," and sometimes even "traditional conservatives." This doesn't necessarily signal confusion. It is often true in politics that you emphasize different parts of your position depending on the battle you're fighting and the identity of your foe. With that in mind, we might today name those who hold this third view as "the defenders of liberal society."

Through all the rough and tumble, its champions have taken a remarkably constant view of the corporation and society throughout the corporate era. For a start, like the populists, they, too, believe that the institutions and practices of private property are fundamental to the good or liberal society. But they don't see the corporations as putting too much property in too few hands. Rejecting the blinkered approach, however, they are prepared to allow government to exercise some regulation over big business. In other words, the system of free-market capitalism should be free of government intervention save in those few and exceptional cases necessary to make it work better. In practice, they've seen two areas that generally require government intervention, one technical and one humanitarian. Government must act in and on the private economy so as to keep it on track and at best performance. In the past, for example, they often thought that progressive tax policies were needed; nowadays the same people in pursuit of the same aim often call for tax incentives for investors. That's not an important difference; if it makes free enterprise healthy it's usually good to do it. In addition, the champions of liberal society have generally supported some minimum of social welfare legislation. For reasons we'll subsequently explore, that humanitarian aspect is at low ebb now and falling fast.

To continue: If, and only if, you have that kind of economic foundation, then a pluralist democracy will follow. A pluralist democracy is more than just any democracy. Formal democracies like the Philippines and, say, El Salvador, use democratic trappings to hide the fact that only a small part of the population holds real power. In contrast, a free-market capitalism allows innumerable people to enjoy economic power and wealth, and this in turn guarantees that the formal democratic political system will work equitably.

Thus the "liberal society" is a society based on private property and capitalism whose economic success provides the basis for pluralist democratic government. It is *the* good society; nothing is better and nothing could be better. Unlike certain other widespread political ideologies, such as historic socialism, the defenders of the liberal society don't generally see a continuing evolution toward a better society, that is, toward a *fundamentally* better society. What we actually have in the Western democracies now *is* the liberal society, and it *may be* the ultimate, best form of society. Some years ago the U.S. sociologist Daniel Bell popularized this idea in a famous essay, "The End of Ideology." In summer 1989 an article in the same mode by a foreign policy analyst for the government and one of the private think tanks excited much press and academic comment. The argument of this article ("The End of History?") holds that the demise of communism in Eastern Europe and the popular impulse there to bring in free markets and Western-style democracy once again confirms the view that liberal society is the unique and final form of the good society.

In my judgment there is little to choose from among these three viewpoints. It is not even a question of their being wrong. Their common problem is that they are utterly out of focus, for they quarrel among themselves about economic and social issues that have precious little to do with the real world of the present.

It is one thing to see a problem, another to solve it. The task of *Corporate Society* is to give a focused account of our own society and of the role of the modern corporation within it, but to do so without falling into the language, the debates, and the stereotypes of the three viewpoints outlined just above. In what follows, therefore, I want to give the reader a preview of an entirely different idea of corporation and society. In part this preview will serve to guide the reader away from the well-worn ruts in the subject, which do have a way of lurching us back into stereotypes, and in part it will point to the deep issues about the nature of modern corporate society, the fundamental debates on how we understand it, and the possibility of changing it. I've placed the names of the main debaters in parentheses in this Introduction, but only here. Readers who want to develop a deeper understanding of these debates and their protagonists are thus immediately directed to the chief contenders.

The Modern Corporation

The modern corporation is *the* central institution of contemporary society. In a way, that is my main point. I stress this because the modern corporation is not simply a peculiar economic organization but a *class structure of production*. In it, we'll find a pattern of class relationships that shape what sort of things are produced and circulated, how and by whom they are produced and circulated, and even the sort of society that consumes them. To put the point a little more technically, the modern corporation consists of a class structure carrying on the production and circulation of goods and services, as well as new social relations, within which the most important social surplus is produced, appropriated, and subsequently deployed. Accordingly, then, we have to study the several classes found within the corporation and the relations that have developed among them in the production process. Because these class relations animate the wider activities of the modern corporation, too, we must try to understand the historical action of the corporations and of the corporate system in their terms.

There are three fundamental corporate classes: a top management that forms the most important capitalist class; a middle managerial, professional, and technical class; and the modern working class. From the standpoint of what they do in the economy—technically, the social division of labor internal to the corporation—there is (1) a top management that presides over the strategic direction of capital and investment and in that fashion provides broad guidance to (2) a much larger class of middle and lower management who monopolize the administrative and technological activities of the corporation or who provide professional services to it. In this way both classes combine to compel (3) a corporate working class to carry out tasks designed, directed, combined, and paced by the middle group.

This three-termed relationship is called *corporate form*. It is the fundamental concept for corporate analysis, much more so than "monopoly," or "limited liability," or "stockholder ownership," or, in fact, any of the traditional ways of distinguishing corporations from other kinds of business. A corporation, properly speaking, is an institution exhibiting corporate form. When I use the term "corporation," that's what I am referring to.

The term then covers all those large, diversified, technologically advanced, international, blue-chip firms that I want it to cover, but it does so by emphasizing their central and distinguishing feature.

The three classes of corporate form have developed within the modern corporation. Their traits must always be grasped in that definite context. Today's corporate capitalists (top management), as well as the middle managerial, technical, and professional class and the corporate working class, emerged out of certain pre-corporate classes and retain certain similarities to them, but far less than is usually thought. In my view, their basic interests emerge almost solely from their relationships within corporate form.

These classes have *both* joint and conflicting interests. This follows because they play complementary roles within a single working institution. Accordingly, their relationships always include both class cooperation and class conflict. As we'll see, class conflict is not something that used to go on in the corporate world and that has now been replaced by class cooperation or, as some have it, by the absence of classes. Class conflict *normally* coexists alongside class collaboration. As I think I can show, the evolution of the corporation has been guided by the way in which these complementary and conflicting classes have worked out their relationships. Corporate society is the result created by their spillover effects upon the larger society and upon the non- and pre-corporate classes that still exist there. In line with the dominant voices in social theory today (as mentioned above), that larger society within which the corporate classes have developed is still spoken of as a liberal society. But one of my central arguments is that liberal society is rapidly being supplanted by corporate society, that is, corporate society modifies liberal society in a process that at the same time erodes and entirely replaces it.

At the center of these changes is the emergence of a new property system, corporate property. This partly or quasi-collective-property system is based in corporate form and replaces the preexisting system of private property.

Class and Property

Here we touch on a big question, what we might call a deep structural issue in social and socioeconomic analysis. It is also the fundamental point at which the present analysis parts company from the viewpoints I described above. All three of them assume a society based upon private property, and all three of them agree that it is impossible to have a good society under any other property system. It is the Copernican earth around which their social universe revolves. My task, like Galileo's, is to get the received opinion to see that they are wrong on this central point.

It is said that Galileo begged his opponents and his critics merely to peer through his telescope. The argument in this book provides my "telescope," but Galileo was, like I am, really asking for more than that. He was asking his critics to reexamine the mental framework they used to order and to arrange their observations—whether of the naked eye or of the telescope. That's what we have to do right here, to re-order the way in which we look at the nature of modern property. Why, in short, say that the modern corporation represents a new collective sort of property system rather than just argue that it has modified the older, private-property system in certain ways? That's the normal way of dealing with the corporation; it's sanctified by long tradition, numerous authorities, and the utter deference accorded to "self-evident" truths. The answer has a lot to do with how we understand "class."

Unfortunately, the term "class" has also become somewhat stale in contemporary discussions. I think it fair to say that most analysts just assume (though they do know better) that private property is an unchanging phenomenon and therefore that familiar private-property relationships, such as link owners to nonowners, capital to labor, upper class to middle class, and so on are more or less equally unchanging. My point is that "class" and "property" go together; change one, you change the other. Nobody would disagree with that as a general proposition. But it *has* been overlooked that one has changed; thus we have to look closely at the changes in the other.

This is another one of those "deep" issues, but Daniel Bell, whose arguments I've belabored at various places in this Introduction and in the book, must be credited with putting the spotlight on the central point. "Private property" is a bit of a misnomer. If you consider the history of systems of so-called private property, you quickly see that they were really systems of family property. That is, families and individuals as members of families, not individuals per se, have been the classic property owners. The owning family was the link tying together the property and class systems. Modern social analysis often loses sight of this basic economic, social, and political fact. An intellectual tradition, particularly strong in sociology in the United States, has tended to exaggerate both the economic and the individual aspects of both "class" and "property." Almost as a rule practitioners in this tradition see "class" as determined primarily and sometimes exclusively by how an individual makes his or her living, perhaps by how much a person earns, whether a person owns or does not own producer property, and so forth. But when you overstress the individual in "class" analysis and lose sight of the property-owning family as the unit of those old classes, the term "class" ceases to have any real use in social theory. And that is precisely what has happened. Having gutted the concept of any serious social meaning, these sociologists then turn around and discover . . . that "class" has no social meaning. Thus the concept of "class" is prevented from performing its central function in social analysis, namely, to serve as an intervening variable, a bridge, between strictly individual behavior and truly social behavior, hence the gateway into the role of consciousness and volition in history, culture, politics, and so forth. Oddly, this "sociological" tradition has emerged as a major force within both Marxist and so-called mainstream social science.

The change from private property to quasi-collective corporate property, then, points to the role family structures formerly had but no longer play in the class system. Essentially, my view is that the corporation—through corporate form—comes to replace the property-owning family as the central institution of modern capitalist society and in its property and class structure. As "individual" private property gives way to quasi-collective corporate property, a radical change occurs in the identity of the different classes, in their relations to one another, and in the nature and characteristics of the society they populate.

There is still another, related way in which contemporary social scientists gut the concept of class. The word "class" is now commonly used as a simple, descriptive term that is, or at least ought to be, easy to apply—as in, "he's middle-class" or "she's working-class." I strongly disagree with that. "Class" is really an historical term, one that should be used as a summing-up concept for complex but related kinds of individual and social behavior *over time*. It will repay us later if we apply some brief corrective right here and now.

The term "class," in the first instance, has a relatively formal, static, even schematic meaning. It is used to mark certain fairly evident features shared, it would seem, by all societies. That is, different kinds of social advantages and disadvantages are not evenly distributed among individuals and groups in society. Nor is there a smooth and uninterrupted spectrum of advantages and disadvantages. Instead, things like wealth or status or authority seem to be stratified phenomena, so that there are for any given social advantage only a few significant strata (that is, levels), each of which exhibits a fairly marked difference from those above and below it.

In addition, the different kinds of strata, for example, authority strata and wealth strata, don't seem to have a random relation one to another. Instead, they seem, at least to a degree, to coordinate with and to strengthen one another, so that it's often true that greater wealth goes with mental work, lesser wealth with physical labor, low status with low opportunity, and so on. "Class" or "class analysis," in one of its most important (static) aspects, represents the attempt to sum up in a single concept this whole phenomenon of differential and coordinated social advantages—the key idea here.

Further, the intellectual tradition in which I work argues that these systems of coordinated and reinforcing advantages arise most powerfully in what are called the social relationships of production. That familiar phrase refers to the concrete and specific relationships that we shape and that shape us as we go about the everyday production and reproduction of our lives. Of course, the daily fabric of people's lives is extremely complicated, so that in a day or a year or even a whole life, no one pattern or pattern of relationships will seem more important than the others. But social distinctions that strongly reinforce one another become noticeable as soon as we entertain historical spans of time, say, two or more generations. When reinforcing class and strata advantages start to reproduce themselves across the generations, we can speak of a class structure. (Hence we can see why families, not just individuals, were so central in class structures of the past.)

Putting all this together, in a class structure the several classes, in coordination with their relationships in the social production process, have different degrees and sometimes kinds of authority, status, wealth, and income. They have differing access to, and ability to dispose of, the social wealth. These tend to be fairly stable relationships. Each class functions, to some degree, as a fairly distinct subsociety within the society, and this may lead its members to identify themselves as a distinct community around issues and events in which their interests and sentiments come into conflict with the other subsocieties. Each has a relatively distinct (expressive or symbolic) culture and, again, *may* come to be self-aware of that. These classes, class features, and class relationships also come to have complementary and supporting links to other social realms, structures, and institutions, that is, beyond the direct production and reproduction of daily social and material life; in the United States at the present time these would include those of government, the media and the arts, the university, and the military.

Consequently, the different classes as well as their individual members come to differ significantly in the degree and kind of power—not authority, but power—they wield in everyday matters and in the ability to modify or stabilize the class structure itself or the place of different individuals within it. And, finally (an embarrassing point for mainstream social science), the different classes and their members enjoy vastly different degrees of freedom to violate established social norms, and, of course, there are vastly different rewards and punishments for doing so.

If stratification features and class structures were strictly sociological phenomena, that is, unvaryingly shared by all societies, the previous account would be complete as it stands. When we bring a specifically historical perspective to these things today, however, sharp changes in the identity and significance of the modern classes begin to emerge: It is pretty evident that the place of the property-owning family within the class structure is weakening whereas that of the corporation is growing. In a private-property system, identifiable families and—as important—certain recurring family structures and arrangements (intermarriage, inheritance, order of birth, biological relatedness, identity of the father, patriarchy generally) have an especially privileged and exclusive place throughout the class structure. Even in the recent past, the nineteenth-century legal-political doctrine, institutions, and practices of "private property" were the central axis of the social relations of production around which one could fully and accurately map the wider class structure.

The private-property system antedated and gave rise to corporate property as its social evolutionary successor and the "solution" to certain of its problems and opportunities (see the section on "Historical Perspectives" below). But, I argue, we can no longer examine modern society adequately by starting from its social relations of production if we insist on giving primacy of place to those relations that rest on the private (that is, family) ownership of the means of production. Family property just doesn't play the same role now that it played in the past.

What does this do to the class structure? On this "big" question, modern writers have tended to fall into two camps. Either with, say, Ralf Dahrendorf they argue that property considerations and property owners have lost much of their influence. This then commonly leads them to some notion of a postindustrial society in which political-electoral democracy is given an exaggerated place and in which class differences *cannot* persist because "class" has, accordingly, lost its importance. Or, with G. William Domhoff, for example, others erect a fairly elaborate theoretical structure to fill in the troublesome space between their observation that the decisive social relations of production *appear* to occur and be reproduced within and around the modern corporation and their *theoretical commitment* that private (and therefore family property) is still dominant.

The concept of corporate form as the genesis of a new quasi-collective property system will help us bridge and solve this dilemma. On the purely theoretical side it will enable us to maintain the view that the class structure is decisively conditioned by the dominant relations of production and to do so within a framework of great theoretical power and simplicity. And, at the same time, it will remain truer to life and the facts of the case than do notions of a post-property or postindustrial society in which social class differences are merely rapidly disappearing relics of the past.

Hence corporate form, which we first find in the social division of labor, is also simultaneously a property form and a dynamic factor in modern class structure. Within that framework, the familiar and conventional ideas and claims about "class" and the role of "class" are easily worked out on the theoretical side and remain entirely apt to empirical and descriptive considerations. The theoretical characteristics, the empirical material in confirmation of those characteristics, and the interrelationships of the three corporate classes are worked out in, I hope, a sufficiently detailed and persuasive way.

Altering the Social Categories

From the nature of the case, that is, because property is such a fundamental category in social analysis, any change in it would tend to alter virtually every area of social, political, cultural, and even purely economic investigation. The following areas are among those fundamentally impacted by the change:

The Theory of the Business Firm. The familiar "market" of the economists reflects their mental picture of a social-economic world made up of independent-propertied families and individuals whose strictly economic (or utility maximizing) relationships are governed by the norm of equal exchange. In this view, the "representative (entrepreneurial) firm" is purely and simply an instrument for carrying out economic relationships arising in that preexisting property system (e.g., Alfred Marshall).

In analyzing the corporation, writers have commonly used much the same sort of socioeconomic model, that is, a model in which class or group interests resting in an existing property system give rise to the corporate firm that then remains more or less instrumentally subject to their purposes (e.g., monopoly theory, finance capital, Adolph Berle and Gardiner Means's "problem" of the separation of ownership and control, and so on).

I turn this model around, so to speak. In the corporate world the firm has given rise to a class and property system whose most important structural and dynamic relationships develop "within the firm." In this setting, the economic conditions necessary for asserting the "market" of conventional ecoomics are lacking and the conception becomes largely an impediment to further investigation of the firm's—and the classes'—various economic transactions. Unfortunately, because of space considerations I can only touch upon these subjects relating to the theory of the firm.

Technology. In this text I try to demystify "technology." I show it not as a quasi-autonomous force dominating the corporation and society (e.g., John Kenneth Galbraith) but instead as the characteristic social productive *activity*—Jacques Ellul's "technique"—of the middle corporate group. Consequently, this middle corporate class enjoys a relatively privileged place in corporate form and a near partnership with big capital, both of which rest on its social monopoly of the historically accumulated knowledges and skills popularly called "technology."

Bureaucracy. In basic social theory, the vast size and bureaucratic organization of modern corporate and other large organizations is often likened (as in Talcott Parsons and Max Weber) to the second law of thermodynamics (entropy) in physics. That's simpler than it sounds. Basically, these writers see the growth of "bureaucracy" as the expression of a lawlike decrease (or entropy) in social spontaneity and therefore an increase in social rationality, which is absolutely and universally characteristic of the development of human society and its institutions. This is probably the single most important theme in modern social theory, widely shared by writers on the left, center, and right. In my view it is wrong. As we'll see, corporate form is *not* a bureaucratic structure. Within corporate form, I portray the relationship between top management and the middle group as a political one reflecting necessary, complementary advantages; an important degree of power sharing; and an attempt not to crystallize the relationship into bureaucratic form but to sustain a dynamic, innovative quasi partnership.

By way of contrast, the relationship between the middle group and the workers within corporate form does have a somewhat bureaucratic flavor, but we'll see that it cannot be *characterized* by that feature. What conventional sociological theory and common prejudice characterize as an abstract rationality governing the internal relationships in large organizations is, in this area of corporate form, an instrumental rationality imposed by one class upon another. We'll see that it is not a Weberian rationality but a Taylorite one, part of a social productive monopoly of the middle corporate class that is imposed upon the workers.

The Corporate Middle Class. This subject is probably best opened by a series of negatives. The middle corporate managerial, technical, and professional class (frequently abbreviated in this text as "middle element" and kindred expressions) is *not*, like Karl Marx's middle classes, a disappearing social formation or formations and hence a declining factor in class conflict. Nor is it, like the middle classes of certain contemporary analyses (e.g., Suzanne Keller), a neutral social group whose power and influence erodes equally the power of capital and labor in behalf of a society based purely on individual merit. Nor is it an Aristotelian buffer and balancing class, pursuing its own property interests independently of both the few rich and the many poor, and equally hostile to both. In corporate form it is a persisting (and, in fact, still growing) class, with its own agenda of interests, which dictate a permanent alliance with capital and against labor. It is certainly no buffer class, as the conventional wisdom has it. If anything, it is the main buffeting class in modern society.

Class Conflict. As already hinted, the main axis of class conflict and the most difficult frontier of class cooperation within corporate form lies along the border between, on the one hand, the capital–middle-element alliance and, on the other, the working class of the modern corporation. From the nature of the case, the most forward positions in this conflict with workers are occupied by the middle group, not the capitalists, and actual, everyday class conflict within and around corporate form is primarily between labor and the middle group, not labor and capital.

This leads to one of the ways in which corporate society is different from liberal society. In it the old class struggle between labor and capital seems to disappear. In my view, this comes about because the modern working class is entangled in day-to-day conflict with the middle group and consequently cannot reach beyond it to engage capital in significant class political battles. This insulation of the ruling class from political class conflict and the consequent growth in conflict between workers and the middle group is one of the system features of corporate society.

Public Sector Versus Private Sector. This is probably the most jaded and stereotyped of all the issues we debate today. Yet out of view of those debaters and absolutely obscured by the fog they generate, it is in the actual relationships between the two sectors that the most profound changes are now occurring in corporate society. In *Corporate Society* I devote a fair amount of space to this very issue. I take the position, roughly, that the existence of any public sector at all, that is, a sector guided by notions of citizen equity and entitlement, is now fundamentally threatened by the steady expansion of the private corporation into "the government business." I say "roughly" because without a digression here it isn't possible to give the precise position I argue in the text. But I can take this occasion to locate that discussion within the broader context of traditional debates about the proper roles of government and business, public and private, democracy and capitalism, society and property.

It is, of course, a commonplace of contemporary social analysis that the differences between the public and the private sectors have been eroding. But to what end? In the classic formulation of the relationship of the two spheres, namely, the way it was formulated in the Marxian tradition, the problem was cast in the following manner: In the capitalist, private-property system there is a fundamental contradiction between the intrinsically social nature of the production process and the purely private nature of its ownership, its control, and the disposition of the resulting social wealth. For reasons not necessary to go into here, the Marxists thought that that contradiction was resolvable in only one way: by socializing ownership of the means of production. Or, more vividly, the contradiction could be resolved only by the victory of the social or public sphere over the private one, that is to say, by the victory of society over property.

"Post-Society Industry"

In the United States, of course, we haven't had a persisting socialist tradition. But the other political and intellectual traditions have been equally interested in this set of "contradictions." Crudely, the populist tradition sees Big Business and the Monopolies as a threat to The People. Big-Business leaders, in turn, see The People, particularly democratic government, as a threat to The Free Market. The champions of liberal society see themselves as the balancers on this issue, preserving free-market economy *and* democratic society. But I argue that the change in property and class relations makes that into an attempt to square the circle. It cannot be done.

Very broadly speaking, the evolution of modern capitalism toward quasi-collective property forms raises an alternative and previously unimagined resolution to the old socialist contradiction and populist nightmare. It raises the possibility of the victory of property over society, more specifically, of the purging of, the absorption of, even the transformation of general social relations into those called for by corporate form and corporate form alone. Some people today write about "postindustrial society"; the nearer prospect, I fear, is the emergence of a post-society industry.

In *Corporate Society* I describe these changes in social relations in detail, but here, before the fact, we must be clear as to the terms of the dispute. My argument is not that the development of the modern corporation poses a threat to democratic government. It does, of course; it's a familiar threat, and much of the effort of the champions of liberal society is devoted to responding, in theory and in practice, to that threat. Instead, my argument is that the producing activities of the modern corporation, the changes in class structure associated with it, and its normal and necessary aggression against the world of private property combine to create a distinctive corporate society that entirely replaces liberal society. In fact, to a much greater extent than is now imagined, liberal society has already largely disappeared. Those who persist in framing political and economic discussions in terms of defending and preserving it, in fact, directly contribute to the sterility of intellectual and political activity today.

Erasing Liberal Society

What I'm saying is that much "normal" social, political, and economic discussion really has its feet entirely in the air. I have earlier described liberal society as composed of free-market, capitalist economic arrangements combined with pluralist political arrangements. Simple, but accurate enough under the circumstances. We can, however, go a step deeper. At bottom the modern concept of liberal society rests on a concept of a social and political "all" that, like the eighteenth-century notion of the state of nature, is unsullied by human greed or even human influence. We can see this in the very arguments of the defenders of liberal society. The characteristic populist fears are the *intrusions* of "big business," "the monopolies," "big government," "bureaucracy," "technology," or some other transgression against what would be or what could be if a basically good society were left alone. Similarly, they share the fears of the ultra-free-market proponents that "socialism" or "the masses" will spoil an otherwise unspoiled society. It's the same stance but with a slight twist. Implicit in all of these fears is the idea that there is an underlying social "all"—the ultimate foundation of liberal society—that, in the last analysis, is not instrumentally subordinated to any single group or institution within it but instead allows every group and force freely to exist and to prosper in a natural harmony of interests. It is a purely natural harmony, in this view, as it exists and persists unless disturbed by some alien force. At the bottom of that natural harmony, all agree, must be a system of private property. In any case, the visible social texture of liberal society directly emerges from the free and unfettered relationships of all groups, institutions, even individuals within it. In this sense, liberal society is purely and simply the negative of totalitarian society.

My general argument is that corporate society does not coexist with private property; it destroys it, supplanting it by its own collective-property forms, and it replaces the classes and institutions formerly spawned and sheltered by private property. This theoretical implication is strikingly confirmed by long-standing and dramatic empirical developments in both the narrowly economic and broadly social fields.

Political Tendencies

Hence we are left with a concept of corporate society that in its deepest structure and tendency is instrumentally and, in fact, radically subordinated to corporate form, for the latter destroys pre- and noncorporate property forms as a matter of course. In this precise sense, corporate society is a negative of liberal society. That shows most clearly and importantly in its stance toward those individuals and groups that systematically occupy the lowest places in it, especially the working class.

In the text of the book, I show in detail that the standpoint and action of the two leading corporate classes permit no "natural harmony of interests" with the working class. There can be no free, unfettered development of the working class because in corporate society more than in previous industrial societies that class must be organized, trained, and disciplined upon purely functional lines. That is, it must be shaped and controlled solely as called for by its place within the network of productive, consumptive, social, cultural, and other relations of corporate form and corporate society. This is not, as, in my view, too many Marxists (James O'Connor, Herbert Marcuse) and their opponents view it, solely a matter of shaping *individuals* through narcotic commodities or social ideologies. Equally or more the *class as class* is formed and shaped by the actions and structures of corporate society.

Historical Perspectives

In saying this, I would warn the reader ahead of time not to consider corporate form, corporate society, and their most important features as an *imposition* by modern capital and its allied middle group upon the working class. From an historical perspective the modern workers' place in corporate form and corporate society represents the repudiation by both labor and capital of proletarianization, that is, of the exclusion of the working class from any share in the social surplus up to and including the full exclusion of the workers from civil society, the culture, and the polity. Instead, I show that the modern working class' place in corporate form constitutes the resolution of the class conflict of the previous capitalist era.

Thus social theories that celebrate the arrival of the workers at "middle-class" status or decry the loss of "class consciousness" to the narcoses of "consumerism" and "individualism" have a basis in fact, although the facts add up to nothing like these stupendous conclusions. That is, such theories often conclude that there is an absolute and final end to fundamental labor-capital conflict, when in fact we see merely an end to certain earlier forms of the conflict. Consequently, this fragmentary perception ends up over-looking the steady development of corporate society, hence of a form of society in which the subordinate place of workers as workers becomes more purely systematic, more purely functional, more purely invidious— and more purely contradictory.

From the perspective afforded by corporate society, two points about modern workers will stand out. First, the transformation of the older industrial proletariat into the modern corporate working class has vastly strengthened the latter's relative social size, its social-cultural level, productive capacities, social cohesiveness, centrality in the social and political systems, and other striking facets. This is as expected. Put most directly, a modern worker is viewed within corporate society as a productive force, purely and simply. Accordingly, he or she is subjected to the same sort of social investments made in tools, science, buildings, and so forth. The social evolution of the working class consequently goes ahead by leaps and bounds. From the standpoint of the leading classes, this investment process is a purely functional affair. The danger arising from the growing capacities of the working class will be blunted, they appear to believe, by social Taylorism, that is, by the increasing social supervision of the middle corporate class.

Second, corporate society destroys pre- and noncorporate classes such as peasants, small artisans, propertied farmers, the entrepreneurial classes generally, which, taking the longer historical view, can correctly be seen as the most resolute social foes of the urban laboring population throughout its modern evolutions (cf. Barrington Moore).

Beyond these two observations, the concepts of corporate form and corporate society provide no further definitive guidance in social analysis, especially and specifically to those who identify their aspirations with the fortunes of the working class. We are left with a problematic that cannot be analyzed in terms of corporate society: an historic working class of vastly strengthened social and political capacity, subject to extremely powerful and intensive social control at both the individual and class level, in a society that is rapidly destroying many of its older and most bitter foes along with the main social barriers that formerly loomed so large in the working class' path.

But what is that path and where does it lead?

The Dictatorship of the Clever

The replacement of liberal society by corporate society, however much the working class may have contributed to the process, nonetheless creates a society in which the working class as a class is still viewed and treated as the least competent, the least advantaged, the least valued, the least free class. What has changed, however, is that the champions of liberal society no longer see this inequality as an unfortunate legacy from the past that can be progressively eliminated. In their view, even gross inequalities must be maintained, perhaps now even deepened, for reasons rationally and functionally necessary for the good of corporate society as a whole. Writers who advocate these changes, such as Bell and Dahrendorf, are wont to argue that there is already enough social mobility so that some individual workers—"the really worthwhile people," one imagines—can escape their class situation. But in the cold logic of corporate society the place of the working class as a class is fixed and all but essentially cosmetic changes precluded. Corporate society, like the corporate form upon which it is constructed, absolutely requires a subordinated class. In the logic of corporate society, it is entirely right and just that workers be subject to the dictatorship of the clever.

As we can see, therefore, in this argument a deep contradiction emerges in the concept of corporate society, not only in the confused "postindustrial" logic of certain theorists but also in the society as it is actually developing. The argument that competence alone should rule, that only merit should be rewarded is an argument for strata differences, not class privileges. It does not follow, in the grim logic of functionality, that the best and most creative designer should also be given a golden key to the only clean washroom, first priority in the corporate jet, exclusive use of the squash court, and privileged access to the White House, but merely that he or she should be given the best facilities and the best supporting opportunities to continue to do the best designing. Bell and other neoconservatives are right when they say that you can't fairly argue against the existence of social strata if the stratification is directed strictly to this or that agreed-upon end. But the leap from this modest point to support for a corporate society in which a clear system of differential coordinate advantages arises and then persists is a leap from legitimate social analysis to flagrant class special-pleading. Such is the end of Bell's ideology.

Insofar as we speak of a fully functional society, it must be a classless society. Not a strataless society but assuredly a classless society. Of course, in this turn of the argument, the category "classless society" is only a theoretical residue or residual concept (Parsons). But it is not a turn toward utopian thinking. Here, "classless society" is used as a category of social analysis that we form from the negation of another familiar category, namely, "multiclass" or "class society." Nonetheless, from the narrow logic of corporate society, and for the working class specifically, the abstract category "classless society" offers potential escape. The concept of a classless society at the present time has important meaning in four distinct yet closely related ways:

Historically speaking, the concept and goal of a classless society can be analyzed out as a constitutive element in the social action of the lowest or laboring classes from earliest recorded times and, with the specific content of the demand for different kinds of equality, as an emerging element in the transformation of the older artisan, through the classic proletarian, up to the modern urban worker.

Analytically, the concept takes us beyond the logic of corporate society by raising the possibility of a social order that would at once transcend corporate society and at the same time resolve its central contradictions.

Expressively, it poses as an ideal a society neither fully and instrumentally subordinate to one or a few of its constituent groups nor, like liberal society, shaped as the chaotic sediment and outcome of purely selfish purpose and advantage.

Practically, it raises in the most urgent way the need to understand and build up the forces, structures, social practices, and values that will act in the present and the close future to bring about a more classless society in a setting in which, it appears, the corporate classes are becoming more and more distinct and in which their attendant rights and privileges are widening—radically so, in my judgment.

If it is true, as Marx argues, that the deep structure of society sets itself no goal it cannot accomplish, then the destruction of class society and the creation of its successor have begun to emerge as practical tasks.

Bibliographical Essay

In *The Structure of Social Action* (Free Press, New York, 1949), Talcott Parsons has argued that one of the keys to understanding a writer is to see what other writers and positions he or she is butting against. In that sense, Daniel Bell's *The Coming of Post-Industrial Society* (Basic Books, New York, 1973) and Ralf Dahrendorf's *Class and Class Conflict in Industrial Society* (Stanford University Press, Stanford, 1959) are important to the present study. Dahrendorf's wholly inadequate, even confused treatment of the role of property in modern society is, logically though not biographically, the point of departure in my argument.

Milton Friedman's views on "the market" and democracy can be found in his and Rose Friedman's *Capitalism and Freedom* (University of Chicago Press, Chicago and London, 1962). Bell's *End of Ideology* includes the famous essay of that name (Free Press, New York, 1960). "The End of History?" by Francis Fukuyama was published in *The National Interest* 16 (Summer 1989). Both Bell and Dahrendorf employ the conception of "liberal society." Dahrendorf particularly emphasizes the decline in power structures resting in private property whereas G. William Domhoff is probably the most prominent of those who argue that upper-class families and social circles— thus private-property structures—remain at the center of the U.S. ruling class, as in his older *Who Rules America?* (Prentice-Hall, Englewood Cliffs, N.J., 1967).

The great Alfred Marshall remains well worth reading because of the largeness of his views and the narrowness of his contemporary followers. His concept of the "representative firm" is developed in his *Principles of Economics: An Introductory Volume* (Macmillan, London and New York, 1930. This eighth edition is considered the standard one for Marshall's views). Paul Sweezy and Paul Baran's *Monopoly Capital: An Essay on the American Economic and Social Order* (Monthly Review Press, New York and London, 1966) remains the best and most influential statement of that position, and Rudolph Hilferding's *Finance Capital: A Study of the Latest Phase of Capitalist Development* (1910; now translated by Morris Watnick and Sam Gordon, Routledge and Kegan Paul, London, 1981) is an unjustly neglected masterpiece. It is far superior in scope, analysis, and accuracy to the later, much more heralded *The Modern Corporation and Private Property* by Adolph Berle and Gardiner Means (Macmillan, New York, 1932). Baran and Sweezy and, especially, Hilferding already see that modern capitalist society is "beyond" private property, as did Marx, but fail to go past that perception. That is, because they do not adequately identify and analyze the new property structures, they fail to see in them the seeds of new class structures radically different from those associated with private property.

John Kenneth Galbraith's views on technology as a quasi-autonomous force are set out in his *The New Industrial State* (Houghton Mifflin, Boston, 1967; 4th edition 1985). Jacques Ellul's useful polemic, *The Technological Society*, originally published in French, appeared in an English edition in 1964 (Alfred A. Knopf, New York).

In his *Structure of Social Action* (cited above), Parsons draws the analogy between the second law of thermodynamics and the decrease in social-institutional spontaneity over time. Although that is his own view, he also attributes it to Max Weber. (It is utterly characteristic of late nineteenth- and twentieth-century social science to counterpose "rationality" and "spontaneity" as contradictory, that is, as logical contraries.) A statement of Weber's central arguments on "bureaucracy" and "class" is found in *From Max Weber: Essays in Sociology*, translated and edited by Hans Gerth and C. Wright Mills (A Galaxy Book, Oxford University Press, New York, 1958). Weber is one of those writers who, like Marshall, far outshine their followers. Parsons and his *Structure* are universally cited but, I suspect, little read nowadays; it is a difficult book but vastly worth the effort to read it. All references to Taylor and Taylorism point to Frederick Winslow Taylor's *The Principles of Scientific Management* (W. W. Norton, New York, 1967).

Critics usually draw Marx's views on the middle class from *The Communist Manifesto*, which was finished in 1847. Yet Marx lived until 1883, during which time he further developed and modified his views. They really have to be reconstructed from several of his writings, especially his histories (*Class Struggles in France, 1847–50*; *The Eighteenth Brumaire of Louis Napoleon*; and *The Civil War in France*) and the brief preface to *A Contribution to the Critique of Political Economy*. (One edition of *Class Struggles* is by International Publishers, New York, 1964. For other writings, see *Selected Works of Karl Marx and Friedrich Engels*, International Publishers, New York, 1988.) Dahrendorf's treatment of Marx's views, taken from those sources, starts out in fine and insightful fashion but then becomes unaccountably obtuse when Dahrendorf comes to the subject of property. The argument that the modern middle class, as it were, stands entirely outside the class struggle is given in Suzanne Keller's *Beyond the Ruling Class* (Random House, New York, 1963). Aristotle's views on the middle class are found in his *Politics*. A sustained analysis of the consequences of working-class "individualism," "consumerism," and other narcoses is presented in James O'Connor's *Accumulation Crisis* (Basil Blackwell, New York and London, 1984). Students may find Herbert Marcuse's *One-Dimensional Man* (Beacon Press, Boston, 1966) somewhat easier to negotiate.

The entry of the modern corporation into the business of competing with and replacing government and the nonprofits in the provision of various services is a tale that can so far be followed only in the newspapers.

"Policy Shift on Access to U.S. Data" (*New York Times*, April 10, 1989, D1) is a fairly typical story in that vein.

The argument that private property is at the root of private liberties is a veritable staple of ideologically conservative literature, as in F. A. Hayek's *The Counter Revolution of Science* (Free Press, Glencoe, 1955). Probably its classic statement is found in John Locke's *Second Treatise of Government* (1690; Prometheus Books, Buffalo, 1985).

The assertion that pre- and noncorporate classes are the most resolute foes of the modern working class is ultimately attributable to my own views on the development of German and other forms of fascism. It is my own extrapolation of the position so cogently argued in Barrington Moore's *Social Origins of Dictatorship and Democracy: Lord and Peasant in the Modern World* (Beacon Press, Boston, 1963).

The notion of "residual categories" is drawn from Parson's *Structure of Social Action*. There he attributes the idea to Vilfredo Pareto.

1

Corporate Form: Organizing the Production of a New Physical World

The Corporation as a Social Structure of Production

The modern corporation is, first and foremost, a social structure of production; that is, it is made up of a unique relationship of different social groups in the production process itself. This is its central characteristic, much more important than its legal form, its propensity to control (and raise) prices, its bureaucratic character, its addiction to up-to-date technology, or even its sheer size. Of course, the size of modern corporations has certainly been an important factor in their success since their organization in the "trustification" movement of over three-quarters of a century ago. But it isn't physical size, it is social size. From their beginnings the corporations were determined to operate in a society-wide manner. More than local firms catering to local tastes, more than regional firms exploiting regional advantages, the new corporate giants were determined to operate with a fully national scope and, as quickly as possible, extend their operations throughout every corner of the globe. We are so familiar with this aspect of corporate behavior that we can forget that no earlier business firms could even conceive of operating on that scale.

The modern corporation has remade modern social structure and the modern social classes. For example, the modern professional class was virtually created at the call of the corporation. Before the modern era there were, of course, doctors, lawyers, architects, civil and military engineers, and so forth. But the technological revolution of the last decades of the nineteenth century vastly multiplied both the number of professions and their economic importance, a process that continues to this day. Moreover, even such older professions as medicine, architecture, and civil engineering were revolutionized by being forced to copy the scientific and technological styles of work being forged within the corporation.

In these changes, the older classes declined and were replaced by new ones formed within the corporation. Thus there has been a radical decline in the size and importance of the pre-corporate middle or (as some prefer) "upper middle" class whose economic role and reward came through its owning and using its own property in professional and business pursuits. This entrepreneurial or small-business class has by and large been supplanted by a new class of corporate employees, the managerial, technical, and professional group or, as I shall often refer to them, the "middle element." Similarly, the class of skilled craftsworkers, on whom the technological basis of civilization had rested since historical time began, have also been supplanted as the most important urban laboring group by the semiskilled factory operative.

It is my argument that the older, pre-corporate structure of classes has been replaced by a class structure that arises directly in the producing (and related) activities of the modern corporation. The division of these newer classes rests on a deliberate, coordinated structure of authority, function, and reward that I term "corporate form." In it a small class of top managers use financial and policy instruments to guide a group of middle managers, technicians, and professionals who, largely by administrative and techno-logical coercion, control a third group, the production workers who, increasingly, only carry out simple labor tasks. This definition is, however, only a first take on corporate form, because the latter is more than just an organizational arrangement within the corporation; it is also an emerging property system and, following on that, the germ of modern social class structure. But to understand those complex matters it is necessary first to get a firm grasp on corporate form as it operates within the productive activities of the corporation.

It is interesting that conventional opinion still speaks blithely and simply of "labor and management," failing to see that a modern corporation has two quite different kinds of management who control two quite different kinds of human effort within the organization. At its simplest, corporations have to manage managers who in turn manage workers; thus the dual management problem: on the one hand to manage workers and on the other to manage their managers or, as it would be talked of today in business circles, to manage systems. The single word "management," then, hides two different historical and practical problems the modern corporation faces.

We can begin with managing the workers. Here there is, in fact, a whole nest of hidden problems. Prior to the corporation, the technological basis of industry rested on the skills and knowledge of craftsworkers, a technology rarely set down in books and manuals but instead passed down the generations by the apprenticeship system. The youthful apprentice worked side by side with the experienced craftsworker or, as he was often called, the master: This was as true of iron-making and of wagon manufacture then as it is of carpentry today. After a several-year period of learning, the apprentice was admitted into the rights and privileges of the craft. In this system the person who employed the craftsworker was not, properly speaking, a manager, that is, a person who exercised close control over the manner in which work was carried out. At best he or she provided a sort of loose supervision that, more often than not, remained ignorant of the secrets and techniques of how the job was actually done. Accordingly, under this older crafts system, the workers organized the work and set their own pace.

But the emergence of a new, science- and engineering-based technology toward the end of the nineteenth century promised much higher levels of productivity and greater profits to industry, *provided that* the work process itself could be reorganized and redirected to that end. Thus to the other emerging technologies there had to be added one more, namely, the principles and techniques of managing workers.

This sort of management is now so familiar to us that we can carelessly assume something like it existed from time immemorial. But, in fact, the professions concerned with the management of work and workers are almost entirely an invention of the corporate era. The most notable pioneer in this management area was Frederick Winslow Taylor, whose active life in the United States in the decades either side of 1900 paralleled the years of birth and then early development of the corporate system. We will turn to his work in a moment.

The problem of managing managers or systems was equally novel and even more complex. Earlier forms of business had primarily been local or at best regional firms operating in a more or less specialized field. But none of those particulars was to hold for the industrial organizations that emerged at the turn of the century. The technical problems posed by the need to control these giant new firms were far more formidable than those posed by the direct management of labor. Accordingly, the process took somewhat longer. In fact, in spite of the considerable difficulties that business still finds in trying to manage labor, this second meaning to the term "management" is the one that preoccupies its students. It has an extremely interesting history, of which we may only touch the surface. It culminated in the work of Alfred Sloan of the General Motors Corporation.

Alfred P. Sloan and General Motors: Managing the Managers . . .

The modern corporation was a U.S. invention, although in the years since World War II it has been copied in other countries as well. Even from the narrowly business standpoint, it grew out of somewhat contradictory impulses. There is no doubt that the rapid bout of stock swapping and stock watering just before and after 1900 that formed the great "trusts" was (as similar shenanigans are now) more often than not motivated by purely speculative considerations. In almost every case, the new trusts brought together by J. P. Morgan, Jr., and other financiers caused steep rises in securities values, handsomely rewarded the insiders, and, not incidentally, paid large commissions to the brokers. But it was another, quite different impulse, personified in part by Andrew Carnegie and Charles Schwab in the steel industry, that concerns us here. They, too, wanted to grow rich, but in an entirely different way. They wanted to seize hold of the vast new opportunities furnished by technological change and by the size of the potential U.S. market. And that in turn meant that they had to give thought to and to solve the novel management problems created when extremely large organizations emerged on the frontier of rapid and highly complex technological change. In the longer run, this latter impulse has been the more important. Its story begins with the Pennsylvania Railroad and, at least to date, ends with the General Motors Corporation.

The Pennsylvania Railroad of the post–Civil War era, then under the presidency of J. Edgar Thompson, was by all accounts the first modern industrial organization. It was in its time the largest business in the world, with a capital of over $60 million, operating some 3,500 miles of track, and employing over 30,000 men in a period in which a firm with 1,000 employees was considered very large. The Pennsylvania was also much attuned to technological change. It led the way in modern financial recordkeeping and cost accounting. It was the first major firm to thoroughly commit itself to the then new steel technology, doing so on the promise that steel would prove superior to the other forms of iron then in use and long before the problem of making reliable steel in industrial quantities had been solved. An important pioneer in the new communications technology, the Pennsylvania Railroad was, in fact, considered the technological marvel of its time, not least because its main lines, from Philadelphia to Pittsburgh, had to pass over the Allegheny Mountains. The Pennsylvania's success in pioneering mountain railroading, as well as its size, profitability, and other virtues, led to its being considered the "standard railroad" of the world, the one against which all others were measured. This was, of course, an era in which railroads were thought the paragon of modernity.

The turning point in Andrew Carnegie's young life came when he entered the service of the Pennsylvania Railroad as a telegrapher. Soon he gained the sponsorship of Thomas A. Scott, manager of the Pennsylvania's Western Division and another of the important figures in the history of corporate management. With Scott's support, Carnegie began a meteoric rise within the Pennsylvania and then, later, using his railroad connections as the springboard, entered into the steel business. Carnegie's claim to fame in the history of management rests, of course, on his creation and buildup of the Carnegie Steel Company. Here, true to his Pennsylvania tutelage, he copied its characteristic pursuit of technical efficiency and cost control. His unique contribution probably was in seeing the economic advantages of rapid, hard-driven investments in technological improvement. In the period under discussion, other iron and steel makers, like businesspeople generally, tried to conserve capital equipment as far as possible. But, trying to extend the useful life of capital equipment may be more costly in the long run if, in the interim, vastly more efficient equipment is developed. But then, like now, U.S. business operated in a system of price agreements among rivals, and these cozy arrangements were disturbed by shifts in productive technology. In the iron and steel industry the technological lag between what could be done and what was actually done was fairly considerable. But not for Andrew Carnegie.

Carnegie understood that improved equipment led to higher productivity. Moreover, he understood the paradox that the way to offset high capital costs was to charge low prices for his products because this expanded the market. Hence he pursued a strategy of reinvesting most of his profits in improved technology so that he could undersell his rivals. This single-minded focus on the linkage among high-priced technology, lower prices, and an ever-expanding market was his contribution to business-economic culture. In that sense, he, more than Henry Ford, is the real pioneer of mass production as an economic strategy.

Carnegie is an important figure in the history of corporate management. But like his teachers, Thompson and Scott, Carnegie only ran a company; they were the sort of highly "charismatic" leaders Max Weber wrote about who led by the sheer force of their intelligence, energy, and determination. The longer-term solution to the management problem, however, was to develop a *system* that would run a company. So long as these imaginative and energetic men remained economically active, there was no need for such system. But this was not true for their (generally) less distinguished successors. This difference came to a head for the first time in the Carnegie Steel Company when it had to make do without Carnegie himself, after Carnegie sold out to the Morgan interests in 1901 and his company became part of the greatest trust of all, the U.S. Steel Corporation.

The problem didn't surface immediately. Carnegie retired to his castle in Scotland, where he became preoccupied with philanthropic activities. His successor and the first president of U.S. Steel was Charles Schwab, Carnegie's protégé, not only a steel man but also one who was legendary for his knowledge of every phase of the business. He had to be. U.S. Steel posed a very different and, in fact, much more difficult management problem than either Carnegie Steel or the fabled Pennsylvania Railroad. It was a diversified business.

Carnegie Steel had been solely a fabricator of basic steel products; it produced ingots, sheets, bars, and other basic steel shapes. Only in the production of rails did it turn out a finished or final steel product. Basically, it was in the business of making raw steel, which it then sold to other companies that made finished products such as nails, wire, tubing, and so forth. In fact, Carnegie's threat to expand into the finished steel industry had finally induced Morgan to give up competing with him and instead buy him out at his asking price. Thus Schwab and the new board of U.S. Steel for the first time faced the problems of managing a highly diversified company—which raised the problem of managing managers in its most acute form.

From the beginning of his tenure at U.S. Steel, Schwab was confronted with more than just the "narrow" problems of engineering, production, and sales. The board of the steel corporation was dominated by financiers who soon came into conflict with Schwab. He wanted to make money by making better steel more cheaply, but the financiers were content to sell the old product at an inflated price. Schwab soon left (or was probably forced out of) U.S. Steel. It meant that the technical-economic promise of the new combine was not to be realized. In fact, it has never been realized, for U.S. Steel rapidly lost its one-sided share of the steel business, lost the technological lead it inherited from Carnegie, and kept up a plentiful flow of dividends only by developing, through its trade association, the American Iron and Steel Institute, the system of price cooperation with its "competitors" that Gardiner Means studied later. It is not beside the point to remark that through all of its subsequent history, right up to the present, U.S. Steel (now USX) has remained an indifferently managed, technically laggard firm. As the twig is bent . . .

Thus it remained for other companies and other managers to solve the problems left unsolved by the financiers at U.S. Steel. More than to any other, the mantle passed to the General Motors Corporation (GM) and its gifted leader, Alfred P. Sloan. When Sloan assumed the role of chief operating executive at GM in 1921, he took over a close replica of the problems U.S. Steel had faced two decades earlier. GM had been founded in 1908 through the paper amalgamation of four predecessor automobile-producing companies. In the following two years, twenty-five additional companies were brought into the Corporation in essentially the same fashion. To all effects and purposes GM was primarily and simply a holding company, that is, it held control over the stock of the subordinated companies, but central management participated little if at all in their actual management. This was, of course, typical practice in the period and is undoubtedly the source of the view, popular still in politics and in the history profession, that the trusts merely represented an attempt to speculate in securities values, monopolize markets, gain big organizing fees, and so on.

Actually, GM had been founded with something like Schwab's original vision for the steel combine. William Durant, its originator and first president, though surely a speculator of the first rank, also wanted to build up an automobile- and equipment-manufacturing enterprise in which a diversified product line offered insurance against market fluctuations and centralized ownership provided resources and overhead savings for technological and product innovation. Thus, contrary to the still prevailing populist conception of corporate enterprise, even in the "trustification" period a modern technical-economic ideology coexisted with the psychology of the stockjobber and high roller.

Durant, like Schwab in a similar situation, ultimately failed to bring the various producing units of GM into an effective relationship, but for a number of years it didn't seem to matter. The centerpiece of GM at the time was Buick Motors, a well-run firm, and its high-priced cars were very popular. The years just after 1908 saw the luxury-automobile market develop rapidly. Thus GM seemed to be doing well in spite of its primitive business structure. Durant continued to add new holdings to his GM empire.

With the advent of World War I in 1914, the corporation prospered further on war orders. GM continued to grow, both integrally and by the acquisition of other companies. In late 1920, however, the onset of a postwar depression brought the Corporation to the brink of failure primarily, in the eyes of Durant's associates, because the Central Office of the company had little practical control over outlays for inventory, the volume of physical output, and the cash reserves of the producing units. In fact, the situation was so bad that central management had to guess how much the producing units were earning, framing its own unstable finances on those estimates. Thus when the shakeup came Durant was ousted, and his successors set out to design a new organization. Sloan was the most important and creative figure in this process. He was so successful that he would dominate the company for the next thirty years.

It is probably to the point that Sloan was an auto man, not a financier. He had been for many years the owner of one of GM's suppliers, the Hyatt Company, a remarkably successful bearing-manufacturing firm. He came into GM proper when Durant proposed that Hyatt be absorbed into the still growing GM empire and, apparently under Durant's sponsorship, Sloan rapidly gravitated to the top of the GM management. Like Carnegie, and Thompson and Scott before him, Sloan was keenly alert to the link between capital investment in new technology, costs savings, and volume sales.

GM was much too diversified in both geography and, especially, in product line to be run by the energy and dynamism of one man. Sloan saw clearly that he had to establish a structure and a system to run the company. The outline requirements of the new organization were reasonably obvious. It should preserve the existing decentralization as far as practicable. But it should select and centralize those business functions necessary to give top management effective control over the company as a whole.

Durant appears to have been a man of large plans but little method. It is clear from Sloan's own autobiographical account that he didn't quite approve of Durant. But his disapproval took a creative form in that it led Sloan into extremely advanced thinking about management problems. Probably as much as any other figure in the early history of management, Sloan may be credited with changing management from an art to a technique. Thus, even before taking over from Durant in the early 1920s, he had given considerable thought to what may be called "organizational technology" as set in the practical context of managing what was already one of the largest companies in the world.

These thoughts were now put to the test. Asked to draw up a series of organizational studies, Sloan put forward two very simple but fundamental ideas intended to clear away the organizational and financial shambles left by Durant. The first was that the creation of policy and the implementation of policy had to be organizationally distinct, that is, carried out by different people entirely. His idea that people who create policy should *not* be the ones to carry it out seems to violate common sense. But, nevertheless, he insisted that control over policy had to rest in a group of executives who had no operational distractions, while operations themselves remained wholly in the hands of still another echelon of executives who worked under separate policy guidelines. Sloan clearly did not conceive of these two worlds as entirely cut off from one another; his method of linking them, as we'll see, made the difference.

The second idea echoed Carnegie. It was that a purely capitalist criterion was the only suitable standard by which to guide the business; that is, the issue was not just how much one made but how much one made *in relation to* how much was invested. As he put it at the time:

> The profit resulting from any business considered abstractly is no real measure of the merits of that particular business. An operation making $100,000.00 per year may be a very profitable business justifying expansion and the use of all the additional capital it can profitably employ. On the other hand, a business making $10,000,000 a year may be a very unprofitable one . . . even justifying liquidation unless more profitable returns can be obtained. It is not, therefore, a matter of the amount of profit but of the relation of that profit to the real worth of invested capital within the business. (*My Years at General Motors*, p. 44)

Sloan was far from indifferent to the absolute size of the profits of the company, but he understood the need for high-volume production in order to offset the costs of the latest, most efficient, and most profitable technology. As he wrote, GM's aim was "to produce not necessarily the highest attainable rate of return on the capital employed, but the highest return consistent with *attainable volume* in the market" (*My Years at General Motors*, p. 141).

By late 1920, Sloan had been installed as chief operating officer at GM and could put his ideas to work. In practical terms these ideas rapidly evolved into the following elements:

1. The operating side of the business was assigned to a number of Divisions, each representing a distinct product line such as Chevrolet, Fisher Body, and GMC Truck. Each Division, in the person of its top executive, was endowed with all the organic powers of an independent business. This was perhaps Sloan's most important innovation. Divisional executives, generally vice-presidents, were not under the administrative supervision of the top officers of the Corporation but were given full authority to operate their Divisions as they saw fit. Sloan was prepared to carry this principle to the limit. If, for example, a Division used products, such as trucks, that were produced by another of the Divisions, the divisional executive was not required to purchase them within the Corporation unless they seemed to be a better buy. All that was required of these divisional leaders was that their actions conformed to certain broad policies emanating from the Central Office.

2. Only a few operating functions were retained within GM proper, that is, not located in the Divisions. These included labor relations, the legal department, style, and dealer relations.

3. A Central Office, actually the top management group, retained exclusive authority over the adoption of policy. Policies, however, were formulated in elaborate, continuous consultation between top management and the Divisions through the agency of an equally elaborate staff organization reporting to the Central Office. Here Sloan was employing an advanced line-staff system originally developed by the Pennsylvania Railroad but in a style that sharply emphasized management by consultation and persuasion, not by command. Basically, Sloan's structure involved two distinct, parallel, and intimately connected management organizations. The first or *line* organization was a chain of command or authority wherein executives were given extensive grants of discretionary authority and were expected to use it. If the currency of the line organization was authority, that of the *staff* was information. A parallel organization of staff officers collected information on the impact of various policies from those who carried them out and conveyed that impact to the top officers of the corporations. Sloan had a veritable passion for decentralized ways of doing things, and this led him

to try to involve virtually every (line) executive in policy formulation for
areas bearing upon that executive's operational responsibilities. In the last
analysis, however, only top management had the power to promulgate those
policies.

4. Sloan correctly saw that this decentralized style of management
demanded a much more elaborate financial technology than had previously
been required in large businesses, when reliance on direct administrative
techniques had managers literally peering over the shoulders of their
subordinates. He and his associates, particularly the comptroller, Donaldson
Brown, began to develop new techniques for apportioning costs and
estimating the profitability of various activities. In time, these financial
techniques became the foundation upon which the Central Office chose
among alternate policies for internal management and external growth.

5. The Central Office became, in effect, the banker and sole investor
for the operating Divisions. The latter had to compete for capital against
one another. Those employing it more profitably gained access to additional
capital, and their executives won increased responsibilities. Less successful
Divisions might be liquidated, their executives sacked. Thus financial matters
were highly centralized and, as a result, administration could be highly
decentralized. Sloan called that "decentralized operations with coordinated
control," but, as he frankly reported, the rigidities of language don't quite
express the dynamic balance he sought between the two terms of the
contradiction.

6. Pursuing that balance, Sloan developed a plan of executive compensation that tied the income of managers directly to GM's profits. A definite
portion of the company's profits was earmarked by formula to establish an
executive compensation fund. Nearly all management personnel were entitled
to participate in the plan, though rewards were structured in such a way
that relatively small amounts were made, available to lower-level managers
with the amounts increasing geometrically, so to speak, as one went up
the corporate ladder. Sloan was consciously trying to give to each executive
a proprietary interest not in the company but in the *profitability* of the
company, the extent of that interest corresponding more or less to the
contribution an executive made to the profits of the entire corporation.
In practice, to become a higher-level executive was tantamount in time to
becoming rich indeed.

7. Although these elements dealt in the first instance only with the
relationship of the Central Office to the Divisions, it was part of Sloan's
design that their spirit should characterize how management functioned at
each level. Executives generally should have the powers of independent
businesspeople but be guided by policies they have helped to formulate.
And they should be judged by a purely capitalist criterion: Did they use
capital effectively? If they didn't they were not to be more closely supervised;

they were to be replaced. Only thus could Sloan institutionalize the positive organizational values of centralization and decentralization while avoiding the sins of both.

These new arrangements showed their value almost immediately, not least in that they freed Sloan and his chief associates from the day-to-day burdens of administration and allowed them to concentrate on the broadest and most fundamental dimensions of corporate policy. The Corporation weathered the depression and began to prosper to an unheard-of degree, soon passing Ford as the nation's leading automaker and eventually becoming the largest and most profitable business in the world.

During the same period in which Sloan reshaped GM, quite similar reorganizations to confront analogous problems were going on at a number of other big companies, notably at Du Pont, Sears and Roebuck, and Jersey Standard (now Exxon). By the post–World War II era virtually all big companies, in the United States and overseas, had adopted such systems, often just copying GM's. The account given of these matters by the chief historian of modern corporate organization, Alfred D. Chandler, Jr., differs in a few particulars from that of Sloan. But the differences are primarily terminological: Where Sloan speaks of the separation of policy from operations, as described above, Chandler refers instead to the separation between entrepreneurial and administrative functions. Essentially, though, with Sloan the modern corporation had developed the most difficult part of corporate form; it had brought system and technique into the management of managers. Before going on into its modern ramifications, however, we should bring up-to-date the other management problem, the problem of the direct management of labor.

. . . Who Manage the Workers: Taylor, Taylorism, and Schmidt

Even from their earliest origins in the 1880s—well before the "trust" movement—the nascent modern corporations pursued a fairly consistent strategy in dealing with the closely related issues of technological change and the work force. The strategy can be stated succinctly: The early corporations inherited a technology based essentially upon the skilled worker and consequently severe limitations upon the degree of practical control capital could exert over labor, particularly as it bore on productivity and hence profitability. Thus the modern corporation has tried to shift the technological basis of industry away from the skilled worker by developing, in cooperation with the educational and scientific systems, an entirely new group of employees fitted into management itself, the modern supervisory and technical professions.

In concrete terms, they have tried to strip technology from the worker, that is, to strip away its mental and skill elements and its elements of control over the work process, relocating all of these within the ranks of management. This particular aspect of the strategy is usually connected with the work of Frederick Winslow Taylor and the "scientific management" movement of which he was the acknowledged leader. Accordingly, that movement is often named after him, though one must always keep in mind that the strategy itself has many sources and ramifications unconnected with his person.

Frederick Winslow Taylor differs in at least one important respect from the other pioneers in the evolution of corporate management: He had actually passed through an apprenticeship, and this experience allowed him to grasp the central problem of his life's work. He was not of worker origin, but for reasons peculiar to Taylor had turned down a university education in order to apprentice as a machinist. On his first job, in a machine shop owned by family friends, he saw that the men were not doing all the work they could do. They were, in his words, "soldiering," that is, more or less consciously restricting output to what they believed was a fair day's work.

This is a nearly universal phenomenon. On almost every job workers evolve a common understanding of both the upper and lower limits of how much work they should do. By and large this understanding is not imposed by a particular worker or by the formal political or economic ideas the workers bring onto the job from the outside world. An informal social group develops that imposes on each worker the obligation to restrict output to what is thought fair to the other workers. In this way, "speed-up," "rate-breaking," and other forms of ruinous worker competition are avoided. At the same time the group normally pressures individual workers to put forward a proper effort, not to waste material or damage tools, and in general to behave in a workmanlike manner. Traditional management theory, naturally enough, emphasizes only the restrictive side of this behavior, but that is clearly only one side of the coin.

Taylor saw that the management of the shop was then not even aware that the workers were working less hard than they could. But the fact could hardly be hidden from a man whose skills were those of a worker but whose loyalties inclined to management. He quickly drew the appropriate lesson: If management were going to bring out "the highest potential of the workers"—his peculiar phrase for forced-draft output—it would have to understand the intricacies of the job better than the workers. Then and only then could it reorganize things so that maximal productivity could be achieved. This, of course, is the social rationale of the new professions and technologies that were then beginning to emerge.

But a second step was required as well: It was necessary to intercept the action of the workers' informal social group that created the "soldiering" in the first place. This is the central strategic idea in the history of the management of labor. The assembly line, time-motion studies, piece rates, merit reviews, titles, bonuses, and promotions—all of these and more are directed to this problem. Some (usually the older devices) simply try to break up the action of the primary workers' group; sometimes the more modern ones, such as "the Japanese system," accept the inevitability of the group's existence and seek to modify individual worker behavior by trying to change the dynamics, values, and ideas of the group. This is the very point of "quality circles" and other social exchanges with management. Taylor's approach was to try to break up the group.

There are many fine accounts of how he did this but none so vivid, so persuasive, and so transparent as Taylor's own. The following longish excerpt is taken from pages 41 and following of his *Principles of Scientific Management*, published initially in 1911 (W. W. Norton, New York, 1967):

One of the first pieces of work undertaken by us, when the writer started to introduce scientific management into the Bethlehem Steel Company, was to handle pig iron on task work. The opening of the Spanish[-American] War found some 80,000 tons of pig iron placed in small piles in an open field adjoining the works. . . . With the opening of the Spanish War . . . this large accumulation of iron was sold. This gave us a good opportunity to show the workmen, as well as the owners and managers of the works, on a fairly large scale the advantages of task work over the old-fashioned day work and piece work in doing a very elementary class of work. . . .

[The pig iron gang] consisted of about 75 men. . . . A railroad switch was run out into the field, right along the edge of the piles of pig iron. An inclined plank was placed against the side of a car, and each man picked up from his pile a pig of iron weighing about 92 pounds, walked up the inclined plank and dropped it on the end of the car.

We found that this gang were loading on the average about 12½ long tons per man per day [that is, just over 300 pigs]. We were surprised to find, after studying the matter, that a first-class pig-iron handler ought to handle between 47 and 48 long tons per day, instead of 12½ tons. . . . Once we were sure . . . that 47 tons was a proper day's work for a first class pig-iron handler, the task which faced us as managers under the modern scientific plan was clearly before us. It was our duty to see that the 80,000 tons of pig iron was loaded on to the cars at the rate of 47 tons per man per day. . . . And it was further our duty to see that this work was done without bringing on a strike among the men, without any quarrel, and to see that the men were happier and better contented at the new rate of 47 tons than they were when loading at the old rate of 12½ tons.

Our first step was the scientific selection of the workman. In dealing with workmen under this type of management, it is an inflexible rule to talk to and deal with only one man at a time, since each workman has his own special abilities and limitations, and since we are not dealing with men in masses, but are trying to develop each individual man to his highest state of efficiency and prosperity. Our first step was to find the proper workman to begin with. We therefore carefully watched and studied these 75 men for three or four days, at the end of which time we had picked out four men who appeared to be physically able to handle pig iron at the rate of 47 tons per day. We looked up their history as far back as practicable and thorough inquiries were made as to the character, habits and ambition of each of them. Finally we selected one from among the four as the most likely man to start with. He was a little Pennsylvania Dutchman who had been observed to trot back home for a mile or so after his work in the evening about as fresh as he was when he came trotting down to work in the morning. We found that upon wages of $1.15 a day he had succeeded in buying a small plot of ground, and that he was now engaged in putting up the walls of a little house for himself in the morning before starting to work and at night after leaving. He also had the reputation of being exceedingly "close," that is, of placing a very high value on the dollar. . . . This man we will call Schmidt.

The task before us, then, narrowed itself down to getting Schmidt to handle 47 tons of pig iron per day and making him glad to do it. This was done as follows.

As the account continues, Schmidt is called aside and the following "conversation" is recorded. Schmidt's "foreign accent" is taken directly from Taylor's book:

"Schmidt, are you a high-priced man?"

"Vell, I don't know vat you mean."

"Oh yes, you do. What I want to know is whether you are a high-priced man or not."

"Vell, I don't know vat you mean."

"Oh, come now, you answer my questions. What I want to find out is whether you are a high-priced man or one of those cheap fellows here. What I want to find out is whether you want to earn $1.85 a day or whether you are satisfied with $1.15, just the same as all those cheap fellows are getting."

"Did I vant $1.85 a day? Vas dot a high-priced man? Vell, yes, I vas a high-priced man."

"Oh, you're aggravating me. Of course you want $1.85 a day—everyone wants it! You know perfectly well that that has very little to do with your being a high-priced man. For goodness' sake answer my questions and don't waste anymore of my time. Now come over here. You see that pile of pig iron?"

"Yes."

"You see that car?"

"Yes."

"Well, if you are a high-priced man, you will load that pig iron on that car tomorrow for $1.85. Now do wake up and answer my question. Tell me whether you are a high-priced man or not."

"Vell—did I got $1.85 for loading dot pig iron on dot car tomorrow?"

"Yes, of course you do, and you get $1.85 for loading a pile like that every day right through the year. That is what a high-priced man does, and you know it just as well as I do."

"Vell, dot's all right. I could load dot pig iron on the car tomorrow for $1.85, and I get it every day, don't I?"

"Certainly you do, certainly you do."

"Vell, den I vas a high-priced man . . ."

"You have seen this man here before, haven't you?"

"No, I never saw him."

"Well, if you are a high-priced man, you will do exactly as this man tells you tomorrow, from morning till night. When he tells you to pick up a pig and walk, you pick it up and you walk, and when he tells you to sit down and rest, you sit down. You do that right straight through the day. And what's more. No back talk. Now a high-priced man does just what he's told to do, and no back talk. Do you understand that? When this man tells you to walk, you walk; when he tells you to sit down, you sit down, and you don't talk back at him. Now you come to work here tomorrow morning and I'll know before night whether you are really a high-priced man or not."

This seems to be rather rough talk. And indeed it would be if applied to an educated mechanic, or even to an intelligent laborer. With a man of the mentally sluggish type of Schmidt it is appropriate and not unkind, since it is effective in fixing his attention on the high wages which he wants and away from what, if it were called to his attention, he probably would consider impossibly hard work. . . .

Schmidt started to work, and all day long, and at regular intervals, was told by the man who stood over him with a watch, "Now pick up a pig and walk. Now sit down and rest. Now walk—now rest," etc. He worked when he was told to work, and rested when he was told to rest, and at half-past five in the afternoon had his 47½ tons loaded on the car. And he practically never failed to work at this pace and do the task that was set him during the three years that the writer was at Bethlehem. And throughout this time he averaged a little more than $1.85 per day, whereas before he had never received over $1.15 per day, which was the ruling rate of wages at that time at Bethlehem. That is, he received 60 per cent higher wages than were paid to other men who were not working on task work. One man after another was picked out and trained to handle pig iron at the rate of 47½ tons per day until all of the pig iron was handled at this rate, and the men were receiving 60 per cent more wages than other workingmen around them.

To our contemporary eyes, Taylor seems a thoroughly cruel master and his goal a system of industrial serfdom. And in fact this is usually the way he is seen. Schmidt himself is a caricature of the foreign-speaking immigrants who then made up most of the industrial labor force. Taylor's racial stereotyping, right down to the "comical accent," shows the deep contempt then imposed on workers by their employers. But most of all, contemporary readers see—as Schmidt supposedly did not—that Taylor would have him work nearly four times as hard for only half again more pay. That and the conditions imposed by Taylor—lift only when told, walk only when told, put down only when told, rest only when told, and no back talk—are unambiguously seen as offensive by the modern reader. In my experience, contemporary readers, even the most conservative and business-oriented, are embarrassed by his account and are invariably quick to point out that things have really changed for the better since. On the other side, persons of pronounced labor or left-wing sympathies are equally quick to point out that nothing has really changed at all.

Both sides in that debate lack perspective. Taylor's homely example is a portent of vast changes in the management of labor that would eventuate in the present system. If (and the point is somewhat controversial) Taylor himself is the central figure in this history, his contributions made for both a much more humane labor system *and* a much more exploitative and dangerous one. The two are inextricably bound.

The worse system is readily apparent in the Schmidt example and need detain us only briefly. Schmidt must work at the physical limit of his health and energy. That remains true for workers in industry today and is one of the reasons employers are sometimes so willing to pension workers who are "too old." Here "too old" often means over forty. Second, Schmidt is made into a functional dummy on the job. That is, the fiction is created that Schmidt is really only a machine whose sole ability is to obey orders. That only a stupid person would do the sort of work workers customarily do and under the conditions they do it remains a widespread management attitude. (Not only is this attitude baseless but it also contradicts what management already knows and fears from its workers. Thus the same manager who is utterly convinced that his "hands" are "of the mentally sluggish type" who must be told in painstaking detail what to do and what not to do is infuriated when the workers become aggrieved over some issue or other and retaliate by "working to rule." Here the workers act just like Schmidt, exactly so, doing nothing save what they are explicitly told to do.)

This point should make us aware that Taylor's ideas are only sometimes a description of what he is doing and what he wants to do. If we take them literally, they result in nonsense—or chaos. In the present instance, "Schmidt" is a stereotype not of what is or even of what could be but instead of a one-sided labor-management relationship at which Taylor aimed and at which the management profession still aims. The goal in question is to maximize the assertiveness of management and the docility of labor.

If the manager can be convinced that he or she is Taylor and the worker and manager can be convinced that workers (like Schmidt) are really stupid, this will encourage the one-sidedness in their relationship that management thinks desirable. In other words, the tale of Schmidt carries with it heavy ideological baggage as to which classes are clever and which stupid; which are prudent and which irresponsible; which class is energetic, committed to dynamic change, and burning with personal initiative; and which class loves to take it easy, has a stick-in-the-mud attitude toward technological progress, and follows herdlike the common opinion.

Third, the worker's job is stripped of much of its mental and moral challenge and he or she becomes a mere cog in an impersonal industrial machine. Much of the modern labor and left-wing criticism of Taylor comes in here, particularly around the point that the world of the skilled worker is thus destroyed and the worker's actual condition on the job considerably degraded. This is undoubtedly true, and yet the changed situation of the worker is somewhat more ambiguous than the point allows. Curiously enough, the condemnation of Taylor's personal influence and of the broader phenomenon called Taylorism actually require that one *not* look at these changes from, say, Schmidt's vantage point. Then a number of elements emerge that undercut both the embarrassment of business-oriented people and the moralism of their finger-pointing foes.

To begin with, Taylor proposes to pay a premium wage, that is, a wage above the then prevailing standard at a time when that was calculated to pay the worker only so much as would keep him or her, adult or child, alive and able to return the next day. Of course, real life, unlike Taylor's account or the theories of the economists of the time, is far too complicated to reduce to formulae. But in the economic practice of Taylor's era, the governing idea was that wages had to hover around the subsistence line. If managers paid more, they felt, those lazy workers would quit as soon as they had saved a small amount, waiting until that was gone before they would take a new job. Or they would carouse with the extra money and thus not come into work. Additionally, there was the usual baleful influence of the economics profession. Wages were then thought of more or less as pure costs, sums that had to be expended to get the work done but that should be minimized as far as possible.

In his story, Taylor proposes to pay more than that, provided Schmidt accepts a style of work guaranteed to be more productive. Here Taylor, at least symbolically, treats wages not solely as costs but explicitly as investments. He sees what other managers (and economists) of his time did not, namely, that labor is a productive asset and like any other productive asset should respond to investments to improve its quality. This, and not the old subsistence-cost theory, is the conceptual framework of the modern wage system. Its down side is that it demands superhuman effort from the worker, only partially recompensed by the additional pay. Its positive and humane side is that it links wages to productivity, as they were then not normally linked, and thereby carries the promise of an improving workers' wage, improved living standards, thus further improvements in productivity, and so on.

It is almost beside the point that Schmidt was asked to work four times as hard. I am not being callous here; the other management systems in use at the time were also trying by every means possible to get more work from the workers. Unlike Taylor's, however, they mostly relied on sheer force and terror or their equivalents. In the late 1890s men and women were fired at the drop of a hat from jobs in which they were expected to work ten- to twelve-hour days, often at piece rates so low that they then had to put in overtime to earn bare subsistence. It was a period in which Pullman in Chicago built housing for his workers so as, in part, to be able to demand even greater obedience than could be demanded if they lived independently. Not at all incidentally, housing his workers in his company town also helped him to steal back in rents, water, gas, and other fees any sum of "excess" wages he might inadvertently have "overpaid" his workers.

In reading of Taylor and his views, we must remember, too, that we are stepping back into an historical period in which workers were frequently abused—often beaten—by their supervisors: It was a chronic problem in the very industry Taylor was writing about. Workers then commonly had to bribe foremen to get their jobs, bribe them to hold the jobs, and even bribe them to receive something approximating the pay scale nominally agreed to. In this context, Taylor is a revelation. To begin with, his mode in dealing with Schmidt is to reason with him or, perhaps more accurately, at him. He proposes to Schmidt an arrangement built upon a concept of equity. To our ideas, four times as much work for half again pay is no equity, but in a time and an industry in which four or even more times as much work was commonly demanded, often enough at *less* pay, Schmidt would have had to be dumber than he is portrayed not to see the advantage. And that's the point; in Taylor's story, and in its implications for the management of labor, new and important elements appear for the first time.

Basically, Schmidt is offered an exchange. In exchange for more effort he is offered high pay, and the offer is made as a positive incentive and not simply and solely with a foreman's cudgel or a policeman's billy club. Further benefits follow: Taylor stresses the importance of choosing the best workers and then of training them. But, having gone to the time and expense of training Schmidt, Taylor is not likely to chuck him onto the pile of unemployed at the next economic downturn. Schmidt, therefore, is being offered semipermanent employment in an industrial world in which job security was then almost unknown save for the highly skilled.

Modern corporations follow this same rationale. They operate with the idea that they have a permanent, core work force; a more or less fixed body of workers who are their employees. That fixed number of bodies can be expanded by overtime (usually compulsory) in busy times and shrunk by lay-off in bad times. For the worker, this means that he or she can earn extra money on overtime and then use that to live on when the inevitable lay-off occurs. The advantage of the lay-off is that it isn't a firing; the worker knows that he or she will be picked up by the company again— the sooner if he or she has seniority—and doesn't have to search vainly and expensively for another job in what will be, by definition, a time when there are lots of idle workers.

I think it clear that I'm not arguing that Taylor's system is a kindly one, nor the only one possible, nor even that it is humanly bearable by the average person. Modern industrial employment, particularly in factory or mine, is a harsh, often life-threatening affair. And surely it is a world in which most of us must put aside our ideas of equality, rights, and so on and accept the dictatorship, pure and simple, of the boss. Taylor's ideas of superproductivity and absolute obedience are very much part of the process that made such work so difficult and dangerous. And his ideas have helped to sustain to this day the evil fiction that the dictatorship of the boss and the subservience of the worker are entirely necessary and natural. But—a cruel yet important "but"—they have also served as the actual historical vehicle through which workers have been in part able to partake of the gains of industrial capitalism. I include here not only the economic gains but also the cultural, social, and political gains built on that secure if brutal economic foundation. But I am running ahead of myself.

Corporate Form: The Corporation as a Technical Productive Structure

Corporate form is the unitary product of both Taylorism and Sloanism. In simple terms Taylorism represents the division of two broad social productive functions within the corporation into two separate groups. There is a steady evolution of technological control and initiative and consequently of de facto power over day-to-day work away from workers and into the management echelon of school-trained supervisors, engineers and other technicians, and certain professionals (e.g., the industrial sociologist, the designer, etc.). Implicit in this same tendency is a steady evolution within the lower rungs of the corporate work force in which the skilled worker, product of an apprenticeship, comes to be replaced by the semiskilled operative as the prototypical working-class figure.

One can describe Sloanism as the separation of management into two distinct groups, one concerned with the formation of policy, the other with carrying out operations. Chandler speaks in parallel terms but with a somewhat different language. He describes a steady and still developing separation of the entrepreneurial from the administrative functions within management. For convenience we can refer to the two distinct groups thus formed as, respectively, top management and a middle element of people with supervisory, technical, and professional functions within the corporation. This middle element clearly includes low-level straw bosses as well as quite important executives.

Two conceptual modifications are necessary before we can go on. I am unhappy both with Sloan's term "policy" and with Chandler's term "entrepreneurial." In its normal meanings the word "policy" is too narrow as it does not call to mind the all-important financial and investment functions of top management. The problem with "entrepreneurial" is just the opposite. It carries an excess of ideological baggage. It suggests risk-taking, for example, a prominent feature perhaps in the local druggist, grocer, or hairdresser, somewhat less important for an executive in a moderately large business, and of infinitesimally little importance for top executives in, say, GM, Du Pont, or Exxon. Top management in a large corporation is dedicated to risk avoidance, not risk. The point of diversification—a point understood even in Durant's earliest ideas about a modern business—is to remove *by structural means* the element of uncertainty from the business. Each individual venture of a large company, it is true, carries a significant possibility of failure, but one of the main tasks of upper management is to counterbalance that possibility with other compensating activities. There is no more risk in the corporate world generally than there is in the insurance business.

We need a more descriptive term for a top management group who are neither only policymakers nor still risk-courting entrepreneurs. I propose the term "corporate capitalists." In both Sloan's and Chandler's accounts of the responsibilities of top executives in the big companies it is shown quite clearly that these leaders have decisively shed all organizational functions that are not those of a capitalist per se. Basically, modern corporate leaders concentrate on two things, high sustainable profits and corporate growth, which is to say they concentrate on growing capital and nothing else. They are, if not pure capitalists, as close to it as any group of business leaders has ever come.

It is important at this point in the argument to make a clear distinction between capitalism and ownership. This isn't normally done, but it should be. From the conceptual standpoint, an owner of a capitalist business has in fact a dual and often contradictory interest in his or her business. As a capitalist, he or she will almost always find it advantageous to reinvest profits to the greatest degree possible. This is the best and often the only way to keep the business alive and healthy. But as an owner the same person has another, entirely contradictory interest, namely, to convert those profits into personal income and enjoy whatever comes of spending them. Of course, such a distinction had no place in the pre-corporate era; it would have been a purely theoretical distinction that pointed to no practical consequences. The capitalists of the time were owners as well as capitalists and somehow squared the contradiction. If the term capitalist-owner hid a conflict of interest it was then analytically unimportant.

But that's not true now. As one can see from Sloan's compensation scheme, now almost universally adopted by the big companies, to be a high executive in the modern corporation is to be, first, a servant of the corporation's imperative to expand and, if successful in this, then to become a property owner. In other words, a modern corporate executive must first contribute to making profits; then he or she gets a share. This is quite unlike the case of the idle son of a rich owner who draws money from a business to which he has never contributed. Or, to put it somewhat differently, the high corporate executive lays a proprietary claim against the profits of the business, not against the business itself. Sloan's organizational scheme and his compensation scheme together aim at making the difference between capitalist per se and owner (of a capitalist business) a distinction of primary theoretical and practical importance. To recapitulate, then, the term "entrepreneur" suggests a property owner who risks that property in a chancy undertaking. For that reason it is singularly inappropriate in the corporate context. The terminology we want is "corporate capitalist."

Sloan's "operations" and Chandler's "administration" are inappropriate for another reason. In their normal English meanings they suggest primarily the supervisory function. Yet, as we saw, the management echelon also contains technologists as well as different kinds of professionals, that is, people who primarily design and often manage not people but machines, products, and physical processes, or who perform highly specialized professional services. Much of the practical point of Taylorism was to locate technical and technological personnel in the management echelon, where their presence helped to transform not only technology but also the nature and extent of the supervisory function in industry. Thus it is incorrect (insufficiently expressive, to be precise) to speak of lower and middle management as having purely or primarily administrative functions, to speak of them just as supervisors. The middle element in modern industry, properly described, is an administrative, technical, and professional group, and we should, accordingly, adopt that terminology.

Bringing these conceptual and terminological changes together we get the following: What we witness in the evolution of the modern corporation, through the past eighty-odd years, is a steady social, functional, and organizational separation of its capitalist activities per se from its administrative, technical, and professional activities in such fashion as to subordinate the latter to increasingly sensitive capitalist controls, or Sloanism. And in the same historical period, a steady social, functional, and organizational separation of these activities from work itself, or Taylorism. Looked at as a theoretical paradigm, what these two developments suggest is not the familiar pair of labor and management but instead the trio of capital, technology (or technique, in Jacques Ellul's sense), and work. This empirically means that we should judge the historical separation of functions among top management, middle or lower management, and workers as the central phenomenon in the development of the modern corporation. In fact, I would go further and argue that what we mean by the modern corporation is that institution *constituted* by that threeway social, functional, and organizational division.

If we adopt that terminology, we recognize that not the legal form of the organization but rather its internal social productive relationships are crucial. Accordingly, the word "corporation" takes on two different meanings. In familiar usage, any business legally incorporated by a state is a corporation. But as I will henceforth use the word, it will refer to any large organization exhibiting corporate form. Generally, I will use it to refer to so-called free-enterprise corporations but later will also extend the concept to include any organization whatsoever that uses corporate form, that is, internally reproduces the same class productive relationships as the large private corporations. So far, however, by "corporation" I only refer to the large, modern, private organizations in which there is an already clear or clearly developing separation of function and authority among three distinct groups of its employees. To repeat, a top management, preoccupied by and monopolizing capitalist functions per se, controls through financial and policy mechanisms a middle element of supervisors, engineers and other technicians, and other professionals who in turn control by administrative and technological coercion a work force that simply labors. Corporate form thus stands for both the reality of today's corporations and their continuing program of evolution.

Corporate form does not represent a simple hierarchy. This is an extremely important point because it enables us to see beyond Weber's notion of "bureaucracy." That term has two erroneous implications brought out by the concept of corporate form. In the first place, "bureaucracy" implies that the hierarchical linkages in the large modern organizations are homogeneous, that is, simply a matter of bureaucrats bossing bureaucrats from top management all the way down to the lowest employee. This is simply not so in the modern corporation: The relation of top management to the middle element is qualitatively different than that holding between the middle group and the workers. Among other differences, one relationship is based largely on the carrot; the other has prominent sticklike elements. And the financial arrangements are also different. To employ the term "bureaucracy" here only serves to obscure the distinctive organizational arrangements that Sloan, for example, built into GM's management and that revolutionized modern business organization.

The other problem with Weber's view is that he depicts "bureaucracy" as a more or less pure technical necessity in modern, large-scale organizations. This usage has also passed into nearly universal currency. Thus Weber and his followers make no real distinction between the "technical necessities" of modern large scale organizations and the sort of class structures clearly implicit in corporate form. This leads them directly to the position that in modern society no class structure is possible other than the one we actually have. Although conservatives may take comfort in this thought, "bureaucracy" is too antiseptic a concept to take account of some of the more troubling class realities of modern social and, especially, social-industrial organization. On that account, it really should be rejected, not as the term to use when we want to describe the red tape and unresponsiveness of certain large organizations, but as a term of fundamental social analysis. We will have to come back to the issue of "bureaucracy" in other contexts, but it is important to understand from the outset that the shaping impact of corporate productive arrangements on society is closely linked to the needs of that particular modern institution and has no necessary connection to the nature of big institutions "in general."

Bibliographical Essay

My own studies of the corporation trace back to Robert Engler's *The Politics of Oil* (Macmillan, New York, 1961). Engler's unique contribution to the subject is his break with the hoary tradition that conceives of the modern corporation as a purely economic institution that blindly stumbles into other, noneconomic areas. Instead, Engler treats it explicitly as a political institution in its own right. Robert Averitt's *The Dual Economy: The Dynamics of American Industry Structure* (W. W. Norton, New York, 1968), an equally pioneering work, analyzes the ways in which corporations differ from small and mid-sized businesses in their use of technology, in productive organization, marketing methods, and several other key dimensions.

In that sense, Engler and Averitt should be ranked with Alfred D. Chandler, Jr., as among the most important pioneers in leading corporate studies to reach beyond the purely economic category of "monopoly" and beyond the legalistic narrowness of *The Modern Corporation and Private Property* by Adolph Berle and Gardiner Means (Macmillan, New York, 1932). Chandler analyzes the specifically U.S. development of the modern corporation in his *Strategy and Structure: Chapters in the History of American*

Industrial Enterprise (MIT Press, Cambridge, 1962). With Herman Daems, he has also edited and contributed to *Management Hierarchy: Comparative Perspectives on the Rise of the Modern Industrial Enterprise* (Harvard University Press, Cambridge, 1980), which extends the study of corporate development to Britain, the Federal Republic of Germany, and France.

J. P. Morgan, Jr., remains an enigmatic and fascinating man. It would appear that he was an industrial and capitalist visionary of the first rank who saw well beyond the economic limitations and political liabilities of laissez-faire. Accordingly, it would be particularly valuable to have a full-length critical study of his social and political ideas. In its absence we must make do with biographies that too often remain embedded within the older, muckraking tradition. Lewis Corey's, *The House of Morgan: A Biography of the Masters of Money* (AMS Press, New York, 1969, a reprint of the 1930 edition) remains the best of these. *J. P. Morgan: A Biography*, by Stanley Jackson (Stein and Day, New York, 1983), and Andrew Sinclair's *Corsair: The Life of J. Pierpont Morgan* (Little, Brown, Boston and Toronto, 1981) are also helpful.

Harold Livesay's *Andrew Carnegie and the Rise of Big Business* (Little, Brown, Boston and Toronto, 1975) and Robert Hessen's *Steel Titan: The Life of Charles M. Schwab, 1862–1939* (Oxford University Press, New York, 1975) rise above that old-fashioned level. Livesay, in particular, has written a veritable gem of a book, which successfully portrays Carnegie's multiple contributions to modern capitalist industry.

I have found it increasingly necessary to separate the work of the late Gardiner Means from that of Adolph Berle. At the time they collaborated on *The Modern Corporation and Private Property*, published in 1932, Berle was already a well-known corporate lawyer and Columbia Law School professor who would soon join Franklin Roosevelt's famous "Brains Trust," while Means was still a graduate student. It is, accordingly, not unfair to read *Modern Corporation* as Berle's book, albeit with some limited help from Means. It is a narrow book, a compendium of ownership information accompanying a series of lawyerly briefs on the common law as it applies to stockholder rights and related questions. It is not—despite its illustrious reputation to the contrary—an intellectually stimulating and pioneering work. A legendarily arrogant personality, Berle was apparently content to write his book in ignorance of (or simply by ignoring) the contributions of other investigators. *Modern Corporation* contains less than a handful of references to the rich literature of corporate studies that preceded it. Particularly striking is the omission of references to Rudolph Hilferding's extraordinary *Finance Capital: A Study of the Latest Phase of Capitalist Development* (Routledge and Kegan Paul, London, 1981) first published in Germany in 1910. Because of this, there is a sense in which *Modern Corporation* set the study of the corporation back from the high levels it had been brought to by men such as Hilferding, Thorstein Veblen (dismissed as a "commentator"), Werner Sombart, Max Weber, Lewis Corey, Louis Brandeis, even Marx himself. That harsh judgment is, I believe, well borne out by the series of undistinguished—and often undistinguishable—tracts on the corporation and society with which Berle occupied himself in the ensuing years.

In contrast, Means went on to produce an important work on his own. *Pricing Power and the Public Interest: A Study Based in Steel* (Harper and Bros., New York, 1962) remains the fundamental study of corporate pricing behavior and its linkage to traditional economic and political theory. This book deserves the lofty reputation wrongly accorded *Modern Corporation*.

My account of the development of GM has relied for the most part on Sloan's own very readable and lucid memoir, *My Years at General Motors* (Doubleday, New York, 1964). I find Frederick Winslow Taylor's *Principles of Scientific Management* (W. W. Norton, New York, 1967) more helpful than any of its numerous commentaries.

Labor conditions in the period under discussion are vividly described in Samuel Yellen's *American Labor Struggles* (Pathfinder Press, New York, 1977). Almont Lindsey's *The Pullman Strike* (University of Chicago Press, Chicago, 1964) is the standard study of that company town and the subsequent strike and boycott. Richard Edwards's *Contested Terrain* (Basic Books, New York, 1979) discusses the evolution of the management of labor and contains an excellent bibliography as well. In this vein, Katherine Stone's fine "Origins of Job Structures in the Steel Industry," reprinted in Richard Edwards, Michael Reich, and David M. Gordon, eds., *Labor Market Segmentation* (D. C. Heath, Lexington, Mass., 1975) is indispensable.

2

The Evolution of Corporate Form

The concept of corporate form argues that Taylorism and Sloanism have created three distinct social productive groups whose several relationships constitute the modern corporation. We might glance briefly at those three social formations, at first limiting our review as far as possible to the organizational setting rather than to the wider social or class setting. Following on that, I want very briefly to open up the picture by looking at some of the broader historical factors that initiated the development of corporate form within industry and that continue to play a shaping role today.

Evolutions I: Upper Management

The evolution of top management into a purely capitalist formation goes on apace. In Sloan's day it still appeared necessary for the top executives in a company to "know the business," that is, to have considerable detailed knowledge of the engineering, management, and marketing problems of that specific line of business. For all his advanced organizational ideas, Sloan himself certainly believed that, even many years later. But that has become less and less true in the corporate world today. The typical modern large corporation is a diversified producer to an extent undreamed of even a few years ago. Modern corporate systems of financial reporting and analysis have developed to such an extent that a single corporate management may now operate confidently and successfully in many different technologies and in various product and geographic markets that may have no common thread. GM in its classic days simply cut, cast, stamped, and welded metal, fabricating it into machines powered by their own engines, whether diesel locomotives, tractor combines, air conditioners, military aircraft, refrigerators, or Chevrolets. Thus one could know the business or at least a great deal of it. But in our day U.S. Steel (now USX) operates Marathon Oil; RCA, ostensibly a communications and electrical manufacturing company, also runs major publishing houses, hotel chains, and so forth. At the extreme of this diversification is the conglomerate, which is in many lines of business, often with no one of them related to any other: TENNECO imports quality cigars, mines zinc in New Jersey, prospects for natural gas, and sponsors the Houston Grand Opera.

In such a company top management clearly knows very little about the specific engineering, management, or marketing problems of most of the businesses they control. They have, in effect, shed virtually all specifically technological functions as well as the administration of those functions. In the last analysis, of course, top management controls the technology and administration employed in these businesses, but *only* to the degree that it compels them to obey the policies and the profit and growth targets it chooses. Here, having developed the policy and financial tools necessary, upper management already acquired an almost purely capitalist function. Very broadly speaking, the phenomenon of corporate diversification is an embodiment of the secular trend in industry to bring technology under the more thorough, fine-tuned sway of capital. The conglomerate represents the frontier of that movement.

We should not confuse this development, the subordination of technology to capital, with finance capitalism. The latter conception, deriving from the work of the Austrian economist Rudolph Hilferding, describes a situation in which big-business firms fall under the domination of bankers and other financial capitalists. Up until the end of World War II, for example, German industry was characterized by just such finance capitalist control. But it would be erroneous to describe the modern corporate system in those terms. The leaders of today's corporations are not financiers. Finance is a distinct industry with its own specific technologies. In order to practice it one must know the business, that is, finance markets, central bank behavior, currency movements, and so on.

That sort of activity doesn't preoccupy top management in most corporations. First of all, they tend to separate themselves from the exercise of all specific technologies, concentrating more and more on the strategic problem of making capital expand. Corporations do engage in finance, a great deal of it, but they have technical financial staff to do that work for them. Second and more important, modern corporate managements are not dominated by banks and financial markets and their decisions are not tied solely to speculative and monetary considerations but to decisions and opportunities provided by a dynamic, social-scale technology operating in a mass, international market for goods and services.

It is, of course, true that many of today's great corporations were created by financial institutions. The famous house of Morgan created the U.S. Steel Corporation, International Harvester, General Electric, AT&T, the Edison system, and several other giant firms. But a promoter's speculative impulse to make money through paper arrangements cannot guarantee a successful corporation. Corporate histories, such as that of U.S. Steel, are replete with instances of conflict between the "money" people and the "production" people. As we saw, the first president and a production man par excellence, Charles Schwab, was quickly forced from office at U.S. Steel by the dominant Morgan interests, which, as it were, wanted to reap the harvest of monopoly rather than sow the seeds of technological and industrial improvement. Schwab managed to gain control of the much smaller Bethlehem Steel Company and proceeded to win away a considerable part of U.S. Steel's business by an aggressive policy of plowing earnings back into the firm for technological improvements and lower costs. The U.S. Steel case is, of course, unusual in that the conflict between the money people and the production people degenerated into more or less open conflict. But even in companies like GM and Du Pont, where the conflict was muted, the production people eventually won in the end. Thus within a few decades of the "trustification" movement, as Berle and Means's famous study showed (1932), the great majority of the big U.S. corporations had freed themselves from outside financial control.

Outside the United States, the evolution of the modern corporation was much slower. Ultimately, the real superiority of corporate form to all other capitalist arrangements to date didn't become manifest until World War II. Before then there seems to have been a tendency in business and economic circles to believe that the unusually large size of U.S. firms in contrast to those in the other two most prominent capitalist countries, Great Britain and Germany, had mainly to do with the unusually large U.S. market. Certainly there was no imputation of *capitalist* superiority.

In pre–World War II British industry, for example, the medium-sized, family-owned firm was still the rule. In 1984 the BBC broadcast an extended series, "All Our Working Lives," that attempted to explain why British industries, technologically far in advance of the rest of the world at the turn of the century have lagged so badly since. In light of my earlier discussion about the differences between capitalism per se and capitalist ownership, the explanations for this backwardness given by British business leaders (often the sons and grandsons of that turn-of-the-century generation) are quite revealing: Their families were "used to" or "satisfied with" the older ways of doing business; German or U.S. "cleverness" couldn't really exceed tried and proved "British know-how"; firms in the same industry had a "live-and-let-live" attitude; when the management "really knew the men" work was done at best efficiency. In general, the findings of the BBC series are quite consistent with the more scholarly (though less vivid) academic accounts of the same matters.

From the standpoint of a person who is supposed to embody the capitalist aggressiveness portrayed by the economics profession, these explanations seem irrational and even aberrant, but understandable and, more's the point, quite predictable from the second- or third-generation owner of a capitalist firm who is satisfied with the size of his income and who prefers the competition of the grouse shoot to that of the steel market or who, perhaps, just wrongly believes that a large number of small, relatively competitive firms are more capitalistically efficient than a few price-controlling giants with monopolistic proclivities. I must add—not without a degree of malice— that such a belief was and is hardly irrational in light of the sort of conventional economics provided to businesspeople by thinkers such as George Stigler and Milton Friedman.

The German case is different again. Up until World War II, German industry tended to be organized in the way described by Hilferding, that is, through cartels directed by the big banks, literally a "finance" capitalism. But this little affected the actual producing units in steel, rubber, automobiles, and so on, which remained well below the size of those then already characteristic of the United States. In other words, the cartels simply took over certain narrow functions from the existing firms in each industry but otherwise let them be. The cartel arranged market shares, set prices and quotas, perhaps enforced standards, battled labor, and even carried on some cooperative research and development. But they didn't change the actual producing structure, which remained in the hands of relatively small, often regional firms. Thus the cartel system permitted some development of a more professionalized management, as the British family-based capitalism (capitalist-owner) did not, and it also appears to have encouraged some departure from technologies heavily dependent on crafts skills. I say "some" because a U.S. reader is as a rule stunned to see crafts-based technologies persisting, as British shipbuilding or German gun-making in World War II, thirty, forty, even fifty years past the point when they had been abandoned by the United States. At any rate, the cartel system appears not to have represented as clean a break from the limitations of scale and technological integration imposed by that older institutional form of capitalism as the departure represented by the organization of the U.S. trusts in the decade 1895–1905 and developed through Sloanism and Taylorism.

From the purely technological standpoint, the differences between a system based on corporate form and one based on a finance capitalism are quite marked. The typical major U.S. corporation, with its large producing units, was geared to mass production long before World War II and thus had acquired the organizational ability to integrate new technologies quite readily into its operations, simultaneously keeping to massive production schedules and maintaining very high engineering standards. From a capitalist standpoint this implies that top management is afforded opportunities for "earnings" that are denied to the family-based capitalist and even the finance capitalist. The capitalist superiority of the firm organized through corporate form has since been confirmed in its imitation by other capitalist countries such as Great Britain, the Federal Republic of Germany, France, and Japan.

These earlier German cartels influenced Lenin, via Hilferding, and undoubtedly Lenin's prestige continues to lend legitimacy to conceptions of a "finance" and, especially, a "monopoly" capitalism, even though they do not adequately reflect some of the most significant capitalist institutional and political economic changes of the past two-thirds of a century.

Evolutions II: The Middle Managerial, Technical, and Professional Group

The men and women in top management are, as they say, coming to know less and less about more and more. Putting the point somewhat more technically, there was a time in industry in which those who owned the business and controlled its investments also actively carried out its technological functions. Henry Ford provides a well-known instance of this. Even at the height of his success, Ford spent much of his time on the shop floor tinkering; he was a gifted engineer who was largely responsible for the high-quality engineering that distinguished his early cars from those of his rivals. Schwab, too, knew more about the technology of steel-making than nearly all his employees. But as corporate form develops it *socially* separates policy and investment from the details of operations and the nitty-gritty of technological information and technique. It creates a situation in which top management does not know and cannot grasp the details of how things are done, can be done better, will be done tomorrow. Of course, this or that top manager often knows such particulars, but top management as a group has surrendered this knowledge and the means to acquire it to another social formation, the middle managerial, technical, and professional group.

Top management has in effect helped create another industrial class, the middle group in industry, which has come to have a social monopoly on the knowledge, training, and technique that constitutes modern technology. Thus as top management necessarily becomes ever more generalist in its function, the middle element of supervisors, engineers and technicians, and the various other professionals becomes ever more specialized. This shows in the proliferation of subspecialties in virtually every management, technical, and professional field, which continues, it seems, at an ever-increasing rate: yesterday just electrical engineering; today countless subspecialties that have grown into full-fledged engineering fields in their own right, such as computer design or military avionics. We find the same process occurring at the supervisory level as well; managers specialize in personnel, office, product flow, transportation, and so forth. The relationship of specialization to the expansion of knowledge and technique in the various fields is too well known to bear commentary.

Looking at these matters from an entirely different level, we can see how the terms "manager," "technician," and "professional" come to be applied somewhat interchangeably. The reason is that, in spite of the often diverse origins of middle-element pursuits, they seem to have a common trajectory aimed at achieving recognition of their professional status, acceptance of their technical training and standards, and a style of work that (recalling Sloan) emphasizes the self-supervision of all those who work within the management echelon. Thus as management subfields proliferate much of what is practiced within them becomes routinized into a technique similarly based on a narrow slice of specialized information. In addition each of the management and the more purely technical subfields eventually organizes itself into a professional society that seeks more or less formal recognition by the industrial, foundation, and academic worlds. In the process each of the professions, even the older ones, actively seeks to strengthen its practical capacities and improve its standing by adopting a management-oriented perspective and as much of a scientific and technical stance as it can. Sometimes the science and the technique deserve the name; sometimes, too, the absence of both is covered over by adopting the appropriate symbols.

For good or ill, we now speak equally of steel-making, office interior decorating, and personnel counseling as technologies, even though the first has a scientific basis in metallurgy, crystallography, and other "real" sciences, whereas the latter pair rest on the often specious "truths" of other fields. For practical, industrial, and organizational purposes, however, the significant point about technologies is not the scientific character of their bases but the predictable and calculable character of their results. The normal result of the metallurgist's technology is steel with calculable qualities. So, too, the personnel counselor gives to employees advice that management can predict and count upon, and a properly trained industrial interior decorator will design an office that, predictably, doesn't vary much from other offices designed by similarly trained people. Technologies, whatever their scientific foundation, are freely deployable by top management only to the extent that they have an ineradicably routine core leading to a dependable result.

Accordingly, the middle managerial, technical, and professional group has become the social embodiment of what Ellul means by "technique" and what in common English is called, broadly, technology. Consequently, it is appropriate to define technique as what this echelon of people does and technology as the physical systems and processes they do it with.

It is important to stress that this middle element, its several techniques, and the physical equipment with which it works are essentially and almost exclusively found *within* the modern corporation and certain other institutions linked to it. The unique character of technology in our era is that it flourishes best only in that structured, institutional framework I've called corporate form, that is to say, within large organizations. I am aware that it is commonly argued that technological innovation occurs much more frequently in the smaller than in the largest firms. It is not entirely clear to me, however, that this is true, for we can find dramatic examples of technological innovation occurring in both kinds of firms. But even if it were true, it hardly bears on the argument here. No matter where a technology, scientific discovery, or product development originates, it gains social, economic, and technological significance only when and to the extent that it is absorbed into the big corporate world. High-fidelity sound equipment, for example, was perfected and developed by relatively small firms, such as the Dyna Company, Harmon-Kardon, Fisher, and Acoustics Research, but this occurred in a scientific and technical context essentially created and supported by the government-corporate-university system. Moreover, had the larger manufacturers such as Sony and RCA not taken up those products and mass-marketed them, they would not have achieved the economic and technical significance they now enjoy. In other words, without the scientific and technical contributions of big institutions, it is most unlikely that high-fidelity technology would ever have been developed, and, even if it had, without the commercial impetus given it by big corporations it would, like the wire recorder, be remembered as an interesting but somewhat unimportant dead end in the history of the electrical reproduction of sound.

The word "technology" (or Ellul's "technique") has become virtually a synonym for the social productive activity of the middle element and of the hardware it presides over, which is itself a product of their social productive activity. For many years now, the middle group in industry has had an almost exclusive monopoly on "technology" within the corporation, which is to say on the most modern, productive, and dynamic technology. It enjoys this monopoly and the social privileges it confers precisely because it performs this unique and important role within the dominant productive institution of modern capitalism, the corporation.

I think the substantive point of the capital-technology relationship can be put as follows: By subordinating itself to capital, technology—in other words, the middle managerial, technical, and professional class—gains two things it cannot provide for itself, namely, access to unlimited physical resources and the obedience of labor. The price paid for this subordination is relatively small; the middle element must subject itself to the principle of rate of return on investment. Meanwhile, by associating itself with that middle group and by deferring to its expertise, capital frees itself to the greatest extent possible from social, technical, and other limitations on its growth and prosperity. This is clearly an extraordinarily fruitful symbiotic relationship.

I think John Kenneth Galbraith—with many others, I must add—is wrong to overlook this identity between the middle group in industry and what we mean by "technology." To define technology as he does, as "the systematic application of organized knowledge to practical tasks" (*The New Industrial State*, 1st edition, p. 12), merely tends to mystify the subject. Contemporary "technology" is the *social activity* of an historic class with a distinctive social role and culture operating primarily within the corporation for its own and corporate ends. Galbraith's definition, by contrast, is far too bloodless an abstraction to grasp what is distinctive in modern technology. His definition could as well fit the ancient Romans or the classic Chinese empire or, for that matter, an inquisitive caveman systematically comparing stone shapes to see which one was best to throw at his near neighbor. His "technostructure" is open to the same objections. Its "scientific generality" is won at the expense of historical accuracy and specificity even though, as Galbraith himself recognizes, the very term "technostructure" was coined in order to grasp what was *different* about the modern corporation in comparison with other, previous business forms. The contradiction between his aim and his formulation could not be more glaring.

There is in fact no unitary "technostructure." Just as there is no unitary "management." The history of the modern corporation and the history of much of its outstanding technical and economic success derives from the division of the management echelon into *two* distinct groups carrying out *two* distinct social productive tasks. One of those groups, the middle element, is a technostructure of sorts. But, contrary to Galbraith's notion, it does not run the corporation. It is only the middle group in industry, not the top. The top manages the corporation; the middle element only manages the details.

There is an extremely large literature about modern middle classes, much of it interesting and informative. Some of it has even correctly identified this managerial, technical, and professional group as a new and important phenomenon. But this literature has failed to locate it in its shaping context, corporate form. The significance of the enormous growth of the nonentrepreneurial middle class in our era, from a small social fragment before the turn of the century to the second- or third-largest social formation in the country, is that it is a creature of the modern corporation, where it increasingly performs a distinct social productive role. The middle element is the bearer of technology in our society, but it carries out this role only within corporate form, increasingly subject to the ever more demanding logic of capitalist profitability that in turn leads to the growing demand for docility of labor. Thus it is simply wrong to argue, as so many do, that technology or technique has become a sort of faceless monster out of control. One cannot support that point of view even if one looks somewhat cursorily, as we have, at the way in which technology functions in those institutions and among those social formations that monopolize and exploit it. Contemporary technology is hardly faceless; it has the smiling, professional visage of the modern, university-trained manager or technician who is paid a good salary, given excellent perks, and provided firm direction by his or her employer, the top management of the big corporation.

Evolutions III: The Collective Worker

The working class has also changed considerably under corporate form. Not only has it grown in size, but the experience of different kinds of corporate workers in different industries has become more similar. In the earliest period of the corporations not only was their work force relatively small, covering only a fraction of all nonagricultural laborers, but it was also confined to those few businesses using large-scale productive systems, employing relatively unskilled labor, and utilizing a capital-intensive productive process based on the use of motorized mechanical equipment. In the 1890s such businesses were limited to the manufacture of producer goods, textiles and the needle trades, certain kinds of food processing (canning, packinghouse), mining, the railroads, and a few others. But warehousing, distribution and retailing, office work, almost all the so-called service industries, finance, and even most manufacturing were excluded.

As a result the number of workers in the main industries was relatively small. They were in fact outnumbered by another group of workers whose conditions of employment and lack of experience with industrial technology led them to view the world quite differently than those employed in industry proper. We can mark this distinction—with Averitt—by referring to corporate-sector workers for the one kind, using the expression "small-business workers" (or "workers in the entrepreneurial sector") for the others. The distinction is of considerable importance. The one has been subject to the influences of Sloanism and Taylorism, its members participating in large-scale national industries under highly rationalized management wherein skilled labor and traditional worker skills were minimized. The other has remained in a work world that is basically unchanged in these respects.

In this sense the word "worker" has too often been employed in a fundamentally ambiguous way. Throughout much of this century in all the industrial countries, there have been two distinct urban work forces, of which the industrial (later corporate) group has usually been the smaller. The differences between the two have been quite considerable, as one might expect where the groups were divided between national and local industries and cultures, between newer and traditional technologies, between workers in great cities like Pittsburgh and Chicago and those in smaller, less cosmopolitan cities, towns, and even villages. In fact, their differences are such that it is at least arguable that they represent two essentially different classes.

Although the workers associated with the small-business sector of the economy remain quite numerous, corporate-sector workers have now surpassed them in number and importance. This is certainly true in the United States, and it is true or is becoming true for the other industrial countries as well. It is easy to see why this is so. As corporate form develops, it enables a single top management to deploy virtually any number and variety of middle-element managers, technicians, and professionals in any number of fields simultaneously. Consequently, the big corporations have been able to expand into business and geographical areas formerly denied them. Probably the most vivid instance is provided by the fast-food business. Not long ago the strong regional and even local food preferences were so many and so varied that only local entrepreneurs could succeed in knowing and therefore catering to them. Naturally, these small businesspeople employed large numbers of waitresses, short-order cooks, busboys, and other workers. But now such national chains as McDonald's and Burger King have replaced them. Partly the result of television, which has reshaped national food preferences, and partly the result of the military, who pioneered in the techniques required for mass feeding (such as inventory and portion and quality control), these national firms have solved the problem of penetrating local fast-food markets formerly denied them. As a result, local foods workers in Arizona and Georgia now have very much the same industrial employment experience as do those in Ohio and Pennsylvania. This change is multiplied severalfold as breweries; dairies; food, clothing, appliance and other retail stores; banks and insurance companies; even real estate firms pass under the control of national corporations and are reorganized by corporate form.

Thus a more or less homogeneous working class is being developed in place of a laboring population that was at one time quite varied in its skills, loyalty to local employers, regional diversity, experience of modern industrial organization, and familiarity with up-to-date technology. From that homogenization emerges the concept of the "collective worker." Within corporate form, workers are essentially only units to be fitted in now here, now there as required by the economic and technical demands of the production process. They are the passive material to be shaped by the activity of the middle managerial, technical, and professional group. That is the point of the fictional character Schmidt: He is human material that can be shifted and altered to fit the company's need; thus he is fully interchangeable with any other Schmidt. Labor cartoonists often seize upon this point to drive home to workers the actual position they occupy in modern industry. There is, for example, a famous Industrial Workers of the World (IWW) cartoon of a massive, strapping fellow who has no head: "The Perfect Worker" says the caption, for being mindless he is simply a unit of great strength and stamina that can be freely combined with other, like units to form a working class of uniformly standard quality.

Modern technology can be freely deployed by central management only insofar as it has an ineradicably routine core: One element of that core lies in the uniform training of each of the members within the modern managerial, technical, and professional class, the other in the uniform, available level of skills and motivation of the collective worker.

These two go together as the two terms of a single relationship. In contrast to the myth of runaway technology, the concept of corporate form emphasizes that the growing technological subordination of workers is merely the other side of the coin to the proliferation of the managerial, technical, and professional groups. Thus as the worker's work becomes more homogenized, that of the engineer becomes more specialized. As the worker becomes more alienated at the growing routinization of the job, the manager is discovering new challenges to his or her ingenuity in simplifying the industrial process. The growing numbness of the worker's life is matched by the growing need for creativity on the part of the professional. The decline of the skilled or polyvalent worker is the negative, in the photographic sense, of the rise of the modern professional, supervisor, or technician. Consequently, "new threats to workers and the environment," "new social dislocations," "new threats to human integrity" do not represent the workings of some technological genii, of either the servant variety (as claimed by Galbraith) or the monster species (as argued by Ellul). These are simply systemic features of the way in which the modern corporation and other institutions influenced by it have organized the social production process. Historically speaking, nothing inevitable is going on here; rather, the process expresses corporate form, the normal social action of the corporation and of the social groups that participate in it.

A Social and Historical View of the Corporation

The modern corporation is the dominant institution of our era and has been a major factor in reshaping the present century. In that sense it is an institution of world historical significance no less than the old Chinese mandarinate, the classic Roman army, or even the Catholic church. The story of its emergence and its evolution, too, requires that we look beyond organizational and related questions and into much broader social and historical phenomena. In the present case, three striking developments that emerged in the last decades of the nineteenth century bear importantly on the origins of the corporation and have played a significant role in the evolution of corporate form. These are, first, the emergence of another, greater and very different industrial and technological revolution; next, the reemergence of imperial rivalries among all the great powers; and third, and perhaps most important, the success of Marxian socialism in the form of the social democratic movement. At this point in our study, we can take up only a brief history of these developments. Subsequently, we will follow their threads into the present.

Origins I: A Second and Greater
Industrial Revolution

Steel—not the steel company but the material itself—is central to the second industrial revolution that occurred in the late nineteenth century. It had been known for many centuries that steel was much the best form of iron. Steel's properties come from variations in its mosaic pattern (technically, a crystal structure) of iron, carbon, and other elements. Some patterns yield extremely hard but brittle steel, others steel that is softer but with more flex, still others steel that is easy to fabricate into complicated shapes. Even in the ancient world, craftsmen had learned to control the crystal structure, but only for quite small batches, not in industrial quantities. The other problem in making steel comes from impurities in the ore. Iron ore is richly available on or near the surface of the earth, but it often contains impurities, some of which, like sulfur, are difficult to get rid of and make the resulting steel extremely brittle. The technical details to the solution of these problems need not occupy our attention. Suffice it to say that it was not until 1878 that the last of these barriers to producing reliable steel in industrial quantities, the elimination of sulfur, was finally mastered.

Consider the implications of this step: Virtually every existing material used in manufacturing, transportation, and construction became obsolete, to be replaced by a magic substance that was better, cheaper, more reliable, and transformed how one did the job in the first place. This victory of technology was the foundation for a second industrial revolution that promised, even at the time, to be much more sweeping in its changes than its more heralded predecessor of the early 1800s.

On the technical side, the story is perhaps familiar enough. The first industrial revolution was founded on steam and cotton; it had important consequences for the society of the time but rather limited ones for industry itself. Cotton cloth is just cotton cloth; it has some industrial uses but only some. Steam is a different story; steam engines developed in the mills or on the railroads could also be used in mines or on merchant ships and naval vessels. Yet steam technology was vastly hampered in its development because the boilers, pipes, and valves were still made of older materials like brass and iron that imposed severe limitations of temperature and pressure. The development of steam's further, frontier uses had to await some other technology.

Steel was different. Steel is a fundamental material. Every industry—including the steel industry itself—uses it for the toughest jobs. It transformed the uses of steam because steel boilers, steel valves, and steel pipes could handle levels of heat and pressure several score times those of iron or brass fixtures. Steam turbines operating at pressures of several thousand pounds per square inch could turn machine tools, propellers, drills, generators, and other equipment of a size, at speeds, and with a precision undreamed of even a few years before. Steel drills, saws, hammers, lathes, presses, and grinders revolutionized the metalworking industry. Thus all manufacturing was transformed in an instant into a new world of opportunity—a familiar story now part of our common industrial folklore.

Had we the space we could also explore two other industries that grew parallel to steel and were in their own ways as pregnant of change throughout industrial life and culture. They were the electrical industry and the chemical industry. For our purposes it is enough to note that in the last third of the nineteenth century, an accelerating pace of technological advance fundamentally altered industrial life as a whole because it radically changed not only what was produced but how, at what scale, and at what price. The modern corporation was developed in part as a response to this series of technological requirements and opportunities. It represents an attempt to create an industrial organization that is at home with this sort of changing industrial and technological situation and can harness it for the benefit of—at least—the owners and managers of industry.

We have yet, however, to get to what is really new about the technological revolution of the late 1800s. That reality can be put with great accuracy and simplicity: The technology was fundamentally a *social* technology. It drew upon the intellectual invention not of this entrepreneur or that inventor but of science itself, a social activity. Unlike the relatively small scale and localization of the first industrial revolution, this second industrial revolution normally operated at scales that demanded the coordinated activities not of small groups but of masses of people, not just at this place or that but over the boundaries of societies and continents. It demanded integrated *organizations* of specialists whose effort was coordinated over time in ways never dreamed of before. It forced changes in culture, urban design, migration patterns, social structure, government, and the financial structure in ways and to a degree that were almost entirely novel. And it brought about the development of a new class—the middle managerial, technical, and professional class—systematically versed in scientific and organizational technologies, freely available to capitalist enterprise, and able to employ almost without restriction the personal, social, and economic resources of society itself.

It is interesting that this point is not emphasized in, for example, business history, which is otherwise quite insightful on these subjects. How can such a simple and fundamental point as a shift to a new, manifestly much more social technology be missed? It's a good question, and it clearly points to the deadening influence of the economics profession and its peculiar ideology. In modern economics "the market" provides the governing conception. In "the market" all economic activity is ultimately shaped by the buying and selling that goes on solely among *individuals.* In economics there is no "social"—"social" for it is just the sum of independent, individual actions.

We see in this a particularly gross instance of business and economic ideology helping to obscure the history of business itself. In the late nineteenth century, business leaders tried desperately to evolve new forms of business organization to cope with what was happening and what they wanted to make happen. Thus they variously devised rings, pools, cartels, holding companies, and trusts as they tried to shape the sort of business firm that could best take advantage of the new technical and social environment they themselves were doing so much to create. They saw, correctly, that there were many different forms of business organization, each with distinct advantages and disadvantages. And eventually they saw that a key feature of modern industrial organization was its ability to deploy vast teams of competent managerial, technical, and professional specialists in new ways. But economic theory, then as now, would have absolutely none of this. The leading economist of the time, Alfred Marshall, systematically ignored all this novelty and complexity in business firms. For him, all one had to do was talk of a single, theoretical "representative firm" whose key actor was the "entrepreneur." This "representative firm" sold its familiar wares to the public pretty much as a small farmer used to sell his grain at a country market. Economics was based on simple, timeless truths, as valid for the small farmer as for U.S. Steel. Obviously, it is difficult indeed to squeeze an account of a social-scaled technological revolution into Marshall's narrow, theoretical picture and harder still to use that picture to trace the wider social and economic effects of that revolution. To this very day, conventional economic theory is rather more an obscuring ideology than an illuminating science when it treats of the modern corporation.

One is tempted to use the rise of Pittsburgh or Essen or even Turin as a symbol of this new, more social technology. That would provide a vast improvement over Marshall. But an even better approach requires that we go up a step. The new steel industry didn't only make a major city out of Pittsburgh; it tied together the whole Midwest into a single, integrated industrial organism. Just as it linked the shores of all the Great Lakes to create this unified, regional industrial giant, so too did it create not just

Essen but the Ruhr, not just Turin but the industrial triangle comprising the entire region of northern Italy bounded by Turin, Genoa, and Milan, or the Donbas, or the Tokyo plain.

The "social" qualifier also takes into account that millions upon millions of immigrants were drawn into these regions, some from their near hinterlands and others from different continents. And it refers to the rise of a new, national class of industry leaders that changed, for example, U.S. politics from a series of local contests into a single political drama. Political scientists even treat the U.S. presidential election of 1896 as the watershed for that very development.

Origins II: Dreadnoughts, Gunboats, and Other White Fleets

The second major historical development closely intertwined with the rise of the modern corporation is the reemergence of international, great-power military rivalry in the last part of the nineteenth century. Most sources of this reemergence are somewhat peripheral to our story. One source, however, was the technological revolution just described, which simply recast the economic-military equation between the powers. What is striking about this awakened military rivalry is that it simultaneously embroiled *all* of the great powers on a truly international scale. The continuation of this imperialist rivalry into the present provides the connection to the modern corporation.

The story is probably best illustrated by the naval arms race of the last part of the century, as powerful navies were the chief tools of colony-grabbing and the other moves in the new imperialist rivalry. It is sobering to be reminded that this is the same arms race that played so big a part in bringing about the disastrous bloodletting called World War I.

The major worldwide participants were the United States, Britain, Germany, and Japan. France, Italy, and Austria-Hungary competed in a somewhat smaller race in the Mediterranean, while czarist Russia tried to cope with the impossible task of keeping up in three largely separate races: in the Baltic against Germany, in the Far East against Japan, and in the Black Sea against Turkey and its variously German, French, and British allies. Even Chile, Argentina, Brazil, Spain, and the Netherlands took part in the race as minor players.

The shift from the relatively peaceful and benign international order of midcentury to the savage environment of the 1890s and after is more or less coordinate with the technological revolution. Accordingly, it can be partially rendered—though only partially—in military-technological terms. The British battleship HMS *Dreadnought* is at the center of the story.

The naval vessels of the 1860s, 1870s, even 1880s, even the all-metal, steam-driven ones, look remarkably like those of the pre–Civil War period. People in the United States, of course, see the famous *Monitor* and *Merrimack* as the first modern ships, but they actually differed little from the conventional, all-wood naval vessels of the time.

HMS *Dreadnought was* different. Launched with great fanfare in 1904, she was the culmination of four decades of extremely rapid change in the naval art. She was bigger, faster, and better armed than any other vessel then afloat because her builders, drawing on the latest advances in British industry and pushed beyond them by the admiralty, created a new and unusually advanced naval technology. This famous ship represented a profound shift in the war-making art. The sort of industry-government-scientific collaboration that brought about HMS *Dreadnought* is now absolutely common for all weapons and weapons systems. Thus it is difficult for us to conceive that wars used to be fought with antique weapons of static design. Much of Napoleon's artillery, for example, was centuries old. Even the U.S. Civil War, the first major war not fought with weapons taken out of musty storerooms, was largely fought with weapons whose technology was fifty or more years old. By contrast, *Dreadnought* embodied propulsion and the latest other systems developed especially for that vessel. The ship was, in fact, so advanced that it was to be several years before the other powers saw similar ships into service. Her technological sophistication, novelty, and impact on the international military balance was symbolic of government's growing number of calls on big industry—a development that would soon create a permanent integration of government and the private business firm in the area of international military security. Obviously, this symbiotic relationship has persisted even up to the present.

To this day people talk of a distinct private sector and another distinct public sector—though I dare say this has never existed in the corporate era. In fact, many famous companies, such as British Petroleum and the Radio Corporation of America, were first organized by government in order to carry out tasks of an international military security nature. Because private enterprise is sacred doctrine in the United States, RCA was later turned over to a private management, much like the space communications company some decades later. We see a historical parallel today in the gradual transfer of space rocket technology to private firms both here and in Europe, or in the subsidies that governments in the industrial countries extend, often sub rosa, to their civil aviation and aircraft manufacturing industries.

The salient point of this discussion is that we really cannot look at the modern corporation as a purely commercial undertaking nor at the modern business class as a purely or even predominantly business- and economics-oriented group. From its inception and at every step of its development, the modern corporation has been integrally linked with government, at first mostly in the international military security field, at present in virtually every field. Governments have variously subsidized corporations, often created them, habitually coddled them, and the companies in turn have played and continue to play a major role in the development of state policies and strategies. The development of modern technology has been deeply impacted, arguably even shaped by military and other government require-ments. There is a frequent exchange of top personnel between government and corporation and frequent consultation on policy, tactics, and other matters. Indeed, when President Dwight Eisenhower "discovered" the military-industrial complex in early 1961, he was already more than fifty years out of date.

Because of this intimate and continuing linkage between the corporation and government, the upper business class has been steadily driven to evolve from a predatory band of so-called robber barons toward greater political consciousness and sophistication. At its simplest, this meant that certain time-consuming and mind-consuming business and technical functions had to be passed on to another, associated class, leaving individual business leaders free to deal with the political-social environment that is, truly, the decisive dimension for modern corporate business success.

But a second and much more important change was also required. This had to do with how the upper class was organized and how it structurally related to society and to the political process. This involves a story that must await more adequate development later in the book (Chapters 3 and, particularly, 4) but can be prefigured here. Basically, the older, pre-corporate capitalist class was founded in a private-property system that encouraged deep rivalries within itself, as well as an intrinsically rapacious relationship to government, other classes, and, indeed, society itself. Thus *as a class* it was poorly suited to cope with the new *integrated* technological and political world emerging in the late nineteenth century. Robber barons had to give way, if not to industrial statesmen, then at least to a new class of business and financial leaders. Modern corporate organization, particularly through its triadic division of social labor and its subsequent intimate ties to government and other social institutions, tends to create a fairly unified upper corporate class with closely linked interests and outlooks. Moreover, this class *as a class* has important shared and overlapping interests with other corporate classes, particularly the middle element. Given the nature of the modern corporation, such an upper class is essential to its success, as its activity within the corporations and with government and other agencies tends to strengthen a common interest and outlook.

Origins III: The Specter of Social Democracy

The 1880s and 1890s represent a period, both here and overseas, of rapid development in worker demands and worker organizations, a development importantly influenced by the spread of Marx's ideas. For example, the shift in worker attitudes during this period away from the view that strikes hinder broader worker interests and toward the modern view that strikes advance their cause was one of the dimensions of Marx's influence. He played a chief role in persuading workers' organizations that their previous ideas on the subject were untrue and even harmful to themselves. This was a Marxian influence as yet untouched by the ideas of Lenin. It aimed essentially at what was in those days called social democracy, what we would today call socialism as distinct from communism. The aim was twofold: Workers tried to establish stable unions in the main industries, nationally federated and cooperating with one another. Upon this solid industrial foundation, social democrats thought, a political party of the workers could be organized to win basic democratic rights. Then, together, the union and the party would proceed to expand the political and social rights of the workers. Their ultimate vision was to do away with capitalism and create an entirely new society based on democratic principles.

In the United States, of course, workers already had the right to vote, but this was usually not the case overseas, and, in any case, the existing Democratic and Republican parties were hostile to trade unions and on other matters of vital interest to workers. At any event, however, the prototype for this two-pronged social democratic strategy was Germany, which until the 1880s was the leading industrial nation. There a unified Social Democratic Federation—which combined the unions and a political party—had been formed in 1875 then outlawed by the Bismarckian government in 1878. Still, it grew stronger in spite of the repression, so much so that the German government was forced to repeal the ban in 1890. In 1892 the unions split away to form a separate organization, but both they and the party continued to grow rapidly. There was a parallel development in Britain, where unions of mainly skilled workers had been active and successful since midcentury and the unions themselves had been legal since the 1870s. By and large these older trade unionists worked closely with the Liberal party, in which they had a minor voice. But their paramount position was supplanted after the London docker's strike of 1889 by what was then called the "new unionism," mixed ("amalgamated") unions of skilled and unskilled workers who, unlike their predecessors, had a social democratic political outlook and were determined to win direct representation for workers in Parliament through their own political party. This eventuated in the organization of the social democratic Labour party after the turn of the century. Italy, Spain, Austria-Hungary, czarist Russia, France, Belgium, Sweden, and the other continental countries enjoyed analogous developments in social democracy within roughly the same time frame.

In the United States, the situation was complicated by the inability of the workers to form and then sustain a national trade union movement. A post–Civil War National Labor Union had failed, as had the Knights of Labor in the 1880s. Samuel Gompers's American Federation of Labor (AFL) had been organized (under a different name) in 1878 and by 1890 stood almost alone in the field. Originally a Marxist, Gompers had gradually drifted over to a quite conservative outlook based on the principle that the prerogatives of skilled, usually white and native-born workers had to be maintained even if—as was often the case—it led the AFL to oppose efforts to bring the newer, more numerous, unskilled and semiskilled immigrant workers into the movement. (Opponents of the AFL referred to it as the American Separation of Labor.) Consequently, the mantle passed to others. Most prominent of these was Eugene Debs, a railroad union leader who had led the famous Pullman national rail strike in 1894. He had been jailed for his efforts, came increasingly under the influence of Marxian ideas, and accordingly attempted to reenact the international social democratic strategy here. By the turn of the century his Socialist party began to play an appreciable role, and, frustrated by what he saw as the myopia of the AFL, Debs subsequently lent his efforts to organize a new national labor organization, the Industrial Workers of the World, in 1905.

The leading U.S. industrialists active in the incidence and initial evolution of the modern corporation were well aware of this international trend toward social democracy, and we can trace various steps they took to defeat it. J. P. Morgan, a dominating figure in his own right, can also function as a representative type. He had extensive international connections, and in them we can occasionally see glimpses of the importance he assigned to checking these pretensions of the workers. He and his firm had risked substantial funds on the infamous Versailles government and army that used them to overturn the Paris Commune, the famous worker-based revolutionary government of Paris in 1871. He also had extensive financial and political connections in both Germany and Britain. In the United States Morgan was a major figure in the rail industry. Thus he was party to its continuing disputes with the workers, culminating in the 1894 strike and, of course, with disputes in the coal industry, which was dominated by the railroads. Andrew Carnegie and his henchman, Henry Clay Frick, had precipitated the famous Homestead (Pennsylvania) massacre. The Rockefellers had engaged in a running battle with miners at their Colorado Fuel and Iron Company from the 1890s onward, culminating in the Ludlow massacre (of miners and their families by Rockefeller gunmen) in 1912. In short, many of the leaders who were most instrumental in initiating U.S. Steel in particular and the modern corporation in general had had long, personal experience of the developing struggle between labor and capital.

These men and their associates were deeply involved in efforts to check or deflect social democracy. The 1894 rail strike had been triggered by a revolt of the workers in Pullman, Illinois, against the dictatorial George Pullman (who had close ties with the Morgan interest). But it is evident from Pullman and other company towns that there were also attempts to upgrade the quality of labor, as well as make it more docile, through the provision of schools and medical services. In this they have much in common with what came to be called "welfare capitalism," a movement in which the companies built housing, provided clinics, sometimes nurseries and schools, offered limited stock-option plans, and in general tried to create positive links of mutual self-interest between themselves and their employees. The Morgan-dominated U.S. Steel was one of the leaders in this field, and much of the early history of Gary, Indiana (which was practically created by U.S. Steel), should be read in this light.

Still another facet of this effort was the creation of company unions. Actually, this dates somewhat later, for it appears that the first attempt to create a company union as a prototype for corporation-worker relations grew out of the Ludlow massacre of 1912. The Rockefellers grew quite enthusiastic about their Employee Representation Plan but the patent duplicity involved in creating and maintaining bogus leaders for the workers limited its effectiveness and the movement made little headway.

For their part the new corporations were resolutely opposed to independent trade unions. At the time U.S. Steel was formed, some of the units still had unions, but the company succeeded in ridding itself of the last of them by 1907. Thereafter, U.S. Steel was a leader in the "open shop" movement (renamed "The American Plan" after 1919), vigorously resisting every effort to organize its workers. One after another, organizing attempts, including an epochal steel strike of 1919, were put down. In fact, by judicious use of the blacklist, company spies, goons and gunmen, closure of plants with union contracts, use of convict labor, encouraging ethnic and racial strife among the workers, control of the press and of local officials, and, of course, through its schemes of "welfare capitalism," U.S. Steel remained an open shop citadel until just before World War II.

The big industrialists took the lead in forming the Citizen's Industrial Association (1903), whose avowed purpose was to fight trade unions. This forerunner of the U.S. Chambers of Commerce consisted of a league of employers' and "civic" groups throughout the country. In this crusade against trade unions and other "un-American" influences, the association joined corporation-dominated organizations such as the National Association of Manufacturers (active in combating unions since before the turn of the century), the American Iron and Steel Institute, and the National Foundries Association.

These early corporate leaders were sufficiently concerned with the rise of social democracy to form and participate in the influential National Civic Federation (NCF) in 1900. The NCF saw itself as the conscious alternative to social democracy, preaching a gospel of moderate reform brought about by collaboration among labor, capital, and "the public." It saw itself as a center political movement, evenhandedly rejecting the attempts both of the social democrats and the forces of laissez-faire to divide society between labor and capital, Left and Right. Prominent among these forces of the center were a number of important corporate leaders including several leading Morgan men. In fact, George Perkins, who worked particularly closely with Morgan, was one of the leading spirits of the NCF.

As is plain to see, the modern corporation was initiated by those with experience in the labor-capital conflict, worried explicitly about the growth of social democracy, and active in a number of efforts to block it. But I have yet to see evidence that the organization of the U.S. Steel Corporation, for example, was explicitly viewed as a step toward the defeat of social democracy. The same is true of the other trusts. We can construct a conclusion that these corporate pioneers *must* have acted with that purpose at least partly in mind. There is no dearth of evidence to support such an inference: For example Morgan had for years preached the necessity of a fully unified rail industry and had made several attempts to actually create in the rail industry a company like U.S. Steel. He had been rebuffed in his efforts, particularly through the resistance of E. H. Harriman and John D. Rockefeller, Jr. Then in 1894 the railroads were forced to improvise a unified instrument, the General Managers' Association, in order to wage their battle with Debs's American Railway Union, the first U.S. union that attempted to bring all the workers in one national industry into a single union. The movement to amalgamate smaller, competing companies into a unified trust, of which U.S. Steel was the most significant example, actually took off only after the Pullman strike had been defeated by government, not industry strength. It is tempting to conclude that the trust movement was triggered by the near victory of the Pullman strike. But the smoking gun—a proposal by an influential industry leader linking the formation of a new firm to a solution of the labor question—is missing.

Nevertheless, there is sufficient linkage between the history of the modern corporation and that of the social democratic specter to make us see the latter as a major influence in its evolution. We are short of evidence, so to speak, only for the connection to the birth of the corporation as a new kind of firm. Thereafter, corporate activities and corporate initiatives are at the forefront not only in resisting social democracy but also in attempting to forge a different relationship between labor and capital than the egalitarian vision of the socialists or the industrial serfdom aimed at by the pre-corporate generation of U.S. capitalists. In fact, the more we look at these matters, the more apparent it becomes that the development of the truly modern corporation in the United States, which far outstretched analogous changes in German, British, and other European industries, has been a major factor in *preventing* social democracy in the United States from enjoying the success it had overseas. Why has socialism been so unsuccessful in the United States? The answer, or at least the core of the answer, may be much simpler than the enormous literature on the subject imagines: The modern corporation developed first in the United States and proved a business and capitalist form much more immune to social democratic inroads than did the much less developed capitalist institutions of Britain and the continent.

There are a number of reasons for arguing this, some well understood, some not at all. Corporate form clearly enables modern corporate leaders to press economic and technological progress to a degree far beyond the abilities of older forms of business organization. This in turn meant a more rapid expansion of the social surplus than was possible under the entre-preneurial and finance species of capitalism. Some of this could be shared with the workers, as the story of Schmidt suggests. The growing separation between corporate-sector and small-business sector workers was also an important factor. The integration of the leading corporate class with government, decisively begun in the Theodore Roosevelt administration (1901–1909) hindered the political success of social democracy, especially as Rooseveltian progressivism freely borrowed many social democratic schemes and proposals. But most important of all, in my view, is the profound change in social structure and deep social alliances brought about by corporate, as contrasted to either entrepreneurial or finance, capitalism.

As Marx pointed out in *The Communist Manifesto,* one of the system features of (entrepreneurial) capitalist society was the development of fundamental social, political, and economic conflict between the middle entrepreneurial classes and big capital itself. In fact, as becomes clear from the rise of German fascism, even the emergence of finance capitalism did not entirely abate this deep system conflict between the middle and upper capitalist classes. But under corporate form, the largest, most influential, and expanding middle class emerges as an ally and partner of big capital. Consequently, under corporate capitalism, the working class finds itself opposed not merely by big capital, with part or even all of the middle sections of society supportive or, at worst, neutral. Instead, it confronts an industrial organization and a society in which the other two main industrial (and social) classes resist its efforts as a single bloc. In short, corporate society has a deep social structure radically different from that of earlier capitalist private property societies. It is to this very subject that we must shortly turn.

Society Re-Created

As this brief historical digression has suggested, the development of the modern corporation is deeply intertwined with several of the most fundamental characteristics and historical features of twentieth-century society taken as a whole. For that reason, I argue, corporate form represents not merely a kind of industrial organization but what I have called a social structure of production. The modern corporation is a social institution in the further sense that it has refashioned the physical-social world we live in by taking the lead in absorbing and perfecting the second industrial revolution. In so doing it has both directly and indirectly refashioned both domestic society and the international political and economic order. In addition, within each of the great modern corporations, three distinct industrial classes have emerged and have continued to evolve, not only in industrial life per se but also as broad social classes. Clearly, then, this new social structure of production has fundamentally transformed modern society.

We should not think of the corporation (as it is often described) as imposing itself on society and the various social classes from the outside. Corporate form, the dynamic social productive structure that historically, empirically, and functionally distinguishes the modern corporation from previous productive institutions, is itself a class structure of production. The emergence of those classes and their relationships—not just the hardware they produce—has transformed modern society, simultaneously destroying pre-corporate society and creating a new world. Technological change as well as social change in the contemporary era comes from the dynamic thrust of the corporate classes operating in a society that is as yet not entirely a product of their relationships and their efforts. Corporate society emerges from the womb of pre-corporate society; it and its classes then slowly grow so as to entirely replace what had been before. It conquers the older society, but as an heir, not a foreign horde.

Bibliographical Essay

Chandler and Daems, *Managerial Hierarchy* has already been cited for the overseas development of corporate form. Additional material can be found in Derek F. Channon, *The Strategy and Structure of British Enterprise* (Macmillan, London and New York, 1973). The chaos of French industry during a hasty rearmament (1938–1940), when still organized into small to mid-sized firms, is truly legendary. For this, see among others William

Shirer's, *The Collapse of the Third Republic: An Inquiry into the Fall of France in 1940* (Simon and Schuster, New York, 1969). Something like the same chaos afflicted German industry until a new armaments minister, Albert Speer, brought order out of chaos starting in late 1942; see his *Inside the Third Reich* (Macmillan, New York, 1970). In Speer's account, it is particularly clear that absent the organizational resources and managerial learning experience represented by the earlier U.S. corporate form, German industrial coordination throughout the war came about more by a perpetual balancing act than by the application of real system and plan.

George Stigler of the University of Chicago has for many years been the ultimate authority for mainstream economists who maintain that the modern corporation requires no particular adjustments to basic economic theory. His views are developed in "Perfect Competition, Historically Contemplated" (*The Journal of Political Economy* 65 (1) [1957]), *Capital and Rates of Return in Manufacturing Industry* (Princeton University Press, Princeton, 1963), and, with James K. Kindahl, *The Behavior of Industrial Prices* (National Bureau of Economic Research, New York, 1970). Milton Friedman, for example, turns to Stigler's arguments in his *Capitalism and Freedom*, with Rose Friedman (University of Chicago Press, Chicago and London, 1962). The theory of the "technostructure" is found in John Kenneth Galbraith's, *The New Industrial State* (Houghton Mifflin, Boston, 1967; 4th edition 1985).

Barbara and John Ehrenreich's "The Professional-Managerial Class" is very good on the general history and sociology of this class, but neither they nor their critics comprehend the essential role of the modern corporation in its formation. The Ehrenreich essay, along with several interesting reactions to it, can be found in Pat Walker, ed., *Between Capital and Labor* (South End Press, Boston, 1979).

Throughout this study I have generally relied for quantitative data on two publications by the U.S. Department of Commerce. *The Statistical Abstract of the United States* is—or was until recently—published annually. It is cross-indexed with a volume that accumulates and, in effect, compares these figures for longer time spans, called *Historical Statistics of the United States*, which is revised and brought up to date every several years. So much information is available in these volumes and so well-indexed is it that I have rarely found it necessary to use more specialized sources for gross quantitative information.

The IWW was formed in Chicago in 1905. For the next decade and a half, it was an important influence in U.S. industrial and labor developments. It was eventually suppressed by the U.S. government, particularly in the second administration of Woodrow Wilson (1917–1921). But the "Wobblies," as they are called, remain an important influence in working-class and radical circles because of their unequalled militance, their songs, their

martyrs, their legends, and, perhaps, because they best embody what appears
to be a central political and social tradition of the U.S. working class—a
kind of radical individualism mixed with quasi-syndicalist theories of
community. One must also, paradoxically, note that the IWW has had an
important effect on the Irish, the Australian, and several other labor
movements. Melvin Dubovsky, *We Shall Be All: A History of the Industrial
Workers of the World* (University of Illinois Press, Champaign, 1988) is now
the standard study of the Wobblies.

I owe the conception of a second industrial revolution to Peter Drucker,
The Age of Discontinuity: Guidelines to Our Changing Society (Harper and
Bros., New York, 1968). Alfred Marshall's *Principles of Economics* (Macmillan,
London and New York, 1930) has already been cited. It remains a curious
historical phenomenon that the theoretical perfection of pure free-market
analysis, by Marshall, W. Stanley Jevons, Leon Walras, and the Austrian
school (making simultaneous and, apparently, independent discoveries in
the field of marginalist economics), awaited the prior development of business
firms that have considerable command and control powers in economic
events. In this the "free market" reminds one of Roman Catholic saints,
who are normally canonized only after their deaths.

The naval arms race of the last part of the century is, of course, parent
to today's international arms race and arms market. Stephen Roskills' *Naval
Policy Between the Wars* (Walker, New York, 1968) and Peter Padfield's *The
Battleship Era* (David McKay, New York, 1972) provide information and
perspective often lacking in the more politicized literature about these
developments.

For labor history and debates in the period under discussion in the text,
I found the following helpful in piecing together a coherent account: Samuel
Yellen and Katherine Stone have already been cited. Charles Gulick's old
(1924) *Labor Policy of the United States Steel Corporation* (AMS Press, New
York, 1968) is invaluable. Selig Perlman's *A Theory of the Labor Movement*
(Augustus M. Kelley, New York, 1928) is the old bible of conservative trade
union history and theory. Like so many books that are characteristically
cited but not read, this one is worth reading as an important ideological
document of its era. Edward Greer's *Big Steel: Black Politics and Corporate
Power in Gary, Indiana* (Monthly Review Press, New York, 1979) contains
much useful information and analysis about "welfare capitalism." *Eugene
Debs: A Biography* (originally entitled *The Bending Cross*), by Ray Ginger
(Macmillan, New York, 1962) and the newer *Eugene V. Debs: Citizen and
Socialist*, by Nick Salvatore (University of Illinois Press, Champaign, 1982)
are the most important biographies of that central figure in the U.S. labor
history of the early corporate era. James Weinstein's fine *The Corporate
Ideal in the Liberal State: 1900-1918* (Beacon Press, Boston, 1968) covers

part of the transformation of the old "robber barons" into a more sophisticated political class and group.

Why Is There No Socialism in the United States? raises a question that is a perennial puzzle to students of U.S. society. Werner Sombart's turn-of-the-century book with that title has been subsequently reissued (International Arts and Sciences Press, White Plains, 1976). Perlman's *Theory* continues the discussion. More recently, there is Louis Hartz's *The Liberal Tradition in America: An Interpretation of American Political Thought Since the Revolution* (Harcourt, Brace and World, New York, 1955). See John H. Laslett and Seymour M. Lipset, eds., *Failure of a Dream? Essays in the History of American Socialism* (University of California Press, Berkeley, 1984) for a wide selection of the debate. The work of the writers cited, as well as that of Daniel Bell and Ralf Dahrendorf, build on Sombart's answer to the question. As the question currently rests, it is cast somewhat as follows: The historic socialist movement of the past century found its real quarrel with the remnants of feudalism and not, as it itself imagined, with capitalism. Consequently, where capitalist *democracy* had already triumphed, as here, the socialist movement was aborted. Moreover, it is now appended, the decline of the European parties of the far left, once so powerful, is a measure of the modernization of European societies, that is, the gradual victory of capitalist democracy over feudal social, political, and economic remnants.

This literature, as is evident, equates democracy and capitalism, although in truth modern capitalism up to the end of World War II generally preferred royal, aristocratic, military, or quasi-fascist dictatorships to democratic governments. Even in the postwar world, the capitalist democracies have generally preferred nondemocratic governments for their wards and dependencies, though that may be (very) slowly changing.

3

Private and Corporate Property

Basic assumptions are, by definition, ideas that we just take for granted. As a result, they can also be ideas that we cling to long after they have become obsolete. "Private property" offers a case in point. The contemporary wisdom is that "private property" is—and ever ought to be—the foundation of U.S. society, but, as I shall show, it has long been superseded by a newer kind of collective property based in corporate form. Ironically, the modern producer corporation, thought to be the very quintessence of modern private property, has actually been introducing this new property system and forming the new classes and systems of class relationships based upon it. To grasp these fundamental changes it will be helpful to consider somewhat more closely than is the custom just what private property is, how we think about it, and, of greatest importance, the kind of social class structure we normally associate with it.

Property as Private Property

Consider from the most elementary point of view what we mean when we speak of private property, when we speak, for instance, of someone's owning a piece of land. Four things seem to be involved in the ownership.

1. The land is in the actual *possession and use* of the owner or, at the discretion of the owner, is in the possession and use of someone else. How the land is used or not used is wholly within the power of the owner and subject to his or her will. The property in question is treated as a direct extension of the owner's person, like an eye or a limb.

2. The owner is in possession and use of any *yield* of the land, such as a crop, minerals, water, or timber rights, as the case may be. He or she can make other discretionary arrangements (renting, leasing, loaning, etc.) involving the yield.

73

3. The owner may *alienate* the land, that is, may sell it for cash or barter it away, give it as a gift to another, or bequeath it through a will.

4. There is a political authority that establishes, recognizes, and enforces a system of property *titles* to the land, as well as procedures for their transfer from one owner to another. Corresponding to this system of titles, there is a converse system of liabilities; that is, a degree of responsibility is imposed on the owner by the legal authority to use his or her property only within the rules of the established property system.

We are so used to thinking in property terms that all of the listed points seem, even upon momentary reflection, "natural" and "normal." Yet the property system they describe is, historically speaking, of fairly recent invention and did not even represent the dominant form of property until well after 1800; moreover, even now, it is not that widespread. For example, in Great Britain, the nation that more than any other gave rise to the modern institution of private property, there are to this day many restrictions stemming from feudal times that limit the rights of an owner (the first attribute listed above) over his or her property. For example, British courts recognize and British hiking clubs are militant in the exercise of rights of passage across land that is to all other effects and purposes private property. In short, the owner *must* grant passage through what is otherwise his or her private property.

In the United States those four attributes usually describe not merely the theory of private property but also its actual functioning. But, even here, they were brought to literal realization only in the last decades leading up to the Civil War. In truth then, the *private* property system—however "natural" it appears to us—is only about a century and a half old.

The "modern" private property system that evolved during the late eighteenth and early nineteenth centuries differed considerably from the preceding property systems. Three differences are particularly noteworthy: First, property rights that had previously rested almost entirely in customs and in practices hallowed by time tended to be replaced by a system of explicit property codes based either on the common-law decisions of judges or on statutory enactments. "Private property" is primarily a legal concept and private property as an institution is very much a legal phenomenon. In that respect, the private property system that came to full development in the middle of the last century made for a veritable revolution in society because it tended to relegate customary property rights and practices to the historical dustbin.

There is another legal dimension as well. It bears on the role of the political authority. On the one hand, the state-created and state-enforced system of titles differentiates legitimate possession and use of property from mere theft, certainly an issue of substantial importance to property owners. But at the same time, private property emerged from a property system in which the legal authority (in Britain, the throne) had long claimed extensive rights to confiscate, regulate, transfer, tax, and otherwise dispose over the possessions of subjects. The modern legal concept of private property has been developed to restrict and regulate the rights of the state over the owner's property. In other words, in a private property system, the distinction "public" versus "private" is utterly basic to the economy and social organization. They represent two different worlds. We often think of the doctrine of laissez-faire as an antisocial movement among *businesspeople* in the last century. In fact, it was the central movement of *property owners* seeking to perfect and bring into full flower the newer, *private* property system that was replacing what they thought were only backward, feudal holdovers.

Second, the doctrine and practices of private property have distorted the way in which we think about economics and related matters. The legal and social world picture built around private property largely concerned land—so-called real property—and this has deeply affected our ideas about property. As argued above, "property" is a shorthand for a complex relationship among people, possessions, and the political authority, but we tend to fetishize it, to think of it purely and simply as "things," erasing as it were the social and political dimensions from our minds.

The third characteristic is that we see property as *private* property, that is, as the exclusive property of a single person. This is straightforward enough when an actual person owns something, such as a field. The influence of ideology and of the legal framework comes in when we have to deal with situations in which two or more persons share ownership. For corporate law this clearly is a major issue, but historically it has been dealt with in a peculiarly distorted way.

Very formally speaking, the law has tended to reduce all the possible cases of ownership to only three forms. There is the "normal" case in which a single person is the owner; if the property is a business that is called a single proprietorship. But for multiple ownership the law recognizes two further ways of dealing with property rights. There has evolved an elaborate body of law dealing with partnerships in which the rights over the property in question are shared. As one might imagine, the difficulties that can crop up when two, three, or two or three hundred partners get into quarrels would be more than formidable. Thus the private property system eventually evolved a concept, that of a corporation.

Here is where the peculiarity arises. A modern corporate enterprise, no matter how elaborate, no matter how large and how varied in its activities is conceived of in the law as a *single legal person*. This means that a corporation itself—above and beyond its stockholders—has independent standing before the courts, can sue or be sued, is protected by the law as if it were a person, can own and dispose over property, and so on. It has all the constitutional and other legal rights and protections you and I enjoy.

The modern legal framework for the corporation was only "invented" in the last decades of the nineteenth century, reminding us again that the complex economic undertakings of the present-day corporation are historically novel. The previously existing world of private property was, basically, content to live with proprietorships and partnerships. Corporations existed but were relatively uncommon, generally operating in areas of interest peculiar to government, although thought inappropriate to and unnecessary for "private" ventures. Then, when the older private property system finally had to contend with elaborate undertakings involving the property of innumerable "partners," it reached back into its own past, seeking for guidance from the familiar: Thus did it develop the doctrine that a corporation was a single legal person. In that way, all the rights associated with a single property owner were suddenly and totally granted to the corporations. We can see a certain magical quality to this solution, but, as the doctrine of laissez-faire was then so powerful, no other legal way of depicting the corporations would at the time have enabled them to so thoroughly exclude government and the public from their private affairs.

This "personal" dimension adds a large measure of specious ideology to our root ideas about property. Purely private or personal property is, in a real sense, a historical fiction. The history of property, as Daniel Bell has pointed out, is a history of family property. This was as true yesterday as it was two hundred or two thousand years ago. To understand this point one has to step back from the hurly-burly world of property as we see it in action every day and look instead to the social forces and groups that shaped and gained advantage from the evolution of our ideas and institutions dealing with property. Bell's point is that property of socially significant size or historical duration, property large enough or long-lived enough to shape and alter customs, the law itself, the political process, the social system, and so on was invariably property belonging to families, not just to individuals. Thus we speak not of the fortune of Lorenzo the Magnificent but of the Medici family; not of this or that Mellon but of the Mellon fortune. Of course, people still think of John D. Rockefeller, Jr., as the prototypical owner of a fortune but the Rockefeller fortune and influence hardly died with that old scoundrel; it continues under the extended Rockefeller clan today. In fact, even John D.'s immense personal fortune was amassed in part with the help of strategic marriages and other family connections.

I do not mean, by the way, to suggest that the history of property is solely the history of great family fortunes. The concept of family property as a social force simply uses the names of the greatest, richest, and most prominent families as a shorthand for a much wider phenomenon. The picture we associate with a society rooted in private property would show a society dominated by many property-holding families, some very rich, some of ample means, and some in the process of going to the poorhouse. It follows in this way of looking at things that the longer-run economic arrangements within such a society represent arrangements of advantage and convenience within and between families. For example, the merger movement of the turn of the century, which created the trusts (forerunners of today's corporations), is often portrayed by historians as the outcome of a rivalry among the Morgan, Rockefeller, Harriman, Moore, and Carnegie *interests*, not just those individual men. The interest in question refers to other men and other families, such as Harkness, Pratt, Flagler, and Aldrich, whose property was allied to or commingled with that of a dominant man or family, in this case, John D. Rockefeller. And, in general, a society founded on the institution of private property is a society in which family property considerations are extremely important. It is a society in which rivalries and alliances between propertied families are the stuff of high politics and of social mores. To this day there is a group of historians and political scientists who are convinced that the most telling way to study modern society is through an investigation of the links between propertied families, particularly the wealthiest ones. In my view we must break decisively with all of this familiar, "natural" social lore and instead try to see and to understand the workings of the now dominant and yet still evolving corporate property system.

Collective Property and Corporate Form

Probably the most striking, even dramatic feature of the corporate property system is that social relations themselves, not merely things and their titles, now appear in property form, generally as the property of this or that corporate institution. Corporate form, both as it appears within a specific corporation and as a broad organizing social relationship, provides a case in point.

In the modern corporation the complex arrangement I call corporate form involves a highly structured relationship among top management; the middle managerial, professional, and technical group; and the workers. That relationship is itself a productive resource, as much so and likely even more so than the physical relationship of the lathe to the stock or the mold to the pour. Initially, I simply defined it as a relationship among the three groups based on a coordinate three-way division of authority, role, and reward. But I want to show that corporate form is also a still-developing, collective property structure, the dominant structure reshaping the modern property system. For that reason, and not incidentally because it will make property issues somewhat less abstract, we should examine fairly closely the new property relations within corporate form as they have emerged within the corporation itself. This will provide the basis for an orderly description of the wider changes in the property system that are associated with it.

Clearly, corporate form is a significant piece of property, in fact and as we've seen, in many ways a more important and fruitful piece of property than the sort found in the family or finance capital forms of property holding. An obvious group of questions follows. Who is in possession and use of that relationship? Who is entitled to the yield from that relationship? Who can alienate that relationship itself or specific individual and group relationships within it? Who is recognized by the political authority to hold title to the right to do all of the above, excluding all others? To dispose over that relationship is to "own" a consequential piece of property indeed. But no individual holds those rights nor can their ownership be ultimately traced to any family or families. They are exercised by a collectivity, top management, which to all intents and purposes exercises the classic rights of property over those relationships. Here, a structured, dynamic *social* relationship is the "property" of top management.

Moreover, it is *collectively* owned by top management. We know from Sloan's pioneering work that immediate ownership attributes are exercised by groups of managers. (We will deal shortly with the position of stockholders who claim pro rate shares of the corporation as their private property.) In Sloan's scheme, copied everywhere, top management has an essentially collective style of work, which is to say, exercises classic property attributes collectively over what are in themselves collective forms of property. Their functional relationships to collective property, such as the middle-element– worker relation, are structurally similar to the functional relationships between an old-fashioned private property owner and his or her physical property.

In light of the foregoing, we can simplify the discussion enormously if we see the essence of collective property as consisting of ensembles of social relationships that own other social relationships—not individuals (or families) owning things, but collectives of people exercising classic property rights over other individuals and collectives of people. In the present case, top management for example, exercises classic property rights over the relationship between the workers and the middle element, that is, it has possession and use of the relationship, can alienate all or parts of it, has possession and use of its yield, and is recognized in all of the foregoing by the political authority. But, at the same time, top management is a social relationship between individuals playing roles that are fully defined by their relationship to the corporation. As I think is now generally understood, the common candidate for a top management job comes to that point because of his or her historical and anticipated contributions to the company and not solely or even primarily because he or she is wealthy, well-connected, or well-born. Hence it follows that top management is likewise a social ensemble structured by the corporation and not the product of an external property system.

Top management exercises the classic rights of property over the physical, commercial, and human assets of the company. Moreover, it is now also widely recognized that human assets, not the plant and equipment, make up the most dynamic and important element in corporate success—thus the significance of the formulation "ensembles of social relationships that own other social relationships."

We are dealing here with property relationships in a *collectivized*, not a private-property system. I want to stress that one cannot treat this situation merely as an extension of private property as, for example, Berle and Means wrongly tried to do. Collective-property forms are not really reducible to private property. In other words, by analyzing backward from owned property through the owning relationships we do not eventually find individuals exercising individual property rights as the ultimate basis for the whole structure.

Surprisingly enough, well before the turn of the century Marx (and, later, following his lead, Hilferding) got much closer to understanding this historical shift in property relations. Both men were struck by the importance of the then newly emerging joint-stock companies. Both saw that private property, as they knew it, was in the process of giving way to a different property form. But both remained within an intellectual framework that didn't quite encompass the radical quality of the change from private to collective property forms. That is, neither recognized that the emergence of collective property forms *also* changes the class and social structure so that collective property is not just private property now controlled by groups or institutions but a new kind of property embedded in a new class structure.

It appears that both Marx and Hilferding failed to make this important intellectual jump because they assumed that the emergence of collective or social property would have to await socialism, collective ownership by society as a whole. Quite evidently, modern collective forms of property are not collective in that larger and ultimate sense. They are forms, I will argue, through which *classes*, not individuals and families, make and exercise property claims—a big step beyond private property but still a long way from collective ownership by society. On grounds of pure logic this last step would require a classless society, as both Marx and Hilferding would agree.

The subject of collective property is complex, I grant, and the final disposition of ownership questions awaits my showing the limited role and property claims of stockholders in this new collective system. Essentially, my argument in behalf of the existence of a collective property system rests on the answer to the question, Who owns corporate form? Notice, this is a different question from, Who owns the corporation? If we answer the latter in the conventional way, we say that owners, that is, the stockholders own it. But if we leave the matter here, the crucial historical and functional differences among capitalist-ownership, finance capitalism, and corporate form are erased. On the other hand, if the system based upon corporate form is, as I have argued, capitalistically superior to one based on simple family capitalism or the more advanced finance capitalism, then those crucial differences must be traced to determine the differences in the social formations that control the corporation as a property form, to what end, and with what interests. Entrepreneurial capitalism rests on the interests, ultimately, of private-property-owning, rivalrous families. Finance capitalism—in retrospect a brief transitional form—rests on relatively small coteries of "insider" individuals and families. But modern corporate capitalism rests ultimately on a class owning and disposing over its common property as a class.

The difference between corporate capitalism and other forms doesn't lie in narrow questions of industrial organization. Berle and Means fall into this trap, resting their analysis of the modern corporation on the differences between entrepreneur-managed firms and professionally managed firms—their famous problem of "the separation of ownership from control." Much subsequent investigation (and obfuscation) of the corporate world and the society associated with it has been conducted within this straitjacket; the work of both Galbraith and Dahrendorf is similarly handicapped.

In our day, corporate form is not just a phenomenon of elementary corporate organization. Sloan, perhaps, or Taylor made only organizational adjustments, but those simple adjustments have helped in the ensuing years to create stable industrial classes, each with a considerable social momentum of its own as well as a momentum stemming from its interaction with the other two groups. Corporate form is thus more than an organizational scheme; it is a property form.

Indeed, this is confirmed when we look at the property relationships of the other two groups that constitute corporate form: the middle element and the workers. Collective property is property "owned" by groups, where the group itself exercises the attributes of ownership. It is a form of property singularly appropriate to the large, social-scale institutions characteristic of a modern economy. Generally, these groups exercise property attributes from their essentially functional position within the institution.

Up to the present, the role of the law has not been to regulate the relations of these groups but to codify their actual practice into precedents.

Notwithstanding the strictures of private property, top management owns the modern corporation because it owns corporate forms. It exercises these property attributes because it occupies the strategic, central position in the corporation or, equivalently, because it disposes over the relationships making up corporate form. The top managers also own the *yield* of the corporation, not in the private property sense that it becomes theirs to consume but in the precise sense that they apportion the company's surplus of income over material costs to the various groups that contend for it. These include the middle element clamoring for higher salaries and for bigger bonuses and the workers looking for better contracts or new benefits. The stockholders are in the same boat with the other groups, too, because their share of the profits is determined by top management.

Already we can see in this an important limitation over the private-property rights of the stockholders. Top management determines, for example, how much of the profits to retain for investment within the business and how much to pay out in dividends. It is clear that this division of corporate proceeds is closely tied up with the further division of corporate monies to wages, salaries, and bonuses. In no case does top management have an entirely free hand, but in every case it has considerable discretion. Here, I would argue, is one of the points where, as I mentioned earlier, we find overlapping legitimate claims against collective property. One exercises ownership of the property, here the income of the corporation, not by taking and consuming it ("capitalist-owner") but by being in the position to adjudicate these overlapping and conflicting claims.

The middle managerial, professional, and technical group also lays property claims against the corporation, claims that rest on its unique and irreplaceable functional role in the company. The technology monopoly held by the middle element functions as its modern form of property and is de facto and de jure recognized as such within the institutional world. Certainly, modern technology can neither be employed nor reproduced without the cooperation of the middle element as an existing social formation. In an older era, for example, the owner of a business "owned" its technology in the sense that he himself could employ it as he or she wished and was dependent on no other specific person or group to do so. Now, however, the accumulated knowledge and technique of the modern world is in the actual possession of a distinct industrial social formation—the middle managerial, technical, and professional group—and can neither be socially used to productive effect nor socially reproduced without its cooperation.

The word "socially" is absolutely crucial to my formulation. A specific engineer or manager can easily be fired by a corporation, but he or she can only be replaced by another equivalently trained engineer or manager, by a person with the same professional training and a similar professional orientation. A company that chronically hired incompetent managers or unqualified engineers would soon be shunned by competent, well-trained people, and this would lead in time to a radical decline in its fortunes. Thus trained managers and qualified engineers enjoy a form of collective claim over the use of parts of the corporate property, that is, those parts that conform to their professional training and expertise. In this sense we can say that the middle element owns a functional monopoly over technology within the corporation. It is a collective ownership because, as indicated, it redounds not to the individual per se but to the individual as a member of a certain profession.

The middle element, however, can exercise its monopoly of technology only *within* corporate form and *subordinate* to capitalist criteria of profitability, because only under such conditions can it be commingled with its necessary productive complements, labor power and physical and organizational resources. No less important, to reproduce this monopoly it needs the cooperation of another institution also characterized by corporate form: the modern university (see Chapter 4). In other words, technique or technology is not the private property of the middle element because it can only be employed as well as reproduced within corporate form. And it is a collective rather than individual property because the individual manager's or engineer's status, function, and reward follows upon his or her membership in a certain profession.

The argument that the middle element "owns" technology as property rests then on the following: it is in de facto possession and use of it, but only within corporate form; it can and does alienate its use to the corporation, but cannot do so elsewhere; its titles to technology are socially recognized by government, industry, and the academic world. In fact, the steady growth of professionalism as a social and industrial phenomenon spreads and enforces that recognition. This is the very point of professional accreditation: The middle element seeks to institutionalize everywhere the recognition of and the rights due its peculiar form of property. Thus an accountant must be certified, an engineer must be a graduate of a recognized engineering school and certified by the appropriate professional association, and so on. This in turn entitles the middle-element technologist, individually and collectively, to a proprietary right against the fruits of technology's employment—but not as a private-property claim, not as an exclusive right. This is where Sloan's compensation scheme comes in: The middle element doesn't lay a claim against the corporation per se but against its *profitability*.

Middle management exercises a property claim against the corporate surplus in the form of a claim to a direct share in the profits. This is normally exerted through bonuses, stock options, or other compensation plans. The historical evolution of modern technology into a de facto monopoly of a distinct social productive formation, the (middle) managerial, professional, and technical class, socially enforces and legitimates this claim.

The position of modern workers in the corporate world also calls into question the older juridical and political economic distinction between the propertied and the propertyless. *The actual and the legal recognition of trade unions within modern corporate industry implies a property claim on the part of those workers against its surplus.* That is, workers can claim no authority against how corporate property is used or alienated, as can the other two corporate groups. But they do make a claim against the company's resulting prosperity, particularly against its surplus. If profits are higher and growth is more rapid, they will feel entitled to bigger wage and benefit gains, and management and government recognize their claim as legitimate. Here again, we are dealing with a property claim that is only partially codified in the law. But both the industrial reality and the now fifty-year-old system of statutory industrial relations grant to unionized workers a socially enforceable claim against increased corporate surpluses arising out of increased productivity. This property right also passes over to non-unionized workers, but only through the change in social customs; that is, as corporate property structures and features become more and more the social norm, even workers who are formally outside the corporate system come to be entitled to a "share" in the prosperity of corporate society.

The workers' claim differs from the claim made by upper management in that the top managers actually make the decisions that divide the surplus among reinvestment uses, bonuses and other property income to employees, dividends to stockholders, and raises in wages and salaries. The workers' claim is exerted only within that context.

The workers' claim against the surplus also differs from that of the middle element in several fundamental ways. The middle element's claim against the surplus is customarily tied to the size of the surplus by an actual formula (within the management compensation plan). For the middle or lower manager this represents a specific claim against the surplus, although one upper management administers with some discretionary room. It is a subordinated claim against the property but no less real for all that. In stark contrast, U.S. capital has historically resisted granting a similar specific claim to its unionized workers; in the auto and some other industries, however, this may now be changing under a newer pay system that substitutes profit-sharing bonus payments for incremental rises in base pay. In any event, U.S. capital has long recognized the workers' generic claim against the surplus, its actual form and amount to be worked out later. That "worked out later" is the collective-bargaining process. This also implies that workers' claims, unlike those of upper management and the middle element are not normally recognized in an annual time frame but rather against the longer-term growth in the size and productivity of the corporation.

Finally, property claims against the corporate surplus for all of management are conceived of and commonly function to bestow rights on individual persons. If one is in the management echelon, one has a contractual entitlement to qualify for a bonus or other reward, the amount to be calculated in whatever way it is calculated for others; thus one has a limited but definite personal claim. By contrast, worker claims—which come normally in the form of secular increases in wages and benefits—are laid by the workers as a group, usually through a union.

Workers make these claims solely as workers, not as individual, juridical persons. Only the *collective* worker has rights against the corporation and, more broadly, the corporation basically deals only with collective labor power, not the individual worker. Often the collective worker is the union. In fact, U.S. law treats unions as juridical persons: The corporate "person" makes a contract with the union "person." The individual worker then has only procedural rights within that framework. That is, he or she has only such rights as are conferred by being a member of the union, and, as it happens, these are as a rule limited to procedural rights only. Thus an individual worker has no right to a raise but *does* have a right to have his or her wages increased by the same procedures as other union members.

In this account of modern capitalist property, the three industrial *classes* each lay distinct property claims against capitalist property and its surplus. Although these are relatively new property relations, they are still evolving and have considerable historical momentum behind them. They represent a hierarchy of claims, but none is exclusive. Upper management lays claim to own corporate form and therefore to preside over the broad direction of the business. Included in this is immediate authority over the division of the surplus as among specifically capitalist (reinvestment) uses, dividends to stockholders, and property claims by all of management, including itself. The middle element claims immense discretionary authority over the employment of technology, including in this a dictatorial authority over the workers. And it claims a "junior partner's" share of the surplus. These eventuate in a set of personal rights against the property or the surplus or both, but these rights are exerted and enforced collectively, often through the profession. The unionized work force exercises a lower-ranked, merely generic property claim against the growth of the company and its surplus, and this claim results only in rights for the collective worker. This is the context within which in recent years management has demanded that workers share in bad corporate times through give-backs and concessions. Thus we can see that dynamic social and productive relationships—not just "things"—are among the most important forms of modern property and that in this century a distinct hierarchy of nonexclusive group or class claims has developed that are normally levied against that property.

As I have suggested, the law still lags behind most of these developments. That is to be expected. Historians of law appreciate that the legal system generally follows and codifies the way things are done; it is only in countries like our own with a written constitution that we can long entertain the fancy that the legal system *creates* the way we do things. On the other hand, the law has not tarried in certain areas. Surely, in consumer law, affirmative action and antidiscrimination law, environmental law, and labor law, to name the most prominent areas, the legal framework has long since formally acknowledged that persons who are not (private-property) owners of businesses may make legally enforceable claims about how that property is used or not used, what social relationships are permitted within it and what not, and so forth. Thus in the strict descriptive sense it is wrong to characterize the U.S. property system as one of "private property." We already live in a mixed property system in which private and collective elements can be found together.

These new rights are rights over the disposal and use of property and are therefore property rights, but they do not reside exclusively with some nominal "owner"; his or her rights over the property must be shared with others. As we've already seen, one of the hallmarks of modern property ownership, unlike private property, is that it confers inclusive not exclusive rights. In antidiscrimination law, for example, certain social relationships, previously thought fully at the discretion of the owner of a business property, are outlawed, and groups of individuals have conferred on them legal standing that, at least in that narrow area, puts their rights over those of the nominal property owner. Here, the nominal property owner is forced to share his or her rights not with this or that named individual or group of individuals but with certain broad categories of people: the elderly, racial and ethnic minorities, the handicapped, women, and so forth.

In the property system now evolving in corporate society, multiple groups make overlapping, nonexclusive claims against the property, claims that are adjusted not only by appeal to the courts (as would be the case in a private property system) but in other socially recognized and enforceable ways. In labor-management relations, for example, the courts even eschew a primary role in governing these often stormy matters. Instead, a special administrative law system, called the National Labor Relations Board (NLRB) has been set up to which the regular courts defer. Sometimes the NLRB settles disputes in a manner reminiscent of the older common-law courts, rendering substantive decisions to disputes. But its primary role is to establish a framework of rules and procedures within which property disputes between labor and management may be settled by the bilateral action of the parties themselves. The resulting decisions, which may involve hundreds of millions of dollars, then have all the force of law, though no court and no legislature have enacted them.

Why is this reality not trumpeted forth by the legal profession and the powers that be? We have the anomaly of a corporate society that refuses to recognize the newer property system that in fact constitutes it and instead doggedly hides behind the rapidly disappearing smoke of "private property." The answer is not hard to discover. The hallmark of private property is the exclusive right it confers on the owner. To acknowledge that collective property is the most economically prominent kind of property and that it is rapidly growing in importance would destroy one of the main defenses corporations and other large "private" institutions employ to keep unions, minorities, the elderly, environmentalists, government, women, and other interested groups at arm's length. "Private property" is not the reality in the United States; as a description of things it is increasingly inaccurate, often just wrongheaded. But as an *ideology* defending entrenched privilege, wealth, private corners of power and influence, it helps to slow down and often stop the claims of outsiders.

We often don't see this ideology at work because we don't fully appreciate how extensively the new corporate-property system has developed. That is, in reality as opposed to ideology, the rights of present-day property owners to enjoy, for example, possession and use of their property has already been sharply limited. We currently live in a society whose reality is constituted by collective property forms, thus a society in which multiple groups make important claims over the use, disposition, and surplus of various properties. The conflicts arising in these multiple claims are the very fabric of the contemporary class conflict; this is the working out of the deep contradiction between the intrinsically social, institutionalized forces of production and the attempt, enforced by a laggard culture and social and legal structure, to deny that already deeply influential reality. Thus it is hardly surprising that the more privileged classes resort to traditional ideological barriers to defeat or at least hold back these emerging claims over the main social and economic institutions. The doctrine of private property is now an old doctrine, hallowed by time, well understood by all. Thus the paradox "private property" is the great barrier behind which the institutions of collective property and their privileged classes try to pursue their collective aims without undue disturbance by outsiders.

Who Owns the Corporation?

There is no question but that the formal legal ownership of the modern corporation rests with its stockholders—and if we were dealing with private property the discussion of ownership would end right there. But, as we've seen, it would be a sterile discussion. That is why the concept of collective property is so critical. Without it we really cannot give a useful account of the ownership issue.

In the contemporary system of collective property, individual stockholders are simply one among several groups that make legitimate and overlapping claims on the corporation. Unlike top management and the middle element, stockholders make no direct claim on how corporate property is used or alienated. Instead, like the workers, their claim is for the most part limited to a claim against the surplus, that is, against the increase in corporate worth that they receive as an increase in securities prices and as dividends. In fact, their claim for dividends does not even come first in the hierarchy of claims against the company. The majority of corporations retain most of their after-tax profits for reinvestment within the business; a 2:1 ratio between these retained earnings and paid-out dividends is common and is the approximate long-term average.

The idea that the stockholders control the business has long since been dropped by most knowledgeable observers. Even in the United States, Berle and Means merely brought the legal and economics professions abreast of what was already widely known by socialists, trade unionists, and reformers. Nowadays it is broadly accepted among those who study these matters that the top management of a corporation is really in control of the property and can often, in fact, prevent the nominal owners from interfering with them. That's obviously true if we are talking of the small- to mid-sized stockholder, for we can read of the latter's frustrations in virtually every newspaper report that devotes more than a single paragraph to a stockholder meeting. Small stockholders cannot control collective property. When they try to play the market like the big operators rather than just enjoying their dividends and stock appreciation, they are invariably fleeced.

The issue of who owns the corporation? may not seem so clear, however, when we move away from the small stockholder. Most outstanding stock in the United States is owned by only a relative handful of people. Perhaps 3 to 4 percent of the population own the great bulk of all privately held shares. But if one follows the financial pages it soon becomes manifest that even the largest stockholders are no longer by themselves a major force in corporate circles. Reviewing various takeover bids, attempts to oust incumbent managements or force fundamental changes in management policy, one sees that private stockholders, even extremely wealthy and influential ones cannot do the job by themselves. Successful takeovers, for example, require the cooperation, even if only passive, of the financial community and can be essayed only by another corporate management. A private person may start a takeover bid, even remain the key figure in it, but unless he or she can gain the support and active help of various corporations (such as bank trust departments or brokerage houses) and unless the rest of the institutional investor world assists in the takeover or at least remains passive, the bid will simply fail. In the same way, individuals or even individual managements that flout the sensibilities of the corporate financial world will be brought to heel. There are any number of cogent examples of this in modern corporate history, as, for instance, the ouster of Howard Hughes from control of TWA in the late 1950s in spite of his holding outright a majority of the stock. Or, more striking, the 1986 episode in which the financial community forced the Hunt brothers, billionaires in their own personal right, to accept sharp restrictions in the exercise of their own property.

It is true, as we have already had occasion to mention, that in an earlier period of corporate history many large corporations were effectively in the control of a single family, like the Rockefellers, or even a single person, like Henry Ford. Moreover, certain financial institutions, like J. P. Morgan and Company (later the Morgan Guaranty) and the old Chase Bank, the creatures respectively of the Morgan and Rockefeller dynasties, exerted control over scores of corporations, this control based on their holding large blocks of stock in the corporations in question and exerted by their nominees on the various boards of directors. During the first decade of this century the elder Morgan controlled so many companies in this way that a special word was coined to describe it: They were "Morganized." The kinship of this form of corporate control with the finance capitalism Hilferding described is quite evident. Morganizing, however, turned out to be an ineffective form of management primarily because the technological, organizational, and marketing complexity of the modern corporation made it increasingly difficult for "outside" directors to be able to preside successfully over the business. The "inside" directors, those who actually served in top management as well as on the board, had all the advantage; they were devoting full time to it, had more and better information, worked together, and so on. Moreover, the power of the outside directors lay in the corporation's dependence on the outside financial world for capital funds. But as the corporation evolved, its ability to earn monies sufficient to pay for its own growth eventually completed the triumph of top management in gaining effective de facto property rights over the affairs of the corporation.

The concept of a collective property enables us to express the facts of the corporate ownership case succinctly. The modern corporation is owned, in virtually every meaningful sense of the word, by its own top management, for it exercises the classic rights of property over the corporation, through its control over the firm. Within that control relationship, top management exercises the rights of property insofar as they can be for a collective property operating at a fully social scale. In fact, Sloan's innovations in corporate organization marked a vast step forward in the institution of collective property because they permitted the owners of the corporation, top management, to materially improve their own ability to exercise the four classic property attributes.

Top management owns the corporation and, within the limits of its own evolving effectiveness, controls the other activities of and determines the rewards of the other groups involved in the corporate universe. But corporate property is a collective form of property and ownership there is rarely exclusive of other groups. In the present context the top management of an individual corporation does not have an exclusive and unconditional right to exercise these property attributes; they are shared with what I call the "corporate public."

By the "corporate public" I refer to the ensemble of all those men and women who play a top management role in a major corporation or allied institution. These people constitute the active capitalist class and the primary capitalist class of modern corporate property. The immediate corporate public of an individual corporation would comprise several different groups. The outside directors (i.e., those directors who are not part of the top management team within that corporation) would obviously be included, as would the top management of those institutional investors who hold large blocks of the corporation's stock, the top lawyers who handle the corporation's business, and the management of its accounting firm and of the banks it does business with. The corporate public would usually include the managements of the firm's main suppliers and customers, leading figures in its trade association, and, often, certain government officials: from the regulatory agency if it is a regulated industry, from the Defense Department if the company plays an important role in national security, or, somewhat less likely, from the Justice Department or Securities and Exchange Commission under specific circumstances.

These different groups and the interests they bring to bear are not hard to catalog. Most outstanding corporate stock in the United States is held by institutional investors, including the trust departments of banks; insurance companies; brokerage and investment houses; mutual funds; pension plan managements; foundations, museums, universities, and other institutions; and so forth. Probably the key group here are the trust departments, for nonprofit institutions and pension plans frequently ask them to manage their stock portfolios, as do large private investors. Moreover, the trust departments tend to hold stock for shorter periods than do the insurance companies and would thus be inclined to look more critically at short-run corporate performances. Each of these institutional investors is answerable to its own corporate public and has as well a number of both practical and legal obligations incumbent upon it. They need and want reliable, effective managements in the corporations whose stock they hold, for they need steady dividends and a steady appreciation of stock values for their own purposes. If the management of the corporation whose stock is held by the investors falters in performance or if there is reason to believe that it will falter, the institutional investors will have ample motivation to move against the management, and, from the nature of the case, they will find many allies.

A relatively small handful of national law firms handles the affairs of almost all the major national corporations. These firms become and remain intimately knowledgeable about the affairs of their clients, particularly because until very recently even the largest corporations did not maintain sizable in-house law departments. Generally, the big law firms are in a position to know if scandal threatens the company, whether the top management works effectively together, and, to a degree, whether top management is on top of its job. A corporate management that fails to impress its own lawyers with its ability or rectitude is courting trouble, particularly if the legal work involves defending the corporation's management from the consequences of its own folly.

The big national corporations tend to generate their own long-run investment funds in the form of hidden "profits" and retained earnings. But they go to the banks for short-run loans, and, naturally, banks handle their accounts, too. Bankers make a point of knowing their clients' business, and in this case it would hardly be possible to remain unaware of financial difficulties almost as soon as they begin to crop up. Because the banker of a given corporation is also the banker for many others, bankers make up a central group in judging corporate performance and, of course, can rather easily become the center of an opposition group interested in ousting a sitting management.

As with the big law firms, only a handful of big accounting firms handles the business of the entire corporate sector. The nature of their business relationship necessarily leads to their being well informed. Similarly, certain government agencies, such as the Commerce Department, the Anti-Trust Division of the Justice Department, and various regulatory commissions watch over individual corporations. Although they don't normally have as intimate access either to the top people or the inner finances of the corporation in question, any hint that the government is unhappy with a corporation, especially if it involves bad publicity or the possibility of legal action, makes government disapproval a factor within the world of corporate management. Something like the same case can be made about the watchdog role of executives in the trade associations or in the National Association of Manufacturers, the Business Round Table, the U.S. Chamber of Commerce, or other business associations.

Finally, there are the outside directors. Unhappiness there, chronic difficulties in finding people to serve as directors, or the departure of an outside director from the board because he or she is troubled by some issue can be very dangerous. In fact, in recent years and because of the revelations that various corporate managements, at Mobil and Lockheed for example, were involved in bribing overseas government officials, there have been some moves to strengthen the hands of the outside directors so that they can better exercise a broad watchdog function. Such individuals are usually asked to serve on the board because they have a prestige in their own right that means that they are also well thought of in other business circles. Consequently, they are an important part of the corporation's outside public.

For the top management team of a corporation, the attitude and behavior of its immediate corporate public is of fundamental significance. In the normal course of events, each member of that corporate public remains well informed about the effectiveness of the existing top management and has pressing personal or, more commonly, institutional interests in the success of the company. Each has a widely recognized right to intervene, alone or in concert with others, *if* his or her interests are or appear to be poorly served. By definition, the corporate public is *not* part of top management of the corporation in question (though it usually serves in that capacity in other institutions). But it acts like a classic public, that is, an informed group with concrete interests, watching from a distance but with a decisive power to intervene on its own initiative. Thus a corporation's top management team is ultimately answerable to its particular corporate public.

There is a strong warrant to extrapolate the concept of a wider corporate public from this notion of a narrow one. Each big corporation generally shares several or more members of its own public with those of other companies, in the form of lawyers, trust departments, directors, and so forth. Here, the image of a single corporate public being woven from the strands of shared lawyers, accountants, outside directors, bankers, and so on is entirely appropriate. But much more important is that each corporation's immediate corporate public is similarly structured to that of the others, by the same sort of people, with the same sort of compelling institutional interests, and the same sort of capacity (and occasional need) to intervene.

The corporate public is the ultimate owner of the modern corporation. This is a collective ownership that traces back not to individual shares of stock but to the institutionalized social productive roles these people play within corporate form. The corporate public is, then, both the active and the primary capitalist class of the modern corporate-property system. Thus we speak of the corporate public as a social class and not merely as an elite with more or less parallel roles in otherwise autonomous institutions.

In the earlier capitalist era, the property-holding family was the significant unit of the capitalist class, and its economically active members were correctly seen as representatives of family interest and family property. This paradigm cannot be transferred to the modern property system based in corporate form. Here the significant unit is the upper corporate management team, which is answerable to the corporate public. Thus a class directly and collectively owns the modern corporation, exercising its ownership through top management units. In this view of the matter, upper-class society, that is, the social ensemble made up of very wealthy individuals and families, is subordinate in its interests and its influence to the active corporate public. That is to say, it is a passive and secondary player in the corporate-property system.

A corporation has, then, a fairly extended corporate public with numerous and detailed stakes in the behavior of top management and the latent ability to topple it. As indicated earlier, there is no question that the top management of a corporation exercises the attributes of collective property over its company. But it is equally true that it is watched over from a distance by a number of groups with pressing reason to pay attention to what top management is doing, ample opportunity to do so, and a number of joint (or at least overlapping) interests that potentially unite them. Obviously (and unfortunately) the corporate public is not *the* public, that is, the vast majority of all those affected in one way or another by the corporation. If anything the corporation's public is unhappiest when the larger public gets involved. But this corporate public acts the way *a* public is thought to act: alertly interested and with the potential for decisive involvement.

As is so often the case with relatively new social phenomena, the language we use to describe them is confusing because it is rooted in the past. That's why I am chary of saying, for example, that a corporation's top management exercises certain property rights *in behalf of* the corporate public that has the ultimate ability to seize those property rights and redispose over them. I don't entirely object to that way of speaking about the corporation because it does express some of the facts of the case, but only some. That method of expression leaves some residual confusion, as the modern corporate system, true to the spirit of Sloan, is both decentralized (in the form of autonomous top managements within each corporation) and coordinated (by the corporate public). In ordinary language, as Sloan himself has remarked, that appears to be a contradictory formulation. It is easier to say that the corporation is owned by its top management, always mentally adding that because the ownership of collective property is not fundamentally exclusive in nature one also always has to take into account the property claims of other groups. The corporate public is one of the groups that has property claims against the corporation; it is the ultimate power in the corporate world, but it does not exercise its power directly, except in the unique case of ousting a management. The moment this power is exercised, however, it is immediately forsworn to another, new top management group.

In addition to the corporate public and the actual individual stockholders, both the middle element and the corporate production workers also have property claims against the company. All of these claims are legitimate and socially enforceable, many overlap, none or very few is exclusive. These ideas of the exercise of ownership rights and of overlapping claims against property necessarily complement each other in the world of collective property. It becomes confusing only to the degree that one does not shed entirely the idea of a *private* property.

Bibliographical Essay

Thomas Cochran's, *Business in American Life: A History* (McGraw-Hill, New York, 1974) is good on a broad range of business and legal issues for the later part of the nineteenth century. Daniel Bell discusses family property in his *End of Ideology* (revised edition, Harvard University Press, Cambridge, 1988), among many other places. G. William Domhoff (*Who Rules America?* Prentice-Hall, Englewood Cliffs, N.J., 1967) remains among the most influential of those who argue for the contemporary importance of a *family-based* upper class. See also E. Digby Baltzell, *The Protestant Establishment: Aristocracy and Caste in America* (Vintage, New York, 1964).

In the text proper it did not seem appropriate to discuss the relationship between the corporate public and the sort of upper social class Domhoff describes. My position is that the interests and the actions of the upper capitalist social class are directly constituted by its active members, the corporate public, and not, as Domhoff holds, by the interests of upper-class society, that is, a league of families bound by various clubs, private schools, intermarriage, intertwined personal networks, and other exclusive *social* (in the narrow sense) institutions. For convenience here, let us distinguish the upper social class as identified by Domhoff from the corporate public as I identified and defined it in the text. I don't doubt that they must be distinguished and that both are important. The fundamental difference, as I see it, is that the corporate public is formed within the modern corporation itself or, to put it more concretely, the corporation rather than the property-holding family furnishes the elemental building block—the significant structural unit—of the upper class. As I suggested in the Preface and develop in subsequent chapters, these differences are basic to social theory, political analysis, and adequate historical description. Here, my view carries the implication that the upper *social* class has more a parasitical than a constituting relationship to the corporate public and that in all but the shortest time frames membership in the class and, especially, influence and prestige sufficient to play a leading role within it stem from one's active role in the aggregate corporate public. In the opposite view, the corporate public is essentially made up of representatives pursuing the interests of a social and cultural league of wealthy, socially exclusive families.

Marx's observation that capital was becoming socialized—"the capital of associated individuals," in his expression—and that this portended even more fundamental changes is found in Chapter 27, Volume 3 of *Capital* (International Publishers, New York, 1984). His prescience is regularly subject to scornful derision by "bourgeois" critics. Yet by the middle 1860s he had already noted a "transformation of the actually functioning capitalist into a mere manager, an administrator of other people's capital, and of the owner of capital into a mere owner, a money capitalist." Surely, he could at least be said to have "anticipated" Berle and Means's famous "discovery" of the separation of ownership from control by a matter of . . . sixty years.

The concept of the collective worker is further developed in my "Modern Capitalist Labor System: Going Beyond Braverman and Edwards" (*Labor Studies Papers: College of Old Westbury*, Old Westbury, N.Y., 1983, mimeo) and "The Labor System," a paper read at the Summer Conference of the Union for Radical Political Economists (Sandwich, Mass., August, 1986). See also Karl Klare, "Judicial Deradicalization of the Wagner Act and the Origins of Modern Legal Consciousness" (*Minnesota Law Review* 62 [1978]) and "Labor Law as Ideology: Toward a New Historiography of Collective Bargaining Law" (*Industrial Relations Law Journal* 4(3) [1981]), as well as Paul Weiler, "Promises to Keep: Securing Workers' Rights to Self-Organization under the NLRA" (*Harvard Law Review*, June 1983).

In general, the development and spread of the various systems of administrative law are among the most important institutional embodiments of corporate property forms. The newer ones, such as the antidiscrimination and environmental protection systems, date only from the present era and are characteristically concerned to establish entitlements in the corporate system for individuals and groups who are outside the corporate management echelon. But the older ones, dating from the Bureau of Corporations of William McKinley's and Theodore Roosevelt's time through the various agencies established in the Wilson administration and culminating in the alphabet soup of agencies under Franklin D. Roosevelt in the 1930s, often have a different point. The Federal Aviation Agency (FAA), for example, has not been particularly zealous in protecting the rights and safety of passengers, but it does force each airline to take an industry rather than a narrow company outlook. Obviously, there are some spin-offs to the public, but one of the basic thrusts of this agency, like so many administrative law bodies, is to police individual companies for the industry so that the collective-property interests of the corporate public will not be irreparably harmed by a single, willful, wayward top management team. The expression "for the industry" is perhaps deceptive, because the top personnel of each of these agencies are normally drawn from the industry the agency regulates and return to it when their "government service" is over. What we really have here is a form of industrial self-government that uses state powers to enforce its will on others. The FAA is no less part of the industry than United Airlines, Boeing, and the various metropolitan airport authorities. Here we have merely one more instance of a single government–private-sector control net that keeps the public at bay with ideological smoke about "private enterprise" and "the free market."

In passing it should be mentioned that the system of self-regulation by industry under cover of a regulatory agency seems, in retrospect, to be a transitory one. Where industry itself, as in the steel or auto industry, had managed to squeeze out the smaller firms, government assistance in regulating the industry was unnecessary. On the other hand, where the technology or economics of the industry requires it or the political influence of smaller business firms is important, the regulatory agency provides government sanction for representatives of the most powerful interests to control prices, establish standards, win subsidies, and so on. Technically speaking, any powerful outside agency can do this if it has the means to bring recalcitrant firms into line with "industry policy." For many years, the International Ladies' Garment Workers' Union so regulated the fashion-clothing industry; the Teamsters under Jimmy Hoffa were trying to win the same dominant, regulatory role in the intercity and interstate trucking industry when he disappeared. Where deregulation has occurred, as in that trucking industry, the myriad of small firms have quickly given way to national, integrated, large and rapidly growing corporations. Thus it would appear that control by regulatory agencies gives way to oligopoly whenever circumstances make the latter possible.

The trade associations for the various industries also play this role of bringing possibly wayward firms into line with the industry. Their great patron was Herbert Hoover who, as commerce secretary through the 1920s, helped organize several score of them. Hoover's claim to be a representative of private enterprise and the free market rests on his distaste for adding government officials, no matter how domesticated, to this system of industrial self-government and price regulation. I am indebted to Murray N. Rothbard for this observation ("Herbert Hoover and the Myth of Laissez-Faire," in Ronald Radosh and Murray Rothbard, eds., *A New History of Leviathan: Essays on the Rise of the American Corporate State* [E. P. Dutton, New York, 1972]). The familiar Hoover biographies tend to gloss over his pronounced "corporativist" outlook. In this respect see, for example, David Burner's *Herbert Hoover: A Public Life* (Alfred A. Knopf, New York, 1979).

Edward S. Herman's *Corporate Control, Corporate Power: A Twentieth-Century Fund Study* (Cambridge University Press, Cambridge, 1981) is a distinguished recent study reconfirming the predominance of management over stockholder control. Beth Mintz and Michael Schwartz, *The Power Structure of American Business* (University of Chicago Press, Chicago, 1985), argue for a theory of bank control over corporations. Despite a faulty thesis, the book brings together useful anecdotal material on the actual role of the big banks. In much the same vein Richard Barber's *The American Corporation: Its Power, Its Money, Its Politics* (E. P. Dutton, New York, 1970) is informative on the behavior of banks, insurance companies, foundations, trust funds, and so on within the corporate system.

4

The Ruling Class
in Corporate Society

Corporate society differs radically from those previous capitalist societies that were based upon the institution of private property. Confining our glance for the moment only to social structural differences, four of them are of paramount importance. First, the corporate public represents a far more cohesive and potentially unified class than is possible under a private-property system in which the property-holding family provides the social unit of the upper class. Second, in corporate society the upper class is allied to the multicompetent middle managerial, technical, and professional class. By contrast, previous capitalist ruling classes characteristically faced political opposition from at least part of the middle entrepreneurial classes.

Third, in a private-property capitalism, the upper and middle classes are essentially entrepreneurs, hence rivals, in the narrowly economic sphere. As a rule their joint political interests are at best very limited, and they normally have available to them only few possibilities for joint social action. By way of contrast, the alliance of the two privileged corporate classes occurs within large institutions that are themselves multicompetent, that is, able to function in virtually any domain—industrial, agricultural, economic, political, social, cultural, regional, national, international.

Fourth, within corporate society the two upper, privileged groups face the working class as a solid bloc. This is, of course a corollary to the second point, above, but it is of such major importance that it should be described in its own terms. In societies founded upon private property it is commonly the case that some significant part of the middle classes casts its social and political support to the laboring class. This was as true in ancient Rome as in nineteenth-century politics. As can readily be appreciated, such middle-class support for lower-class aspirations and interests can result in severe social destabilization. In corporate society there is no parallel social structural source of instability.

Because each of these remarks bears on a fairly complex phenomenon, it is worthwhile to consider them further. As previously observed, the history of private property is the history of family-based property. Characteristically, then, the dominant class of such a society consists of numerous wealthy families whose interests are necessarily somewhat discordant. Abstractly speaking, such a class would be unified by its desire to avoid internecine conflict and to present a united face to its social adversaries. Yet in actual history as against pure theory, such classes, both before and during the capitalist era, have been traditionally riven by conflicts between the representatives of landed as opposed to other kinds of property (as was nineteenth-century British and French capitalism) or by regional or sectoral differences (as was Germany prior to Bismarck) or by religious and social differences (as was Italy's north and south). In the acute case, these differences can even lead to civil war, as they did in the United States. Relatedly, a family-based private-property system can also be split by dynastic differences that encourage other, rival classes to challenge the power of the warring dynasties, as happened in the United States in the late 1800s. There are only a few structural remedies for these systemic sources of upper-class instability; the arranged marriage between rivalrous families is perhaps the most important. But, as we know from the histories of the squabbling monarchs of seventeenth- and eighteenth-century Europe, blood is thinner than dynastic ambition. Essentially, blood-relatedness can limit but hardly erase rivalries between great propertied families. All in all, an upper, propertied class founded in private property faces serious obstacles to high-class cohesiveness and has only a few, relatively weak methods of combating it.

This is in extremely sharp contrast to the class I described as the corporate public. As I have already pointed out, the corporation itself through corporate form replaces the property-holding family as the elemental unit constituting the upper class. By its very nature, corporate property integrates and harmonizes the interests of the property owners. The wide diffusion of upper-class stockholding, celebrated by business writers, obviously reinforces and extends the class-integrating nature of corporate property. But it is not merely a question of the property interests of both individuals and families becoming merged within the conventional business corporation. Even more than that, corporate forms of organization permit the upper class to operate successfully in numerous lines of business as easily as in a specialized field, regionally as well as internationally, in private-sector activities as well as public-sector ones, and so forth. Thus a corporate ruling class has no built-in sectoral or other structural fault lines around which conflict must eventually emerge. I have no doubt that differences of opinion and of interest disturb the serene face our upper class presents to its fellow citizens. In this century, in fact, there have been a number of major differences within the upper class, of which the most prominent and, probably, most important involved their reactions to the domestic and foreign policies of FDR's New Deal. But under the corporate property system, such differences, even when they lead to fissures in upper-class unity, remain *situational* rather than structural. That is, they may emerge as various elements of the upper class react to this or that policy, these or those events, but they are not based on fundamental, constituting, and recurring features in the upper class itself.

In corporate society, the upper-class–middle-class relationship is also radically changed. Essentially, a relationship that historically intermixed social cooperation and social rivalry between the two classes becomes radically tilted toward the pole of cooperation. One does not have to read *The Communist Manifesto* to appreciate the historic conflicts between great and modest property within earlier property systems. From Aristotle's *Politics* (written in the fourth century B.C.) up to any conventional political science book today, the conflict—or lack of same—between the property interests of the very wealthy and those of the middle classes is understood to be the fundamental factor governing social stability. Aristotle's view, from which this perennial conversation proceeds, is that the middle, propertied class stands in the social balance between the rich propertied few and the poor propertyless many. By tilting as occasion demands against the avarice of the rich who would impoverish everybody or, alternately, against the resentment of the poor who would destroy private property entirely, the middle group in society prevents either of the extremes from overthrowing the good society. That is one pole of that historic discussion. Marx and Engels represent the other, to the effect that under capitalism, the middle group is being destroyed so that many of its individual members go over to the social side of the rapidly increasing poor. As this process goes on without limit, Marx and Engels wrote, it must eventually destroy both capitalism and private property.

Corporate society changes this relationship. Within corporate form, a fundamental complementarity of interest unites the corporate public with the middle element. For the former, its alliance with a multicompetent middle managerial, technical, and professional class erases all practical limits to the expansion of corporate activity and the increase in the corporate surplus. For the middle element, corporate form provides unlimited access to liquid, physical, commercial, and other resources as well as the docility of labor—hence, as I have already argued, the maximally favorable environment for the social interests of the middle corporate class. (This is, of course, intimately related to my third point above.)

The alliance between the upper and middle corporate classes occurs within a single functional institution. The alliance is therefore omnidimensional, and there is a virtual absence of limits on the kind and size of corporate activity. By contrast, in a private-property system the alliance between the upper and middle classes is by and large limited to defending the unholy trio—as Marx would put it—of "family, property, religion" (*The Eighteenth Brumaire of Louis Napoleon*). And, given the paucity of instruments with which to do this, that trio has historically been defended by the indiscriminate use of force and, of course, by the deliberate imposition of religious and other superstitions.

Within corporate society, the alliance of the two privileged corporate classes faces the working class as a tightly knit bloc, capturing and directing the latter's energies within corporate form. Given the comprehensive nature of corporate activities, especially the almost fissureless public-private relationship in corporate society, this places the working class in a socially isolated and unsupported position. Again, the contrast to pre-corporate society will make this clearer. Within societies based on private property it is common at least for parts of the middle (propertied) classes to make common cause with the lower class and against the privileged part of society. For situational reasons, this or that middle-class figure may side with the modern working class against the upper-class–middle-element alliance, but no significant part of the class does so as a rule. U.S. historians, for example, typically define the early twentieth-century Progressive movement in precisely those terms, and it is not difficult to find analogous middle-class–lower-class alliances in the ancient, Renaissance, and modern worlds. In fact, it is not uncommonly argued that the prominence of figures from the privileged classes within the modern democratic, socialist, and revolutionary movements, such as Debs, Marx, Lenin, and Castro, can be cited as evidences of just such a social alliance. Whether that particular point can be sustained is debatable—but that the historic socialist movement, for example, has frequently enlisted whole sections and strata from the middle classes is not. No such structural weakness exists in corporate society.

More than that, however: In the purely industrial setting of corporate form, the historic movement of Taylorism has tended to withdraw from the working class the mental and skill elements of its labor, thus creating Schmidt as the desired class prototype. A similar situation is recreated in corporate society as a whole under the rubric of social Taylorism. As we must explore this in greater detail later, here it is sufficient to characterize it as a phenomenon whereupon the broad social life of the modern working class, in analogy with its narrower work life, comes to be shaped in its mental and control elements by the middle corporate class. Given the utter domination by the upper corporate classes of political, social, cultural, as well as economic life, this creates a situation in which the working class, in practical terms, faces not merely two oppositional classes in a single, hostile bloc, but confronts society itself.

Within societies organized under the older private-property system, there has historically been social room for the lower or laboring class to develop and sustain its own semiautonomous social structures and symbolic cultural systems. As Edward Thompson has argued in *The Making of the English Working Class*, these structures and their cultures have frequently stood in explicit opposition to the dominant social system and its culture. This possibility is radically reduced within corporate society. To the degree that it tries to create and sustain its own social structures and cultural systems, the modern working class finds that these latter, no matter how pacific, how timid even, stand outside of society and are viewed as threatening to it. Throughout the modern capitalist world, the political and cultural authorities' increasingly hostile and derisive treatment of trade unions—even if they are "class collaborationist"—and of the values they represent stands as sharp confirmation of this troubling feature of corporate society.

A Ruling Class

I have been employing the concept of a ruling class, an idea currently very much in disfavor within mainstream social science. As a clear understanding of this issue is central to much of my subsequent analysis, it is necessary to digress somewhat to examine some of the problems in using such a concept, to clarify how my usage differs from that of other writers, and—most importantly—to vindicate the concept as a fundamental element in the argument I present in this book.

We should begin with some elementary clarification. I don't know of any writers about contemporary Western societies who deny that each of those societies has an "elite" or an "establishment" comprising leaders of business, government, the military, perhaps the arts, too, who enjoy social and other advantages not shared by the middle and lower groups. Nor do any seem to be of a mind to deny that those advantages are relatively comprehensive, that, for example, members of the U.S. establishment normally have access to the highest incomes and other economic perquisites, often enjoy extensive inherited wealth, high status, significant political influence, and all else we associate with an upper class. If conventional social scientists don't employ the expression "upper class," it is perhaps more from sensitivity to our democratic ethos than from any substantive measure of disagreement among themselves that the United States, like the other capitalist countries, does in fact have an upper class.

But it is not—in the standard view of the matter—a ruling class. Again, some further distinctions are in order. There is no doubt in any quarter that our upper class enjoys a predominant role within the political system. Both the House of Representatives and the Senate, especially, are made up largely of quite wealthy men (and a few women) who must have access to hundreds of thousands (sometimes millions) of dollars to win reelection. The great majority of these people either come from the corporate public or have close relationships to it. Most of their campaign money comes from a relatively narrow group of wealthy individuals and, especially, from corporate-type institutions. Top cabinet and other government officials, particularly in the national security area, are customarily drawn from a very narrow range of men and women who are also associated with large private organizations, usually business corporations. Federal judges, including those for the Supreme Court, are chosen from a small group of elite law schools and establishment law firms. The presidency, of course, is often occupied by men of relatively modest background—but to reach it candidates must at all stages of their advance win the concurrence, assistance, and financial support of members of the establishment, who then occupy virtually all the top management and other sensitive posts in their administrations. Finally, in *every* area of the federal government the top management and other policymaking positions are, as a rule, staffed by men and women only recently arrived from top management jobs in the private sector and who will soon return to it. Most state governments and the governments of the larger cities and counties are similarly influenced, often staffed, by persons whose interests and views are basically identifiable with those of the establishment. In short, on the basis of simply overwhelming evidence it is clear that an upper class of men and women hold a vast predominance of political power over any and all other groups.

Why is this not a ruling class? Theoretically speaking, the answer is extremely simple: The establishment within the United States and other Western countries, it is argued in the conventional view, enjoys and employs this political power subject to an effective system of controls operated by the society as a whole. In contrast, a ruling class is a class that not only has a preponderance of political power but uses it against the interests, and often the actual sentiments, of all the other major classes and, of course, of society as a whole. Consequently, in this view of the matter, the United States, like the other capitalist democracies, clearly has an upper class, elite, or establishment, but it does not have a ruling class.

The reader will notice that I have not stressed the hereditary character of membership in a ruling class as one of its defining characteristics. I think the issue almost utterly irrelevant. As a rule, social science writers in the United States confuse the presence of social mobility with the absence of rigid class lines; that is, they are willing to accept the importance of class divisions only if individuals cannot freely pass from class to class. Historically, the position is nonsensical: In some of the most powerful, untrammeled, and rigid ruling classes of the past (such as the aristocracy of eighteenth-century France) there was a constant exchange of faces and families with the other classes. What marks a ruling class is that it monopolizes political power, using that power to aggrandize itself at the expense of the rest of society. Barriers to social mobility are another issue, for they have precious little to do with how a class acts toward the rest of society. In fact, an upper, ruling class with an unstable membership may be more dictatorial and act more the predator as well on the entirely familiar principle of "getting yours while you can."

Like so many other questions of social analysis, issues surrounding the existence and identity of a ruling class are deeply muddled by the failure of social scientists to factor in the rise of corporate property as the dominant property system underlying various class relationships, including the political ones. The path away from this muddle requires fairly careful analysis of the secondary changes wrought by that rise. There are historical and two distinctly methodological elements to these changes. We can examine them in that order.

The Western societies based on private property had their heyday during, roughly, the middle two-thirds of the nineteenth century. It is now widely accepted that the capitalists of the time were truly a ruling class. Not only did they have an overwhelming predominance of political power, but they used it ruthlessly to prevent other classes from interfering with their interests. In the United States from 1850 through the end of the Civil War, for example, capitalists were *given* public lands equal to about 15 percent of the current territory of the United States. "Given" is perhaps the wrong word; they took it mainly by bribing those in Congress and other government offices, by threatening their critics, even, here and there, by outright violence. Analogous happenings can be found in Britain, France, and the other European countries, where the upper class sharply limited both proletarian and middle-class influence over government by restricting the franchise and through bribes, threats, military coups, dictatorships, and free-swinging use of the police.

It is important to underline here the twofold historical elements that went into making those upper classes into ruling classes: first, the evident inhibition or exclusion of the other major classes from influence over the actions of government and, second, the subsequent use of government office to despoil government and society of wealth and other perquisites for the sole benefit of the upper class. Marx was clearly in the right (in *The Communist Manifesto*) to call the typical capitalist government of midcentury nothing more nor less than "the executive committee of the capitalist class."

But, of course, the historical situation has changed in Europe, North America, Japan, and elsewhere, most importantly in that at present the other major classes do have a recognized and active political role, typically won over the bitter historical opposition of the capitalist classes. And, because of that, it is argued, the sort of utter spoliation of government and society characteristic of mid-nineteenth-century politics is now sharply inhibited by the political influence of the other classes acting through democratic institutions. Consequently, the upper class, no matter how great the differential advantages it has within government and gets from government, is not *the* ruling class. Quite literally speaking, the other classes also rule, not always effectively, of course, but in every case enough to bring upper-class advantages into at least some degree of harmony with the needs and desires of the rest of society.

This change in historical situation is impacted by the two methodological issues mentioned earlier. The first of these concerns the difficult problem of making a systematic link between government and the dominant property-holding class within a purely private-property society, that is, a link powerful enough and clear enough to enable the social investigator to make judgments about the political role of the dominant class and the extent of its political influence.

Consider an imaginary (and very simple) case in which a society is dominated by a number of wealthy, private-property-holding families. Assume further that they, like most wealthy families identifiable in the past, spend a great deal of time waging internecine war, each pursuing its perceived interests against not only the other classes in society but also against each of the other wealthy families. On such an hypothesis, the effects of this propertied class on the political mechanism will not be the result of the intended, unified actions of the whole class so much as the residue created by the underlying conflict within the class. In fact, on the given hypothesis, are we even entitled to speak of *a* class as if it were a unified ensemble and not a crazy quilt of squabbling families? To speak of a ruling class in such a circumstance, we must make various judgments as to which subgroups of the class are most representative of the interests of the class at any time. As is clear from the terms establishing the problem, these judgments must be inferential and only partially reliable. This shaky foundation underlies all the rest of the analysis.

Now the point I would make is that shaky methodological foundations are endemic to political analysis of ruling-class dominance in a private-property system, necessarily following from the need to create a conception of a single theoretical class with a single will (or at least a single residue of its will) out of a host of diverse, often sparring, propertied families. For the historian of the middle of the last century, the problem is not acute. If, as was the case then, the political role of the other classes is sharply delimited, the actions of government can *only* represent the influence of this or that part of the propertied class, muddied but never entirely obscured, of course, by the usual career maneuvering among ambitious political individuals. Generally, the historian will have sufficient memoirs, letters, reports, diaries, and other documents upon which to draw the necessary distinctions.

A number of writers dealing with our own times—I have G. William Domhoff particularly in mind—have tried to get around this powerful methodological barrier to identifying and judging the specific role and influence of an upper-propertied class within a democratic or multiclass political system. His analysis makes a number of telling observations, but, in my view, he does not succeed entirely in his aim because he must necessarily assume the burden of proving, in effect, that no other classes have the ability to significantly alter the political action of the upper-propertied class. This considerable burden cannot be overcome if one assumes, as does Domhoff, that private property and its class structure is still dominant. The central problem is as I have put it above: How does one identify a unitary ruling-class will and establish that it is exclusively dominant over the political process, when the upper class is normally torn by dynastic and other conflicts and the other classes have at least formal access to the political process?

In the way in which these issues are currently argued, writers like Domhoff are commonly dismissed as relying upon "conspiracy theories." I think the charge unfair, but, given the burden of proof he accepts in assuming that private property is still dominant for society, the accusation is almost inevitable. That is, he must show, against all sorts of possible counterevidence and argument, that the real significance of one or another event is that it was brought about by the upper class, serves the upper class exclusively, and is invidious to the other classes, regardless of whether or not the other classes see it that way. In a real sense, the harder he tries to prove his case, the more susceptible he is to being accused of reading meaning and direction into political situations that, on their surface, do not exhibit it.

Moreover, the vital linkage between the ownership of vast property and exclusive political power is further obscured if one factors in the famous "separation between the ownership and control" of corporate enterprise, drawn from the work of Adolph Berle and Gardiner Means. The German sociologist Ralf Dahrendorf has most clearly argued for the nullifying effects of this development. To accept Berle and Means's thesis is tantamount to arguing that the wealthy don't even control the companies they own; how then can their economic power be used as an argument that they have exclusive (or even predominant) political power? This is precisely Dahrendorf's tack, and it sets up the intellectual framework in which the question of upper-class political power now resides.

That framework, in its broadest, structural intellectual features, is accepted by most contemporary Marxist and mainstream investigators. In conventional social science, the dominant influence has been that of the U.S. sociologist

Talcott Parsons. Modern Marxists generally look to the Italian communist leader and theoretician Antonio Gramsci. For Parsons, the rise of modern bureaucracies in the business world has vastly weakened the economic power of the wealthy classes. This weakening has in turn been furthered by the spread of democratic values so that the older, once very powerful business class has become only one among a host of competitors in the political system. In Parsons's view, the political system is the arena in which these conflicts among the different parts of society are worked out. Subsequent writers, mostly in the United States, have developed a theory of political pluralism, to the effect that in a modern capitalist society many different groups have important degrees and kinds of power. The significance of the political system is that it balances and adjudicates these different, conflicting powers and interests within a common-value system that is at bottom democratic and egalitarian.

Since Gramsci, the most dynamic of the Marxist analyses have taken a similar tack but use it to reach diametrically opposite conclusions. Conceding the point Berle and Means made about the separation of ownership from control of the most important kinds of property, they argue that the private-property system, though importantly modified, nevertheless undergirds a "hegemonic" (or dominant), specifically capitalist culture. Within this—to use Parsonian language—common-value framework, government and the political process guarantee that the interests of the other classes are subsumed within and consequently exploited by the property-owning capitalists.

As one can readily appreciate from the way in which this complex dispute is framed, the Marxists must be prepared to claim—and the anti-Marxists to deny—that the democratic political process is ultimately fraudulent, that is, subverted by non- and antidemocratic forces and means. These are precisely the basic differences separating modern Marxists such as Marcuse and O'Connor, for example, from their foes on the other side, such as Dahrendorf and Bell. Given the framework of the discussion, writers like Marcuse and O'Connor must assume a much heavier burden of argumentation. A supporter of the status quo merely has to argue that Western democratic political systems are sufficiently powerful to check and redirect the *worst* excesses of an upper class that has, at any rate, lost control of its corporations to bureaucrats. By contrast, the Marxists are placed in the far from enviable position of arguing that, appearances and exceptions to the contrary, modern Western political systems can't be—it is not possible for them to be—democratic.

In my own view one can bypass virtually all of the foregoing structure of argumentation. At bottom, that structure rests on cardinal features of private-property systems that have no place within the world of corporate property. Two are particularly noteworthy and have already been cited. First, in a private-property system the distinction between the public and the private sectors is both theoretically and practically fundamental. By assuming that private property is still dominant, one assumes that distinction, and that in turn prestructures a problem into one's analysis of politics. How are the two sectors bridged? If one class dominates both, how does its overwhelming power in one sector allow it to win and hold similarly one-sided power in the other, formally different and separate sector? Given this theoretical framework, the public-private problem is a difficult one, *whatever the facts of the case.* In a corporate-property system, by contrast, the theoretical problem disappears, and one is left merely with the empirical problem of determining the relationship of the dominant class to the political process, a formidable task to be sure, but not the nearly impossible task imposed when one assumes a private-property system.

The second methodological problem also stems from the distinction, fundamental to a private-property society, between the "public" and the "private" realms or sectors. At several points in my previous discussions, I have indicated that in a private-property society the upper or wealthiest class has historically been in conflict with all or at least many of the other classes. In the middle of the past century, that conflict frequently took the form of trying to exclude all of the other classes from the political process. Hence the problem of the two sectors, public and private, has usually been depicted as one in which the upper class has it in mind to rule alone, to sharply limit the power of all other classes and segments of society, in short, to try to win power and prerogatives over government that are analogous to the power and privileges it enjoys over its own property. Given those terms of argument, the existence of formally democratic political institutions per se is often seen as evidence of middle- and lower-class success against this upper-class ambition, as historically it was.

In corporate society, we employ a very different social model. In such a society, the upper class must be viewed as joined in a social, economic, cultural, and political bloc with the middle element. This is understood to be not merely a situational alliance or a temporary honeymoon but a constituent feature of the society. Moreover, this alliance of the upper and middle corporate classes occurs within an institutional arrangement— corporate form—that is not only common to both government and the private corporation but also makes any fundamental distinction between the public and the private sectors obsolete. By contrast, private businesses limited by earlier capitalist institutional arrangements necessarily had to leave certain tasks to government, particularly in the broad social field. Both in theory and in historical development, this is no longer the case. Modern corporate forms of organization in the so-called private sector are increasingly encroaching on what used to be thought government territory. Jumping ahead a bit, if there is a public-private problem in corporate society, the problem is not one of accounting for private influence in government but instead of retaining a public sector within which non- and anticorporation values can continue to exist.

"Public" and "Private"

A great advantage of the concept of collective property is that it enables us to deal succinctly and fruitfully with the relationship between government and so-called private industry or, as the issue is sometimes posed, between the public sector and private property. As the previous discussion indicates, in the contemporary world the relationship between government and the private sector has proven difficult to characterize in a formula or a theory, though it is relatively easy to describe. One can, of course, simply follow out the logic of "private" property and treat them as two different, more or less hostile worlds, governed on the one hand by an ethos of public service and on the other by the profit motive, but linked only by the legal system and, perhaps, the tendency of modern government to meddle everywhere. However theoretically neat that position is and however attractive to certain, usually conservative and free-market ideologists, it simply won't hold water.

The simple facts of the case fly in the face of an absolute public-private distinction—as C. Wright Mills argued years ago and even Galbraith has been forced to conclude. No modern industry can operate without intimate assistance from government and no government in a capitalist country can govern without extensive assistance and cooperation from the so-called private sector. In fact, it is highly unlikely—in this country nearly certain—that any major public official can either be elected or appointed unless he or she is viewed as nonantagonistic by the aggregate corporate public. And it is equally unlikely that any business executive can prosper in the corporate world unless he or she has considerable expertise in dealing with government.

This discussion of the public-private relationship must also acknowledge that the modern corporation itself has never been a purely commercial enterprise. From their very beginnings corporations have had intimate relationships with government, first in the national security field and including most of the overseas ventures of the imperial countries, such as the United States. Thus the absolute public-private distinction, as it is commonly understood, is largely irrelevant to the corporate world. The concept of private property demands that we draw a clear line between the public and the private sector, but there is no such clear line, not a legal line, not a practical line, not a line that anyone can live with. Ultimately, the social nature of modern production and consumption would and does erase all such imaginary lines.

Given the muddied waters of both methodology and substance in which this issue has been submerged, there is a certain merit in going back to basics as we try to characterize the relationship between the two domains. Further, because in the United States the relationship is both the most strained and at the same time the most advanced of all the capitalist democracies, it may serve as a prototype. Without in any way assuming that the U.S. experience will be repeated elsewhere, the situation in the other countries can be clearly typed and described in terms of similarities to and differences from the U.S. case. With that caution in mind, we might set forth certain main points in a modern theory of the public-private relationship:

The problem is not really an abstract one, however often it is cast as such. Basically, we must characterize the relationships between two concrete historical institutions, the modern, "private" profit-oriented corporation and modern central government.

Throughout the corporate era, the two institutions have more or less agreed on a clear division of labor. The sense that there is a profound public-private problem emerges now because of certain crucial changes presently developing in what had been a stable division of tasks. The U.S. case is the most helpful to our investigation. For nearly 100 years, the United States has had private, profit-oriented business organizations of unusually large size and broad commercial-technical competence. I have already had occasion to comment on this with respect to the steel industry, in which U.S. producers—even before the creation of U.S. Steel in 1901— dwarfed the normal German and, especially, British firm. Because of the size and multiple competency of U.S. corporations, government and the corporations rather easily fell into a three-way division of labor that has lasted almost to the present. One can even speak of three distinct models governing their historic relationships, to wit, a social need model, a commercial model, and a national security model.

Most traditional public tasks, such as mail delivery, the justice system, and the emerging social welfare system (at the turn of the century), were relegated to government. Private business was not entirely excluded; the railroads and, later, the airlines were subsidized to carry mail from city to city. But the central, controlling role belonged to government. We can call this the *social need model* of the corporation-government relationship.

The *commercial model* stands in sharp contrast to this. Traditional commercial undertakings became the exclusive province of the new corporations, which acted as a rule on their own initiative, though with government assistance. The extreme and even distorted case of this kind is, of course, in South and Central America, where the big companies enjoyed blanket, uncritical government support for their efforts at reducing the fate of whole nations to the desires of this or that company (United Fruit in Nicaragua) or this or that industry (sugar in Cuba). The European business experience was entirely different. Prior to World War II, German and British industries were averse to copying the U.S. penchant for huge corporations and were accordingly penalized for their backwardness. Because European companies lacked the assets and the multicompetency of U.S. corporations, their governments had to enter into commercial and related undertakings that were and are, in U.S. thinking, the pure province of the private firm. In chemicals, for example, the British industry resisted consolidating dye-making firms, explosives firms, acids manufacturers, and so on into a single, large, diversified chemical producer in spite of overwhelming technical and commercial imperatives to do so and in spite of the evident success of the U.S. Du Pont Corporation, which had taken this step in the early 1920s. In this case, the British government, under pressure by the Labour party, forced the formation of the diversified Imperial Chemical Industries, Ltd., during the mid-1930s.

As a rule, and because of the early development of corporate form in the United States, no commercial undertakings whatsoever were beyond the technical, financial, and organizational capacity of the U.S. companies. In contrast, the European and Japanese governments have had to assume commercial initiatives right up to the present.

A third, *national security model* has historically coexisted with the social need and commercial models. In the national security field an extremely interesting partnership developed in which the initiative and dominant influence rested sometimes with government and sometimes with private corporations, often with no overriding pattern. Thus during the first two decades of this century, the government compelled recalcitrant companies like Westinghouse Electric and Bethlehem Steel to manufacture new products (turbines and armor plate, respectively) for the navy. On the other hand, the government's inability or unwillingness to impose its demands on the GM Allison Aircraft Division led to widespread reliance on an inadequate aircraft engine, with disastrous military consequences between 1940 and 1942.

If one looks for historical trends in the overall corporation-government relationship, it is evident that in the years since World War II government has been less and less able to control corporations in the national security area. At the present time, national security tasks are frequently "discovered" or created by private firms, weapons systems devised to accomplish them, and specifications for the weapons settled upon more or less unilaterally by corporations and industries. In fact, this very development is reflected in the popular notion of a military-industrial complex run amok. What is not widely appreciated, however, is that this is only the tip of an enormous corporate iceberg in the murky seas of national security. Frequently, the technical training and task indoctrination of the soldiers, sailors, and airmen and airwomen who use these weapons is carried out directly by "manufacturers' representatives." These representatives often remain on the military base or naval vessel to service the weapons and to modify them in the light of new technical and tactical developments. From the nature of their task, it is not uncommon for these corporate employees to participate in combat operations—field testing—so that the substantive distinction between military personnel and corporate employees virtually disappears. With developments like these so common, the fear that government is entirely ceding a "public" interest and a "public" responsibility to "private" hands is hardly groundless.

This erosion of a controlling government influence in the national security field is not limited to dealing with weapons systems. Companies like the Rand Corporation and the Hoover Institution play an important role in considering and adopting the broadest national security policies. It is not at all clear that their influence does not challenge, often modify, and sometimes overturn that of the Joint Chiefs of Staff and other, purely governmental strategic decisionmaking bodies.

Two closely related developments are clearly comprised here. On the one hand, government's ability to make and carry out national security policy is inhibited by the profit-making and related "privates." On the other, these "privates" have been able to absorb what were conventionally thought to be public functions into their own ambit. Consequently, if we look at our earlier historical models, we can see the portent of significant changes. The trend in the national security field is *toward* the commercial model: U.S. defense and security policy is not governed by purely commercial factors—but it is becoming more so and, in the opinion of many, alarmingly so.

More troubling still, something like the same development is now occurring in the government's traditional civilian and social need field. In short, both the older national security model and the social need model appear to be declining in importance in the face of vastly expanded corporate influence and activity in the military and social sectors. Before we can fully gauge the impact of these developments, however, we should consider another enduring feature of the government-corporate relationship that in turn will make them more readily understandable.

By and large the United States has never had a distinct public-sector elite. In Britain, in France, and—legendarily—in Germany, the higher members of the civil service have been an extremely influential and prestigious cadre, products of distinctive, illustrious schools and universities, who train for and then serve out a full career at the highest posts within the public sector. They constitute the "permanent government," having long since developed an esprit de corps, an ideology, a tutelary relationship to private-sector institutions, and a prestige that makes them, in their own eyes and in those of the overall national elite, the most responsible and highest-ranking representatives of the enduring interests and values of the nation itself. There is no parallel group in the United States save the professional military cadre, with perhaps scattered pockets in the diplomatic and intelligence services. Generally, U.S. civil servants occupy only the lowest rungs of policymaking posts and, of course, the ranks of middle management and clerical and other lower-ranked positions.

In the U.S. system, the highest posts of the federal government, called the administration, consist of 3,000 to 5,000 presidential appointees, most of whom are brought in from outside government and who serve for all—or even only part—of the president's term of office. They, not the professional civil servants, monopolize policymaking in the government. In the case of middle management there is frequently a parallel influx and outflow of men and women from private industry who actually carry out those policies. Thus there is an immense two-way traffic between the executive department of government and the managements of private corporations. Policymaking positions in the national security apparatus are in fact monopolized by Wall Streeters, by people from the big corporations that get most of the defense contracts, and by ideologues and other mandarins from the advising agencies associated with them, such as the Trilateral Commission, the Foreign Policy Association, the Asia Society, and so on.

In addition, influential retired politicians, military figures, and government administrators find high, well-paid positions in industries of which they were "disinterested" regulators and purchasers just prior to retirement. Consequently, it is difficult to speak truthfully of an integral public sector elite distinct from and counterpoised to a private one—in Britain, yes, or in France or West Germany, certainly, but not in the United States. Obviously, we do have vast numbers of people who choose to make a career in government and from time to time, now in this agency and now in that, these men and women have managed to form a distinguished and influential group (as in New York City under LaGuardia or in Washington under Franklin Roosevelt prior to 1940). But they do not occupy the highest posts, they do not make or have serious impact on policy, and they do not have in aggregate the prestige and the real esprit we find in certain European countries.

Thus, if one is at all inclined to a conspiratorial view, the sort of government-industry cooperation outlined here, which is so often to the advantage of industry, can then be used to buttress one's case. Government, in this view, is the captive of private business, which staffs its offices and then uses those offices against the public trust and for private gain, either personal or, more usual, corporate. Obviously, there is some truth to a conspiracy view of these matters, probably far more than centrist and conservative writers are willing to admit, though recently the evidently limitless rapacity of President Ronald Reagan's appointees opened many eyes.

As a general theory of the corporation-government relationship, however, conspiracy theory isn't especially helpful because its basic theoretical idea goes little beyond observing that public officials and public officers can often be traduced by old-fashioned greed and dishonesty. Moreover, certain key facts don't easily fit into this view. Private industry is not always happy with what government does; the Vietnam War, for example, never elicited much enthusiasm from the private sector, whose representatives were among the earliest voices calling for U.S. disengagement. Similarly, private industry doesn't always have one voice, even on matters of the greatest concern: The high-interest policies pursued by Paul Volcker at the Federal Reserve in the 1980s harmed and were opposed by large numbers of important business institutions and their leaders. Even the Reagan administration, ideologically committed to the private sector to a degree surprising in a country in which such enthusiasm is the norm, could not always do what business wanted. The reaction of the federal government to the near failure of the Continental Illinois Bank led it inexorably to assume regulatory powers over the private banking industry that are positively socialistic in their scope and implications. I could go on listing examples, but the substantial point about conspiracy theories of the public-sector–private-sector relationship is that government isn't always just the servant of big business.

People who take this populist, conspiratorial view often try to explain away the Volcker policy or the Vietnam War by arguing that the business forces who supported and got advantage from them were "really" more important than others, or that a divided business voice gives government some room for maneuver. (We've already discussed this from the methodological viewpoint.) But there are too many well-documented historical cases in which even a unified business voice of the highest power and prestige couldn't get government to act as it wanted. Probably the most memorable (and amusing) of these occurred throughout the conservative administrations of Warren G. Harding, Calvin Coolidge, and Herbert Hoover, which were adamant in refusing to help the oil industry restrict domestic oil supplies in order to drive up prices. Apparently, the oil executives were somewhat lax in their faith in the true religion of "free markets." Hoover, the commerce secretary for most of the period, is even reputed to have delivered pious homilies on the subject to the oil executives. It took the irreverent and "antibusiness" New Dealers of Franklin Roosevelt to provide the necessary legislation, in this case the Interstate Oil Compact, through which an industry-dominated agency limited the availability of domestic oil so as to keep up the price. There is a more contemporary parallel to this fundamental, conservative government-business opposition: The Reagan administration was notorious for refusing to provide funds that might in any way support either contraception or abortion not only here but also overseas, even though the business community views overseas population control as one of the central issues of the era. At any rate, this sort of unevenness in the government-industry relationship sits ill with theories that make government into the pure-and-simple servant of business.

Government agencies, too, are organized by corporate form. I have already described part of this, namely, the near exclusion of middle-level civil servants from policymaking posts and their monopolization by presidential appointees only recently arrived from the private sector. Top management in government has much the same powers as top management in industry. And the various relationships among top management, the middle group of government administrators, technicians, and professionals, and the workers are also structurally similar. For example, since the acceptance of public employee unions by John F. Kennedy's administration in 1961, the laws and practices of both the public and the private sector distinguish lower-level employees from those just above them in the same way. Basically, if a public servant performs managerial functions or has access to confidential management information, he or she is ineligible to join a union. All other employees, with a few exceptions not relevant to this discussion, must come under collective-bargaining agreements. In short, the triadic division of labor we found in the private corporation has also developed in public agencies. And, as this has occurred, the social, economic, and other paraphernalia of corporate form have also developed within government. Zero-based budgeting (which forces each budget item into direct competition with all others) and the growing stress on productivity measures for the output of employees as diverse as teachers and secretaries may serve as indices of the growth of corporate form within the public sector.

It follows that the top managers of government policy and those of the private corporations are related by more than their frequent interchange of faces; they play identical functional roles in both organizations, enjoy many of the same perquisites, have access to comparable resources (including a diligent, multitalented middle management group), deal similarly with their respective labor forces, and so forth. It is within this striking shared context that their interchange of personnel must be considered. There is a definite and distinct sense in which this class of people exercises proprietary rights over government policy and behavior. In saying this I mean nothing more nor less than what has already been described: basically, that at the policy level of government agencies and private corporations alike, the aggregate corporate public exercises rights and enjoys privileges from which they distance the members of all the other classes.

This brings us to what seems to me to be the crucial difference in the present day between the public and private sectors. Individual government agencies and individual corporations are increasingly nearly identical in their division of labor, hierarchical relations, attitudes toward productivity, and so forth, that is, in their purely internal structure and functioning. Top government figures are thus full-fledged members of the aggregate corporate public and subject to the same sanctions. In that sense they are responsive to the aggregate corporate public much like top private-corporation managers. But there is this difference: Governmental managers must also respond to the general public—you and me, the press, and everyone else— within a public-sector ethos, buttressed by legal and institutional factors, which emphasizes the rights of that broad public both collectively and in detail. Corporation leaders are far more insulated from the public—as much as anything by the continuing importance of the myth of private property and, of course, by the powerful social and economic forces that find comfort, solace, or crude advantage in that myth.

This broad analytical framework lends itself to the sort of careful distinctions one has to make to deal with the intricacies of the public-private question. It is a way of embodying most of what we know, for example, that the executive department of government is more insulated from the public than is Congress or that agencies linked to especially powerful industries are much more resistant to public interference than others. Thus one can influence the Civil Rights Commission or the Environmental Protection Administration from the outside, but the Defense Department is more insulated, and the Federal Reserve Bank is an invincible fortress. I think the logic of the position is clear enough: The difference between government agencies and private corporations rests not in any fundamental internal structural or even value differences but instead on the nature of the external publics to which they must be responsive and the sorts of sanctions those publics can exert.

I would analyze the large nonprofit organizations such as universities, foundations, research institutes, and kindred institutions now so influential in the United States, in much the same fashion. At their policymaking and budgetary levels, each has linked interests, perspectives, and personnel both among themselves and with government and industry. Their top positions are rather thoroughly integrated with those of both the private and the government sectors; there is a steady interchange of personnel. Each top management deals with a more or less permanent cadre of middle-element specialists with skills and interests fundamentally similar to those of middle groups in the private and government sectors. And each has its own "labor problem." Each must cope in its own way with its various publics, including, of course, the general public. In any case their top management groups must be considered integral members of the aggregate corporate public.

Here it is useful to remind ourselves of the ultimate significance of corporate form as an institutional feature governing the relationship of institutional leaders to other people and forces. The development of corporate form *means* the gathering together of policymaking powers into a relatively small group. It means that that group is provided with the most efficacious methods of carrying out those policies without being inhibited by those who actually carry them out, especially by those at the lowest rank. In general, it means that the upper management enjoys considerable influence over policy and budget questions, that the middle rank has some such influence and, of course, direct contact with the policymaking echelon, but that the lowest rank has little or none. These are all normal system features of corporate form.

I earlier described three distinct models of government-corporation relations in the United States for, respectively, traditional governmental activities bearing on so-called social need, purely commercial activities, and the mixed case of national security. Further, I argued that the older national security model was evolving *toward* the commercial model. So, too, is the social need model. That is, one can now discern a movement on the part of profit-oriented firms to move into the "government business." Already, important parts of the postal delivery business; the provision of children's day care and care for the elderly; the administration of prison systems, school systems, technical training and retraining of workers; sanitation and water services; and many other traditional governmental functions are being carried out by profit-oriented corporations. Sometimes entire functions are spun off to private enterprise: The growing security industry, which already employs two-thirds of all security and investigative personnel in the country, is agreeable to contracting for a town's police functions. Or this or that government agency will subcontract out part of its tasks to a private company, typically for program development, training workers, part-timers, computer programming, and so on. This major development still awaits its chronicler.

The deeper significance of the Reagan administration here, as of Margaret Thatcher's and other conservative free-market-oriented governments overseas, bears heavily on these changes. Liberal and social democratic critics typically charge these reactionary governments with having a nostalgic view of the past and a desire to return to a golden age of free-market individualism, self-reliance, and other mythological virtues. Nothing could be further from the truth. Whatever may be the conscious perceptions of politicians like Reagan and Thatcher or of acolytes like Milton Friedman and the Young Tories, this rhetoric of free-market individualism is *the* ideology rationalizing and extending a corporate takeover of the "government business." I cannot refrain from adding that one must be truly myopic to judge the conquest of public health, social welfare, and other traditional governmental tasks by immense international corporations as a victory for old-fashioned, individualist values and free-market entrepreneurship.

The commercial model of the corporate-government relationship is replacing the others, as already indicated. This radically changes the public-private problem, especially as it bears on the issue of a ruling class. Traditional discussions of the issue have looked to see if there is undue corporate or upper-class influence on government. Given our earlier discussions, it is evident that this is the wrong question. The major problem now is not that corporate leaders unduly influence government leaders to act thus and so in this or that policy area; for many years now they have been composed of members of the same class. The real problem is that private corporations are bringing those policy areas directly under their sway by absorbing traditional governmental national security and social need functions, policies, and activities. Or, the same thing from a slightly different standpoint, it is not a question of the private sector distorting the public sector but of an older public sector being absorbed into a radically expanding private sector. The ultimate question today is, Will there continue to be a public sector in the near future?

Very broadly speaking, this development has two nasty features. It is, of course, heralded as an emerging victory for individualism over bureaucracy and for efficiency over muddle. Perhaps that may even be true from time to time. I don't doubt it. But by the terms of my analysis it also lifts both national security issues and social need issues out of an arena within which the public and its supporting democratic institutions had fairly considerable power and legitimacy to intervene against the aggregate corporate public. National security and social need issues are tossed into an arena in which the corporate public is insulated from intervention by "outsiders." Especially in the area of traditional social need, it changes the services that are offered from matters of citizen right into matters of commercial privilege. To take an extreme case, of the roughly two million police and security personnel now in the United States, approximately two-thirds are employed by private firms, and their numbers continue to grow. Security of one's own life and property in the "public" world can less and less be guaranteed. One must instead go into "the market" and create a "private" protected sphere—a building, housing tract, or store—resting on one's ability to pay. Thus citizen safety joins day care, medical insurance, and employment security as a privilege uniquely enjoyed by the better-off. The broad social programs of both the Reagan and Thatcher governments must be written into this ugly equation. But the metaphor is inaccurate, for we are dealing here with a social inequation that becomes increasingly imbalanced.

Is there a ruling class in the United States? Obviously, there is an upper class that wields vast discretionary power, allied with an omnicompetent middle class, within an institutional and property form that is limitless in its potential application to social and political tasks, in a structure designed to minimize the mental and control capacities of other classes, including in particular the most numerous class, the corporate working class. By the very terms of our discussion, the aggregate corporate public dominates policy in this setting and thus composes an unusually powerful and influential ruling class. And, what is worse, the scope of its influence and its freedom from sanctions imposed by the public appear to be growing.

It is worth remarking here that the so-called privatization movement represents a ruling-class counter to the familiar "welfare state," that is, to many of the historical victories won by the working class of the last generation. This is a topic to which we will subsequently return. Let it for the moment suffice to observe that by all traditional measures, our upper corporate class is more and more a ruling class, although with a radically different long-range approach to government. It seeks to supplant it, not direct it. This is perhaps the most striking, most novel, and most troubling feature of today's ruling class; we must now contend with a ruling class that can increasingly *create* a world in its own image and to its exclusive liking.

Corporate Society: The Fabrication
of the Social World

The technological revolution in the steel, chemical, and electrical in-dustries I described earlier in this book led to changes in industrial society far more sweeping, I believe, than is usually realized. Important enough in their own right, they were also omens of the changes that subsequently occurred in virtually every existing industry of the time and in the many brand new industries their success has since encouraged. Taken together, these technological revolutions remade the physical world we live in. This has obviously been a source of indirect change in the social world as well.

For example, if we could make a list of the physical items now in everyday use, most people would be surprised to find that in almost every case they were either introduced or brought into common use only through the modern corporation. I raise this point because the conventional wisdom usually attributes to the corporations only the phenomenon of mass production, suggesting that what they mass-produced was already being made before the corporate era. But that is not the case; essentially the objects we live with arrived only with the modern corporation. This is true both for grand items like steel bridges, which made it possible to cross defiles, rivers, and bays that simply could not be spanned before the corporate era, and for petty items like telephones, plastics, electrical hand tools, aspirin, and diet ice cream. It is essentially true to say that the physical-social universe of items with which we live—buildings, tools, vehicles, chemicals, food products, medicines, fabrics, and so on—is almost entirely a creation of the modern corporation.

The social effect and the effects on individual consciousness of the technology and productive effort of the modern corporation are obviously quite enormous. Taken in conjunction with the class and property changes I have been describing, the modern corporation has refashioned the social and cultural world quite as extensively and quite as profoundly as it has refashioned the physical-social world.

But at least to date this has been for the most part an inadvertent effect of corporate activity. The basic paradigm has been that the corporations introduced new classes, technologies, or products so that we as individuals have been forced to react, to readjust our ideas, habits, values, life-styles, and so forth. Government, the schools, and cultural institutions have been placed in much the same reactive position, so that, taken together, both individual life and social-institutional life have been thoroughly altered.

Now, however, it is becoming evident that the ruling class is mounting a conscious drive to further remake society in a certain way; essentially, to extend into society the sort of class relationships that emerge within the corporation. In a clear and definite sense they wish to "perfect" corporate society, ridding it of its pre-corporate residues. In short, they are trying to fabricate society itself as a corporate and capitalist product.

One of the main, intended victims of this drive has been the public sector, that is, the social need model of government behavior and government programs. This is hardly a subtle development that must be teased out of tangled and ambiguous evidence. The ruling class increasingly sees social welfare as a set of programs to give away social services the class wishes to produce and sell for a profit. Accordingly, this class has acted to cripple the public sector's ability to compete with it. For example, it has quite literally forced an alteration in, especially, the federal tax system that in principle renders it incapable of supporting an effective public sector. As I have elsewhere argued, this has been achieved by a simple strategy: In the past several decades there has been a wholesale shift in the tax burden away from business and onto the shoulders of the individual taxpayer. Liberal critics of the tax system tend only to stress that there has been a shift of individual taxes from richer to poorer individuals. This, too, is important in discrediting the public sector but nowhere near as massive in its effect as the other. Essentially, the shift in the tax burden has created a situation wherein the individual taxpayer finds he or she is paying more and more taxes into a government that offers fewer and fewer—and those shoddier—services. Meanwhile, the wealthiest part of our economy escapes effective taxation. It follows as night from day that this must ultimately lead to taxpayer revolt against government activity in the social field, hence right into the hands of the ruling class' plans.

The scale of this tax shift is quite enormous; the amount of taxes on business that government forswore in the years roughly 1945 to 1980 was *greater* than the rise in the national debt for the same period. In other words, had there been no such shift in the tax burden, all factors holding equal, we would have come into 1980 not with a huge federal deficit but instead with a considerable federal surplus. One can multiply dramatic incidents like this, but the substantial point is that we live in a society in which large institutions exhibiting corporate form continually expand into new areas at the expense of older ways of doing things and of the groups and classes associated with them. Part and parcel of this process has been a growing deference of governmental agencies to the profit-oriented corporations. More and more, the role of government is to tend to those problems created or left over by the aggressive though planless expansion of the private corporations; this is the way I would analyze poverty and many other kinds of social dislocation and social problems in the United States.

Presiding over these developments is an apparently highly unified, aggregate corporate public that increasingly sees that its opportunities and interests require getting into the "government business." Allied with the multicompetent middle element, this corporate public has discovered that no human social activity is beyond the scope of corporate competence and that in principle no domain or sector under the sun cannot be made to turn a handsome profit. Society itself can be and is now being fabricated as a capitalist product by the modern corporation.

Thus there tends to emerge a distinctive corporate society that mirrors the internal structure of the modern corporation with its three-way division of classes, function, authority, reward, status, responsibility, and entitlement. In such a society, as in the corporation itself, the broadest contours of policymaking come to take in the top management, here the corporate public, while the everyday, more mundane affairs increasingly become the prerogative of the middle group.

And then there is Schmidt. I confess that it is tempting to see "his" hand in the fecklessness of the present-day mass electorate and the obtuseness and social irresponsibility of most present-day democratic political leaders, especially on the liberal and social democratic side. Of course, the point of the figure Schmidt is not that he is a dunce but that he is required by the system to behave as one, whatever his personal merits. I am not entirely convinced one can turn Schmidt into a useful theory of electoral-political behavior but neither am I convinced that political, dunce-like, Schmidt-recalling behavior is entirely unrelated to the practice of Taylorism in industry and, of course, to the wider phenomenon of social Taylorism.

Corporate society is only an *emerging tendency* in contemporary affairs. It is only too easy to take these few ideas I have used to characterize corporate society and to extrapolate them into a full-blown nightmare. But we have not yet addressed whether the reality is as uncomplicated and as lacking in countervailing tendencies as the intellectual model. It is evident that we must look much more closely at the other two corporate classes and their development before we can arrive at a balanced picture of the net historical tendency of modern society and class structure under the impact of the modern corporation.

Bibliographical Essay

Richard Hofstadter's *The Age of Reform: From Bryan to FDR* (Random House, New York, 1960) points to the primacy of the middle classes in the development of the Progressive movement. People in the United States have legendarily assumed that they have much more by way of social mobility than Europeans, though it has long been known that that is entirely illusory; see Seymour Lipset, *Political Man: The Social Bases of Politics* (Doubleday, New York, 1960). In an eminently readable study, W. H. Lewis, for example, attributes considerable social mobility to early eighteenth-century France in his classic *The Splendid Century: Life in the France of Louis XIV* (Doubleday Anchor Books, New York, 1957).

Antonio Gramsci's major work, a series of *Prison Notebooks*, was written while he was imprisoned in fascist Italy during the 1920s and 1930s. Partly because the original was in Italian, it took some thirty years for the *Notebooks* to become widely known to the English-speaking world. In addition, Gramsci had to write them in compressed form and in a cryptic style that disguised their import from his jailers; it was only with considerable difficulty that they were smuggled out of prison in the waning days of his life. Portions of his work are now available in a number of translations and formats as, for example, *Prison Notebooks: Selections* (edited by Quintin Hoare and Geoffrey Smith, International Publishers, New York, 1971). Herbert Marcuse's *One-Dimensional Man* (Beacon Press, Boston, 1966) is quite well known; James O'Connor's *Accumulation Crisis* (Basil Blackwell, New York and London, 1984) is somewhat less so.

On the surface my argument seems very similar to that of C. Wright Mills's *Power Elite* (Oxford University Press, Oxford and New York, 1956). As an undergraduate product of the mid-1950s, I owe a great debt to Mills. His vivid intellectual commitment and his willingness, in behalf of a liberating vision, to beard the stuffed shirts at Columbia University and other prestigious but smug centers of "humane learning" provided a powerful moral example to the few of my generation who would listen. Nonetheless, my own analysis differs in substantial measure from his. Two aspects are particularly noteworthy. Mills normally stays within the intellectual framework provided by conventional sociological "elite theory," wherein an individual joins an elite that remains influential only to the extent that both it and the individual are functional to the institutional and value framework of a specific institution in a specific society. In this sense, elite theory emphasizes that individual members of the elite perform specialized functional tasks and have differing, perhaps conflicting, institutional obligations. It is hardly the ideal framework for Mills's purposes in *Power Elite* in that he wants to emphasize the functional similarity of tasks and the convergence of interests of the various members and kinds of national elite. As I pointed out in the case of Domhoff earlier, the harder Mills tries to demonstrate these similarities and convergences, the more open he is to the (baseless) accusation that his views amount only to a conspiracy theory. Like Domhoff, Mills works within an intellectual framework that perhaps cannot be overcome by certain kinds of empirical evidence, no matter how much of it is advanced. Our present emphasis on class and linked property structures is precisely the element necessary to carry Mills's argument, but it is missing in his work.

Second, Mills had an entirely inadequate conception of the middle group in modern society. Essentially, Mills saw the middle group as white-collar workers contrasted to blue-collar ones. Analytically speaking, the distinction is neither fundamental to industry nor does it accurately identify the distinctive industrial-social role of the middle managerial, professional, and technical class. As his main study of this group, *White Collar: American Middle Classes* (Oxford University Press, Oxford and New York, 1951) reveals, he did not see (1) that the diversity of administrative and technical tasks within modern institutions was assumed by the middle group, leaving top management entirely preoccupied with tasks, experiences, values, and interests that are socially convergent by their very nature, and (2) that the middle corporate group occupies not a politically and socially ambiguous role in the class structure but a firm alliance with top management based on fundamentally complementary interests.

Mills is also among the numerous writers who have described the constant interchange of personnel between government and industry. See his *Power Elite*.

Alfred D. Chandler, Jr., and Herman Daems's *Management Hierarchy: Comparative Perspectives on the Rise of the Modern Industrial Enterprise* (Harvard University Press, Cambridge, 1980) is the source for the Labour party's role in the creation of Imperial Chemical Industries, Ltd.; Wesley F. Craven and James L. Cates, *The History of the Army Air Forces in World War II* (Ayer and Company, New York, 1948) for the material on the inadequacy of GM's Allison aircraft engine.

Mainstream U.S. historians as a rule are cautious about attributing excess *contemporary* political influence to business; such things are chronically portrayed as past abuses now commendably corrected. Thus it is often the case that historians who are by field or outlook somewhat out of the mainstream are much more informative about business-government relations.

A case in point is my source for the Hoover policy toward the oil industry: Gerald D. Nash, *United States Oil Policy, 1890–1964* (University of Pittsburgh Press, Pittsburgh, 1968).

My article on taxes was given the (slightly overheated) title "The Great Escape: The Secret History of the Deficit" by the editors of *The Nation* (August 21–28, 1982).

5

The Modern Middle Class

Corporate form consists of three classes of employees within the modern corporation: top management; the middle group of managers, technicians, and professionals; and the production work force. These last two, the middle element and the workers, form the bases not only of separate social classes but also of classes with sharply opposed social interests.

In the Middle?

Not every observer treats these two groups even as separate productive classes, much less as separate social classes. Instead, they're often spoken of as two kinds of workers, perhaps white-collar as opposed to blue or brain as opposed to brawn out on the plant floor, but workers all the same. Under a system of private property this made sense, partly because there the owner and entrepreneur customarily knew the business well enough to understand the technology or technologies employed or presided over a work effort whose details were controlled by skilled craftspeople. There was no numerous or important middle group. The owner might, it is true, employ a small office staff, perhaps a clerk like Bob Cratchit in Charles Dickens's *Christmas Carol*. People like Cratchit are the prototypes of the term "white-collar worker," but prior to the corporate era their numbers were so few, their roles so unrewarding and, relatively speaking, unimportant in the production process that one could simply dismiss them as another kind of worker, well out of the mainstream of capital-labor conflict, hence of no further theoretical or practical concern.

This option is no longer open to us. People who serve within the middle and lower management echelons of the corporate world, and others closely akin to them, now make up about 25 percent of the work force and are paid nearly half the sum total of wages and salaries. In fact, both their relative size in the work force and their share of wages and salaries have been more or less steadily increasing throughout the corporate era. Thus even from a narrow economic standpoint alone it would be folly to dismiss them in favor of turning our attention exclusively to "more important groups."

There are a number of significant ways in which the middle element and the workers are different in their relationships to the productive system and economic organization. Among the most important are that the two groups sell a fundamentally different product to the corporation, have fundamentally different experiences of industry and industrial life, have a fundamentally different relationship to top management, and, as is too often unappreciated in these discussions, face each other as the prime antagonists in everyday industrial conflict. Taken together, these salient differences between the two groups argue against the idea that both are simply workers who share a common interest in opposing top management over the long run.

Modern, corporate production workers sell undifferentiated labor power to the corporation. In this, one eighteen- to forty-year-old male, in good health, malleable to discipline, and with a high school education is really as good as any other, and, in fact, such workers can be and are routinely substituted for one another by the company. This is part of the meaning of the collective worker. The middle-element monopoly on technique makes this possible because the worker's individual intellectual and creative role in the production process is minimized. But middle-element people do not sell undifferentiated labor power to the corporation; they sell highly specialized and well-developed skills and knowledge that top management could acquire within its own ranks only at the dire cost of limiting its ability to function as a capitalist class.

The attempt to combine the functions of entrepreneur and technologist distinguished and radically limited the capitalist abilities of the older-style entrepreneur or small-business owner. The work of Henry Ford, for example, the very prototype of the successful owner-entrepreneur shows the limitations of the type. Ford was a talented engineer, salesman, and executive with enough of each of these skills to build Ford Motors into one of the leading firms in the world. But Sloan's GM organization radically changed the auto business. Even Ford's monumental abilities were not sufficient to out-engineer, out-market, and out-administer his GM rival, which had adopted Sloan's proposed collective style of administration, in which marketing and engineering problems were assigned to teams of specialists while central management focused solely on expansion and growth. Modern corporate industry is founded upon the assumption that the middle-element group will provide an almost infinite variety of knowledges, techniques, and skills as a fodder for corporate expansion.

The middle-element specialist *as a specialist* is essential to the modern capitalist *as a capitalist*. Of course, hardly any middle-element technologist, whether manager, technician, or professional, is unique and irreplaceable in his or her skills. But the class is irreplaceable, as are the professional and related organizations that make it up. The highly developed nature of the skills and knowledges; the ever-present change in technology, science, and related areas; the personal difficulties of acquiring these skills and knowledges; and social restrictions on the opportunity for acquiring them tend to group the people and their abilities into distinct professions. These professions, in all their multiplicity, are essential to big capital.

The industrial experience of the workers and the middle element is also vastly different. For example, middle-element employees and production employees are different both in their career tracks and in the ways in which they are paid. Despite the possibility of promotion, undifferentiated labor power (the collective worker) doesn't have a career track. Basically, the companies recruit workers just to be workers. The company wants workers to stay with it and consequently grants relatively modest pay increments for seniority. The company wants only a long-term association with its work force, but it does not offer constant employment to its production workers. It lays people off even for a week or a month if they're not needed. If the company's work force must be permanently cut back and not just adjusted to seasonal or cyclical variations in the economy, production workers are much more likely to be fired than people within the management echelon. Finally, the companies consider a forty- to forty-five-year-old worker to be at the end of his or her useful life, but that's often the very point at which they believe the middle-element employee becomes most useful.

That comes because the middle-element employee really does have a career, that is, a long and uninterrupted job history that starts at some bottom rung and then normally proceeds upward toward greater responsibility. The form in which these preferred employees are paid is arranged accordingly. The pay raises they get from successful service within the management echelon are considerable, the curve showing a geometrical character, that is, not straight-line increases but a growing rate of increases. Some of the lowest rungs of management pay less than the jobs of production workers, but as employees climb higher in middle management a combination of salaries, bonuses or other property income, perquisites, and so on leads to gross-income levels that are multiples of the highest worker wages.

Management-echelon employees are rarely laid off, and firing without cause is rarer still. This follows from Sloan's ideas because the modern corporation really does aim at a relatively collective style of work. This is as true for the middle element as for the top management, as the former are essentially technological specialists who must be combined into teams in order to function. People within the management echelon generally are coddled more than just a little. The company may even retain those who are deemed to be unpromotable at a certain point in their careers, reducing their responsibilities but not their pay. Lay-offs and, worse yet, groundless firings would have, according to corporate thought, a devastating effect on the morale of middle management as a whole.

Workers are kept to an industrial style of work, that is, a style with a severe, military-like discipline. In factory work it is not unusual, for example, for management to enforce rules of attendance and behavior that might seem familiar to a high school gym teacher or even to a drill instructor in the marines. Often there are systems of demerits, and a worker who acquires too many demerits is in danger of being laid off or fired. In general, workers are treated as if they were errant, undisciplined children; the old proverb about sparing the rod and spoiling the child would serve as well to describe a real factory as a fictional orphanage. The going assumption in industrial labor relations is that the workers don't know what to do, wouldn't do it without close supervision, and would do it badly unless under severe threat. By contrast, middle-element people are granted a professional style of work in which the employee is assumed to be able to work with only the lightest supervision, is expected to show initiative as a matter of course, and is thought to be a responsible person able to function effectively within a peer group and not solely when under hierarchical discipline.

Top management has what I would call a political relationship to the middle managerial, technical, and professional echelon, that is, a relationship founded directly upon the understanding that both have many common interests and share at least some degree of power. By contrast, their relationship to the production work force, mostly exercised *through* the middle element, has—or they try mightily to give it—an ineradicably technical and administrative nature. That, of course, is the very point of Taylor's story about Schmidt. Meanwhile, middle-element employees are viewed, used, and paid by the corporation as a sort of junior partner class, as well they are because they exercise an effective monopoly over technology and technique. In addition, top management sees them as allies in disputes with the workers. Historically, they have loyally served in this role.

In fact, the familiar argument that middle-level "workers" and production workers are all "really" workers and will accordingly join together "over the long run" is demonstrably false. The middle element has been in existence as a significant industrial group for about a century now. Throughout the stormy history of corporate industrial conflict, it is hard to find a single instance in which they supported the workers against top management; their solidarity with top management is a constant, not only in the United States but also overseas. Consequently, people who want to argue "all workers . . . together . . . in the long run" are either just wrong in their expectations or have far more patience "over the long run" than do ordinary mortals.

Perhaps the most telling if overlooked argument for the view that these are separate industrial classes stems from their conflict with one another. When the modern worker suffers speed-up or is replaced by a machine, that speed-up is first calculated by and then introduced by a member of the middle element, as is the new machine or the new process or the new work organization. Thus the same event that discomfits the worker is a positive achievement for the manager or engineer. If the worker resists a change of assignment or, as has been known to happen, tries to "soldier" to defeat a management-induced change, he or she is observed and disciplined not by upper management but by whatever middle-level manager or straw boss has been placed over her or him. If, then, there is an everyday industrial class struggle, a point that can be attested to by just about anyone who has had industrial experience, that struggle is de facto fought out by production workers on the one side of the battle line and managerial, technical, and professional employees on the other. From the very terms of the conflict, one's victories are more often than not the other's defeats.

The argument that the workers and middle or lower management are both "really" workers usually assumes that their conflicts are misguided and can be erased if only both sides (especially middle and lower management) come to understand their real interests. That, frankly, is a fairy-tale argument. It stems from a failure to see that the modern middle group is not, as in Marx's time, a class that rivals and is destroyed by the growth of big capital but is now instead a class nurtured by corporate capital and locked in a mutually advantageous embrace with it. Corporate form demands a high degree of conflict between the middle managerial, technical, and professional group on the one hand and the workers on the other; in a real sense that is why the middle element was "invented." It is a class designed, as it were, to absorb the working class' historical industrial levers into its own ranks and then to use them to erect an administrative and technological dictatorship over the workers in behalf of more profitable results.

The conclusion that workers and the middle element are different and opposed productive classes seems to me extremely powerful. When we factor in their different property relationships within corporate form, it strongly establishes the presumption that we are dealing here with two different social classes as well.

The Professions and Professionalism

The organized profession and the wider phenomenon of professionalism are the key to the class position and role of the middle element. In them the individual member of the middle managerial, technical, and professional class enjoys a collective property claim against the corporate surplus and a collective protection of his or her interests. This view of the middle element contrasts with and, I believe, should replace the view popular among economists that the middle-element man or woman is the private owner of a piece of "human capital" that he or she then freely sells in the market place.

Until about a century ago this view of professionalism was not true. Then the existing professions were entrepreneurial in their nature, that is, their occupants sold their skills much like small-business people sold their wares. We may use the legal profession, which still is largely entrepreneurial, as an example of that older professionalism, and it will serve as well to give us an idea of the scope of the change to the modern system. According to legend, when Abraham Lincoln wanted to be a lawyer he presented himself to a practicing attorney and asked to be allowed to clerk. He had few formal qualifications for the post, but such things were not required in those days. Literacy, perhaps an engaging personality, and a willingness to earn little pay while in the apprenticeship were all that were required. When both the attorney and Lincoln himself were satisfied that he had gained an adequate knowledge of the law and of court procedure, he was admitted on the judgment of other lawyers to qualify as one of their number and in that way joined the bar. Admission requirements were somewhat informal. Once admitted to the legal profession, the responsibility fell on Lincoln to drum up business and so on—just as if he were a traveling merchant or a land developer. He could have been removed from the bar for this or that crime, but this decision, too, would be made by lawyers and would in that distant time have been based on somewhat informal criteria, at least as compared to today's way of doing things. Lawyering in those days had elements of technical knowledge and technique, but it was predominantly an entrepreneurial endeavor in which success or failure rested much more on the arts of the huckster or the conjurer than on formal, technical attainments.

Law was not the only profession practiced in this way. Nowadays we think of medicine as the apogee of a scientifically based profession in which at least a certain technical competence in recognizing and treating diseases is requisite. But that is the result of victories won by the scientific medical profession around the turn of the century. Before that, one could qualify to be a doctor through a process akin to the one Lincoln went through to become a lawyer. In some cases and places even less than that was required. So-called doctors who rendered "cures" for this and that (real or imaginary) disease, based on whatever ideas were most salable to gullible clients, were a commonplace in the nineteenth-century United States, so much so that their brand of charlatanism even got its own special name in folklore: "quack medicine."

The premodern professions, then, were organized somewhat after the fashion of guilds of skilled workers. These organizations reach back almost to the prehistory of mankind. Basically, guilds were organizations of artisans who possessed a monopoly over the knowledge of some craft. They established apprenticeship programs both to pass on the knowledge of the craft and to limit the numbers of people who could practice it. Parts of this system had also evolved for the several professions; it was this that Lincoln took advantage of to become a lawyer.

On the purely technical level, it was probably less challenging to become a lawyer or a physician in the last century than to become a carpenter or a brewer because one's peers in those crafts would have been far more demanding than in most "professions" of the time. The carpenter and the brewer were then much more technically competent in their fields than the lawyer or physician in theirs. In that time and for many years before, the artisans really did possess useful knowledge and effective skill in dealing with woods and tools or corn and yeast. But the other professions, with the possible exception of civil and military engineering and architecture, shared a low estate. The entrepreneurial nature of the professions clearly exerted as much pressure to get by on whatever bogus services could be passed off on the public as it did to upgrade their purely technical capacities.

The modern professions date from the simultaneous birth of two great institutions, the profit-making corporation and the modern university, also a corporation and with no less a technical bent than its profit-oriented first cousin. Thus, although today's professions present themselves to the rest of us as if they were always as they are now, they are practically a new social creation. (They are certainly no longer organized as entrepreneurial groups. In this, lawyering, which used to be representative of the other professions, is now the great exception.) We should conceive of the modern professions, then, as existing at the point where the corporations and the universities intersect. Here the paradigm is that the university monopolizes the training of the modern professions whereas the corporation has a near monopoly on their use. Or, because the scientific and technical foundations of nearly all the professions are funded almost exclusively by government, it is useful and accurate to consider the modern professions as existing at the intersection of those *three* institutions. In a real sense, a profession is the intersection of those institutions. It is within that definite and demanding institutional structure that the professions retain traces—but only traces—of their past.

Contemporary professions tend to have highly formal procedures for entry, training, certification, and review of the work of their members. The profession's own standing within the university, corporation, or government depends on its gaining legitimacy from all three, with the university insisting on exercising a strict rein on entry to the profession and a somewhat looser control on training and certification, and the corporations seeing that the profession can deliver the reliable, already trained, immediately usable personnel the profession claims to be made up of. Except in the national security area, the government is pretty much willing to fund whatever professional-technical directions are agreed upon by the corporation-university nexus.

The demands of this institutional structure have shifted the modern professions away from an entrepreneurial model in which the individual professional could win his or her success based largely on grit, hard work, a smattering of knowledge, and a winning personality. Increasingly, modern professions cannot be exercised by independent entrepreneurs. The would-be professional person must gain the formal approval of some institution of higher education in order to join it. Then he or she can practice the profession only within the corporation or nonprofit agency, which alone can provide the expensive equipment and the docile workers it requires. Even medicine, which but a few short years ago was one of the entrepreneurial professions par excellence, has more recently become a profession essentially rooted in and carried on within the ambit of the modern hospital.

This sea change in the meaning of professionalism stems from the same period as the birth of the modern corporation and is associated with the foundation of the modern university in the 1880s. Universities, it is true, are ancient institutions, dating in some cases well back to the Middle Ages. But the modern university is a copy of certain developments in German institutions that began toward the middle and end of the nineteenth century and in which a classics- and theology-based curriculum was replaced by the product of modern, secular scholarship, particularly in the sciences and, later, in law and language. Civil and military engineering have had a long history as professions based either on verifiable scientific information or on long-established and thoroughly reliable practices. Architecture, too, appears to have enjoyed a long and honorable history. But these fields were profoundly transformed by the burst of new engineering and materials knowledge and technique that occurred. As for the other modern professions, virtually all of them grew up in the latter decades of the nineteenth century, usually within the university, which shed its older preoccupation with educating "gentlemen" (or perhaps parsons) and turned to the more demanding task of turning out technical specialists, knowledgeable in the latest scientific and engineering discoveries and useful to industry and government. In fact, most of the modern professions didn't even exist at the turn of the century but were spawned by the scientific and technical discoveries of the modern university, the production needs of the modern corporation, and the acceptance by governments everywhere that economic growth, political stability, and military power have technical roots.

Changes also occurred in the way professions are practiced. A modern professional experiences a different world than that of the private entrepreneur, although he or she still retains certain of the privileges of the independent, self-guided businessperson. In practice, to be a modern professional is to enjoy self-supervision. The contrast between this and the dictatorship exercised by middle-element people over workers is too vivid to require extensive commentary. As in the old guilds, self-supervision represents more than just the claim that one knows how to do the work without supervision. One of the recurring arguments made by professionals is that overseeing is not only technically unnecessary but also superfluous in the moral or quasi-moral sense. Professionalism connotes that the professional will in fact work responsibly and at the optimum pace because he or she is a professional.

In somewhat the same way that the corporate public organizes itself as a class through the corporation and exerts its power and influence through that particular social institution, the middle element organizes itself through the phenomenon of professionalism and similarly uses the professions to project its power and influence within corporate society. In this the middle-element employees differ fundamentally from owners of purely private capital, human or otherwise. They cannot hope to extend their social and political influence through family-based mechanisms because the middle element doesn't exercise its most potent social possession, the monopoly on technology and technique, through the family but rather within the corporate world and through participation in the profession. Those in the middle element can leave property to their children, but, again, their most important property can only be bequeathed by preparing the next generation to enter that professional world.

When the professions and professionalism are transmuted into general social relationships, they continue to show their origin in corporate form. Even within the productive process, middle-element people insist that so-called professional values be recognized. The peer principle among professionals—that is, the notion that hierarchy among themselves is justified solely if and to the extent that it is functionally based—is crucial. As we can see, this value fits well with Sloan's pioneering management style and its emphasis on consultation among all concerned executives, persuasion rather than command, and allowing specialists to work without excessive supervision.

This blend of peer equality, hierarchy determined by knowledge or ability, and self-supervision characterizes not only the narrow economic but also the wider social world of the modern professional. It is often combined with an ideology about the primacy of technology, which we've met before, or of scientific or social rationality in general in order to justify the claim that the middle element is the most important class for economic growth as well as for the foundation of a democratic polity and society. Notice that the middle element's claim to an important economic, social, and political place is not argued on the basis of the ownership of physical property but in terms of its supposedly central role in the effective functioning of our overall institutional structure.

Within the class, the philosophy of professionalism functions to legitimate the activity of virtually any and all subgroups, whether these are narrowly professional or have an ideological, special-interest, or public-service character. Unlike the ruling class or owners of private property generally, who place a high value on class unity, or the working class, which would like to be able to do the same, the middle element almost revels in its own diversity. Ultimately, I believe, this underlines its sense that it and no other is the class of last resort for democratic political institutions. For this reason, too, the middle element is the class within which the greatest variety of political activity occurs, and it is the most active, visible class in the overt party political process and in various issue-oriented organizations.

From the broadest ideological and even practical standpoints, the middle element therefore comes to embody not only technology per se but functional rationality in general. In fact, had Ellul happened to single them out from among the other classes in modern society, the whole of his critique might well have been thrown at them, for they are the most potent bearers of such purely functional values today. Their ideal is "meritocracy," the idea that superior *personal* achievement—as they (mis)conceive it—and it alone confers superior privileges. Their concession to the other classes is "equality of opportunity," which is often confused with "equality." "Equality of opportunity," by contrast, means quite literally that everyone ought to have an equal opportunity to win a place of special privilege and, too often, in Orwell's famous phrase, to be "more equal than others."

The High Costs of the Middle Class:
A Digression on Economic Class Conflict

The failure of economists and sociologists to distinguish the middle managerial, professional, and technical class as a distinct class has contributed to a number of harmful economic myths about modern industrial and social life, almost always to the detriment of the workers themselves. These myths play a considerable role in the conflict of interests of the two classes. In fact, in a situation somewhat akin to the failure of analysts to distinguish private from corporate property, the failure to distinguish middle-element income from specifically worker income plays a considerable ideological role in contemporary class conflict.

Analysts generally merge, for example, the incomes of the two classes into a single category, "wage and salary income." But, using a rule of thumb, roughly 25 percent of those employed in the big corporate world are members of this privileged middle group, and *their* share of corporate payroll has reached nearly half. Thus by collapsing these figures into a single income category, one creates the impression that workers earn far more than they actually do. This spurious "merging" distorts many sensitive economic categories: In recent years it has helped to hide the steady real *growth* of specifically worker productivity and the simultaneous *decline* of specifically worker income. The percentage of middle-element corporate employees has recently appeared to stabilize, but their impact on payrolls continues to grow. In short, this is an exceptionally large and well-paid class of corporate employees. There is even suggestive evidence that they may be overpaid, that is, paid out of proportion to their contribution to the aggregate surplus.

The manufacturing sector of the economy, one of the most heavily corporatized, provides perhaps the most striking picture of the middle element's economic impact. Over 35 percent of all employees are within the middle managerial, professional, and technical echelon, yet they are paid over 47 percent of payroll. In short, in U.S. manufacturing there is roughly one manager or the equivalent to every two workers, and that manager is paid just about what *both* workers together are paid. In fact, because bonus and other proprietary income is often not counted under the payroll category, the 47 percent figure is deceptively low as a measure of the managerial, professional, and technical class' income in the corporate sector.

From the purely economic point of view, the middle element and the corporate working class are no less antagonists than are capital and labor. As suggested, this issue is little understood because of the widespread failure to distinguish three, not merely two, fundamental classes in contemporary society. The following describes some of the main frontiers of specifically economic class conflict.

As already indicated, separate industrial, but not social, statistics are maintained for corporate workers and the corporate middle element. Thus the economic identity and impact of this large and wealthy class are relatively easy to trace within industry but not in the wider society. The reader will appreciate the ideological implications of this omission.

U.S. labor law and industrial practice sharply separate all middle- and lower-level corporate employees into separate, entirely non-overlapping groups. As I mentioned in a previous chapter and will subsequently analyze in the next chapter, people who carry out managerial functions or who have access to confidential information about such things are sharply distinguished from those who don't. In law and in practice the distinction closely follows Taylor's principles. The two groups are often shorthandedly referred to as "management and management confidential" on the one side and those "eligible for a (collective) bargaining unit" on the other. Following on this, the Commerce Department and other statistics-collecting agencies normally distinguish the same two groups in their data as "nonproduction" and "production workers," respectively. The legal and the statistical definitions do not designate precisely the same groups, but the differences are unimportant and, for our discussion, miniscule.

But Commerce and other departments do not parallel these statistics on the social side. There we meet "male," "female," "black," "white," "rural," "urban" as statistical categories or the same people ranked, let us say, by income and then distinguished into fifths, tenths, or twentieths for purposes of further study. Of particular importance to us is that these *social* statistics tend to obscure the very classes we find so clearly evident in the industrial statistics and, of course, in actual and legal reality. Thus the fairly smooth gradations of income we see on the social side are a poor indicator of what we know from the industrial side, namely, that there is an income overlap between what are in fact radically different classes of people with radically different economic prospects. That is, the young executive in this year's figures is lumped in with the middle-aged welder, even though we know that two or five years from now that executive will be earning some multiple of the welder's only slightly improved wages.

More broadly, this statistical anomaly is part of the reason the conventional social science can point with self-satisfied self-deception to a U.S. working class that is reaching or has already reached secure "middle-class status." Social scientists fail to see that there is a dual structure and result in pay and other rewards in industry and that the contrasts between the two groups are more often than not quite striking—now apparently widening. This blindness provides the foundation for a veritable host of economic and social superstitions.

The Commerce Department statistics also give a crude breakdown of all income into two kinds: "private property incomes" from interest, dividends, entrepreneurial profits, and so forth as distinguished from "wages and salary income." Given the massive increase in the middle managerial, technical, and professional class in this century, it is perfectly evident that the category of wage and salary income would vastly outstrip property income, especially because the son of yesterday's entrepreneur is so often today's corporate middle manager. Here, too, the failure to mark off the middle corporate class from those below it leads to wildly absurd social and economic conclusions. In particular, this statistic about the shift toward wages and salary income and away from property income is often used as the basis for the peculiar conclusion that the workers themselves are the major economic beneficiary of modern capitalism.

Had I time and space, I might readily show that industrial productivity data in general, data about worker productivity in particular, about union wage gains and their impact on inflation, and a host of other substantial economic questions with important practical and theoretical ramifications are distorted by the failure to take account of two distinct and different lower corporate classes. In almost all cases that I know of, this neglect of the economic impact of the middle managerial, professional, and technical class leads investigators to conclusions hostile to the economic situation of workers, mainly by exaggerating their income and its growth. These conclusions then become the basis for payroll, tax, trade union regulation, and other policies that ultimately contribute to a further widening of the economic and social prospects of the two classes.

It is clear that this middle element is a major factor in the expansion of the private corporations into "the government business." They can afford to pay for education, retirement, health, cultural, and other services once provided by government on an equal basis for all. But with a large and apparently unending growth of their share of relative income, the middle element, I would argue, doesn't want these services on an equal basis for all. They want a privileged basis, better services of an exclusive kind that government, from the nature of the case, cannot provide. Again we find the middle group in society closely allied with the aggregate corporate public on a substantive issue in which their economic interests and intent are at sharp divergence from those of the other, lower corporate class.

It is an open question whether the expansion of the size and the income and other advantages of the middle element at the nominal expense of the workers is economically necessary. That is, in an earlier period when U.S. industry led the world, one *could* argue that the reason U.S. industry was so advanced and its workers the highest paid in the world was correctly associated with the relative expansion in the size and rewards of the middle corporate class. Now, however, when certain European workers typically earn more than their U.S. counterparts, even though the relative size of their middle elements is less than ours, such an association seems patently erroneous. In fact, the same argument can then be turned on its head to maintain that the middle-element class in the United States is appreciably larger than is economically desirable and necessary, that its economic reward, exceeding its economic contribution, rests in part on its purely *political* assistance to capital. If so, that would go far to explain the relative decline of the United States, especially in manufacturing, in relation to the rest of the developed capitalist world. Of course, the conventional social science doesn't see it that way. By their peculiar lights it is perfectly clear that the *workers* are overpaid and insufficiently productive.

All in all, then, that the economic impact of the middle corporate class is rarely and only episodically explored constitutes a major hurdle to our gaining even minimally adequate answers to many familiar and vexing economic issues. At the same time, it leaves the intellectual and policy terrain wide open for economic arguments, theories, and practices that are unabashedly hostile to the interests of modern workers, their unions, and their families. In fact, economists in general, perhaps out of implicit loyalty to their own class and its interests, have managed to ignore in their quantitative calculations the very middle corporate class they themselves so often credit for the remarkable qualitative advance of Western, capitalist technology.

But it is surely empirically true that over the past eighty-odd years, the advance of Western capitalist industry has benefited from the division of labor between the middle element and a Taylorized working class. It is beyond dispute that this aspect of corporate form imposes a harsh and dangerous experience on the workers but at the same time can be plausibly associated with vast advances in productivity and consequently with higher worker living standards. Whether the radical improvement in worker living standards is sufficient to counterbalance the occupational hardships of a Taylorized factory or office is another question. Conventional social science, ignoring the presence of two different classes, furnishes itself with more than enough spurious material to conclude as a certainty that the equation balances. An intellectual movement among Marxian writers, most prominently influenced by the late Harry Braverman, has argued the contrary position, namely, that modern, Taylor-like management systems have imposed net harm on the working class.

Standing aside from both these antagonists for the present, it seems to me to be nevertheless *possible* that Braverman is wrong and his foes right. If so, it represents a deep and unalloyed tragedy for the mass of mankind in the advanced countries. That is, there may be some necessary connection between a technologically sophisticated society with high and perhaps improving standards of living and the condemnation of something like two out of every three employees to unceasing industrial purgatory. I say this *may* be true because although many claim that technologies exist or can be devised to allow workers a humane industrial environment, the claims are typically airy, their protagonists marked more by hope and goodwill than by social and technical inventiveness. So far as I know that surmisal has been seriously challenged only by the ideas and actions of parts of the Italian working class.

There seems to me little doubt that the modern corporate middle class and the conditions of its social and technological existence represent an enormous qualitative drain on society and, if the European-U.S. contrast is to be taken at face value, a quantitative drain as well. Nevertheless, it remains an open question whether such a social class, using its social-technical position to gather a vast share of the social surplus unto itself while inflicting draconian conditions on its worker subordinates, is ultimately necessary to a thoroughly modern society.

An International Class

The middle element is a truly national class, and there is reason to believe that it is also the first genuine international class. We can take up these points separately.

Economists sometimes talk of *a* national labor market. There is one of sorts for workers, mostly because the nationally based unions and the national companies all react to one another's wage and benefit agreements. There is even some interregional migration of workers in search of jobs, but practically speaking not enough to justify the concept that we have *only* a national labor market. Even to this day there are still any number of regional and local labor markets for workers, so that jobs that are oversubscribed in one part of the country go begging in another. There are also key regional and local disparities in wage rates, conditions, benefits, and other important items. These differences are being ironed out— dramatically so—but we don't yet have a single market for labor. There is, however, just such a thing for middle-element people.

It is now common for would-be middle-element managers, technicians, and professionals to grow up in one region of the country, attend college in another, take postgraduate training in a third, and then move to still a fourth region to start out in their professions. For many years now that pattern has become more common. Geographical mobility doesn't end with the first job either. Many companies routinely shift their rising executives from place to place in order to establish their loyalty to the corporate "community" and not to some town or district. All of this has tended to erase regional and local differences in salaries and perquisites. Related to these changes, there has been a decline in the difference of the quality of professional training offered in different parts of the country. Not too many years ago certain state education systems, particularly in the South, were thought distinctly inferior to those in the rest of the country.

Nowadays a middle-element professional can easily move from city to city without fear of entering an alien, provincial, highly regional culture with unexpected peculiarities in food, social customs, schools, race relations, religious tolerance, and so forth. With some exception he or she can expect to find in the new locale pretty much the same life-style, shops, school system, and potential friends and colleagues that he or she had had in another part of the country. This in turn has helped to erase further the social, cultural, and political variations among professionals in different parts of the country, creating a more or less unitary class acting on a national basis.

I would venture the hypothesis that the resurgence of the Republican party in the past few decades is based upon this nationalizing of the middle element. It is well known, for example, that much of the impetus for the

New Deal and other liberal initiatives came from parts of the middle managerial, technical, and professional class, which was deeply embroiled in social, cultural, and even economic conflict with what it felt was Babbitry, Main Street, small-town provincialism, and so forth—that is, with the power and influence of the small-business or entrepreneurial class. The steady expansion of the corporate sector of our economy, along with its concomitant social and cultural victories, has essentially settled this older conflict between the different middle classes in favor of the middle element. Accordingly, we would normally expect such a privileged group to forget, as it were, the rebellious impulses of its youth and settle comfortably into the more conservative of the two parties, perhaps, in the manner of converts, becoming "even more Catholic than the pope."

There has also been fairly considerable internationalizing of the middle element. For example, in recent years it has become common for middle-element people to live and work overseas for long periods, sometimes broken up by stretches in the home country. Similarly, nationals who have middle-element qualifications now travel to other countries in search of work. As a rule these strangers are welcomed—often positively recruited—by the host country in a kind of reverse "brain drain." In the United States the immigration laws have even been reshaped several times in recent years so as to make it quite easy for foreign professionals to come and work— provided they are not "tainted" by left-wing ideas or associations.

What is happening here is relatively straightforward. To borrow from our earlier discussion, the middle element is the social embodiment of "technology" as a form of productive capital. Each economically active class member represents a unit of some technical knowledge or ability that can be easily joined with others to form a productive social mechanism. He or she, like physical resources, labor power, and financial mechanisms, is a form of modern productive capital that must be combined in order to create or recreate pockets of modern corporate economy. The development of an international middle-element class made capital more mobile than ever before. Capital in the form of machinery and materials was, of course, always transportable, but where it could go was limited by the technological backwardness of the labor force of certain areas and by the lack of an adequate economic and financial infrastructure. An international middle element solves both those problems. Because this class embodies and monopolizes technology, the relative backwardness of the local labor force ceases to matter. Interchangeability among workers today extends across borders. The collective worker isn't losing his or her nationality, but from the economic standpoint that nationality is irrevelant. One can now make steel in Lagos or microchips in Seoul, whereas until recently places such as these were limited to the production of agricultural commodity crops or straw hats. That same middle element also brings its organizational and financial technique with it, so that every country in the world can support an infrastructure adequate to the needs of the corporations.

It is not clear that there is yet a truly international capital. There are, of course, international capitals, but they seem to be employed with more than a hint of national rivalry. But every capitalist uses or wants to use the same technology, that is, the most advanced. In that sense technology is above politics.

I don't think we have as yet a fully developed international class of middle-element people, but we are going rapidly in that direction, most notably in Europe. In almost any city in the world it is possible to observe the international middle-element life-style. People in places as diverse as Paris and Hong Kong, Khartoum and Tokyo, New York and Brasília wear, drive, and drink the same brands. They watch the same movies and television and, more often than not, can speak to one another in the same language, English. To a startling degree all these things either are true or would be true in the communist countries as well, save for their restrictions on purchases from the Western, hard-currency nations. Instead of using the same brands as in the West, therefore, they make their own. But in doing so they try to ape the existing international middle-class style.

It should again be noted that this national and international development has had an enormously corrosive effect on the small-business or entrepreneur class. This effect is particularly marked in the United States. By definition, such a class remains basically a local and, at best, regional grouping. Still, they are not an inconsiderable group of people. To this day they employ nearly half the workers in the private sector and generate something near to a quarter of the national product. But as a class they are in rapid decline. In fact, the decline of the class takes so many forms, some not readily apparent, that it is hard to calculate its size and therefore the approximate rate of its reduction. Basically, however, the growth of a national and international middle element interrupts the social reproduction of the small-business class by attracting its children away from local and regional life and into the more challenging and prestigious world of the multinational corporation and its more cosmopolitan social and cultural ways. My impression is that, until two or three decades ago, the small-business sector retained enough economic muscle to hold its own against the corporate classes in the social, cultural, and even political arenas by dominating local power structures of the less metropolitan areas. But the continuing national development of corporate form has undermined this influence, accounting for the erasure of regional cultural and social differences and the rise of a more truly national and even cosmopolitan culture than the United States has previously experienced.

There are suggestive parallels to this overseas. I have already mentioned the similarity of middle-element life-styles in the industrial countries and the frequent exchange of individuals among them. Similarities in their respective political movements have also developed. On this basis I would in part explain the intimate ideological and programmatic relationship between Reagan's Republicans and Thatcher's Tories as well as the burgeoning ecology and antinuclear groups in the industrial countries. All of these movements appear to find if not their social basis, then certainly their leadership cadres in the middle corporate class of managers, professionals, and technicians.

Bibliographical Essay

The concept that modern employees own and hire out their "human capital" has even received systematic treatment by the economics profession. See, for example, Gary Becker, *Human Capital: A Theoretical and Empirical Analysis with Special Reference to Education* (2d edition, National Bureau of Economics Research, distributed by Columbia University Press, New York, 1975). The Ehrenreichs' article, already cited, has much interesting material on the evolution of the modern professions. See also Christopher Jencks and David Riesman, *The Academic Revolution* (University of Chicago Press, Chicago, 1969).

The intellectual movement led by the late Harry Braverman (*Labor and Monopoly Capital: The Degradation of Work in the 20th Century*, Monthly Review Press, New York, 1974) has an unfortunate tendency to romanticize skilled workers. This is partly a matter of overlooking the invidious relationship such workers typically enjoyed vis-à-vis their nonskilled apprentices and helpers. For example, in the Homestead (Pennsylvania) strike and lockout of 1892—the death knell for skilled-worker power over modern U.S. industry—the members of the Amalgamated Association of Iron and Steel Workers had a peculiar relationship to the employer, Carnegie Steel. As was not atypical prior to the development of the managerial professions, the skilled workers managed the details of making iron and steel, much as modern construction workers still manage the erection of a building. Accordingly, the members of the Amalgamated were paid not a wage or salary but a tonnage rate. The skilled workers themselves then hired, trained, supervised, and paid the wages of their helpers. The unromantic reality of skilled-worker domination of the labor process becomes apparent when we see that only 800 of the 3,800 workers at Carnegie were members of that exclusive craft union and that they maintained a pay differential between the best- and worst-paid workers of about 9:1. Of course, that *is* the point: In a technology dominated by skilled workers, the vast majority of workers are not skilled and do not have many industrial and other levers to exert against either their nominal employers or their skilled-worker bosses and in behalf of their own interests.

The other side of the romantic view of skilled workers is that such a view simply does not take into account that the accumulated and rapidly changing science and technology of the modern era is effectively passed on and developed by institutions dedicated to that purpose, that is, the modern university system. A return to an apprenticeship system such as characterized industry, say, 100 years ago is clearly beside the point. One may rue the social values lost with the demise of the skilled worker, but that is not tantamount to understanding how to deal with even the coarsest, basest consequences of Taylorism. People who follow Braverman really leave themselves only a Hobson's choice—a choice from a set of unsatisfactory alternatives—for industrial organization and work environment.

In July 1989, according to NBC, workers in the Federal Republic of Germany earned on average 30 percent more than their U.S. counterparts. In general, U.S. standards of living, especially for workers, have for a number of years been surpassed by Germany, the Scandinavian countries, France, Switzerland, the Netherlands, Belgium, and—to drive the point home—by the Grand Duchy of Luxembourg. Progressive, even neo-Marxist economists are, apparently, not immune to blaming the deterioration of U.S. industry on overpaid and underproductive workers. This is one of the major themes implicit in, for example, Samuel Bowles, David M. Gordon, and Thomas E. Weisskopf, *Beyond the Wasteland: A Democratic Alternative to Economic Decline* (Anchor/Doubleday, New York, 1983).

In the fall of 1969, workers in Turin, Milan, Genoa, and other northern Italian areas carried out one of the most remarkable and innovative labor struggles on record. As Joanne Barkan makes clear in her *Visions of Emancipation: The Italian Workers Movement Since 1945* (Praeger, New York, 1984), there was a conscious attempt to devise alternatives to the management domination of the labor process, and workers made a number of dramatic gains. In general, the Europeans are far ahead of U.S. laborers in the attempt to end the shop-floor dictatorship of the middle element. Even the standard comparative study of the labor systems of the capitalist democracies by Benjamin Aaron and K. W. Wedderburn, *Industrial Conflict: A Comparative Legal Survey* (Crane and Russak, New York, 1972) shows how marked this tendency has been. Some of this material is brought up to date in *Comparative Labour Law and Industrial Relations*, edited by Roger Blainpain (3d edition, Kluwer Law and Taxation Publishers, Deventer, Netherlands, 1987).

6

Managing the Collective Worker

Members of the modern working class are subordinated both as individuals and as a class within corporate society. Accordingly, we should begin our study of the workers by describing and analyzing the main mechanisms that shape and control them. These include social Taylorism, the phenomenon of socially compulsory consumption, and the transformation of trade unions from organizations representing workers into controlling arms of the state mechanism. Each of these replicate socially the class relationships we found initially only within corporate form. Thus in each of them the modern working class faces the middle managerial, professional, and technical group as its immediate class superior and direct social antagonist. As a preliminary to looking at the first of these phenomena, social Taylorism, we must clear from the path the unfortunate legacy left to us by the Weberian analysis of "bureaucracy."

"Bureaucracy" and Class Domination

Max Weber's concept of "bureaucracy" covers much the same ground as my "corporate form" but does not sufficiently emphasize the scope and importance of class dominance within modern institutions. This mars an analysis that is otherwise useful, although far too sweeping in its claims. "Weberian" ideas on bureaucracy and modern social organization have become a veritable commonplace of almost all modern discussions about large organizations and are routinely employed by newscasters reporting on the sins of the "Soviet bureaucracy," conservative politicians pointing with alarm to the "swollen bureaucracy" in Washington, left-wingers diagnosing "the collaborationist bureaucracy" as the cause of labor's ills, or the plain citizen complaining of "the bureaucracy" that sent out the wrong item from a buyer's catalog. "Bureaucracy" has become a kind of perverse philosopher's stone able to recreate its sins and errors in every time and clime and under all political colors. To the critical reader that very elasticity should sound an alarm that something is wrong with the concept.

Actually, Weber's basic insight and analysis are so cogent and useful that one is inclined just to accept them and go on. His argument—somewhat simplified—goes as follows:

The main social institutions of the modern world dwarf those that immediately preceded them. Nowadays (for Weber, the two decades on either side of 1900) government, banks, manufacturing companies, political parties, and unions have grown enormously and, in so doing, have tended to reorganize themselves into bureaucracies. That is, the various functions they perform are broken down into a systematic arrangement and division of tasks and assigned to functionaries who work under an appropriate hierarchy of authority. Often these functionaries—bureaucrats—perform very narrow and specialized tasks and hold their positions, as a rule, because they have acquired particular qualifications to perform them. They operate under a system of well-defined rules and are accountable to their superiors, who pay them a salary. Often they come to see themselves as having a special and honorable calling that distinguishes them from other wage earners and confers upon them a certain status.

To the modern student of society, all this is so familiar and so commonplace as hardly to bear comment. Yet we must realize that the triumph of "bureaucracy" as we know it has occurred only in the past 100 to 150 years in the industrial countries and hardly at all in the rest of the world. For example, in the South Vietnam I knew so well in the 1960s, the government, the army, the unions (such as they were), schools, the police themselves had all the faults that Weber considered endemic to the premodern way of organizing society through what he called "charismatic" authority. Basically, in South Vietnam each of the institutions mentioned was run by a strongman who assigned duties, often without systematic order and plan. In fact, government leaders and high officers in Vietnam customarily gave overlapping assignments and responsibilities to their satraps, who were thus forced to quarrel with one another in pursuit of their duties and had little time to engage in plots to remove their chief. In addition, anything at all controversial had to be referred to the top for settlement. Thus, though the South Vietnamese army, police, and so on had what appeared to their U.S. "advisers" to be a modern bureaucracy, all the main players had a personal relation to the chief that glued things together.

In such a system the old saw "It isn't what you know, it's who you know" becomes more than a cynical observation; it is *the* rule of the game. People achieve high office almost solely because they are loyal to the chief or can be made so. Whether they can lead the division, manage the national bank, run the police, or edit the newspaper hardly matters at all. These cronies are accountable only to the top boss and, in fact, in Vietnam more often than not they saw their posts as rewards for loyalty to their chief, rewards they mined for all the graft and pay-offs imaginable. Finally, these cronies had no separate calling; when the leader fell or (as was the custom) was pushed from power, they fell with him, to be replaced by the cronies of the new chief.

Weber generally was of the view that the rise of bureaucracy was a good thing, better than previous social practices. But, of course, it needn't be better, and it can be far worse. As he himself pointed out, it is more or less endemic for a large bureaucracy to acquire a life of its own and to function as if it—not the tasks assigned to it—were the be all and end all for which it was created. This phenomenon tends to attach the adverse connotation to the very word "bureaucracy" in everyday usage. Moreover, this negative note is reinforced by the most knowledgeable analyses both of Stalin's terror and Hitler's mass-murder programs, which argue that they were inspired by small numbers of zealots but largely carried out by numerous bureaucrats "just following orders."

Weber believed—at least in theory—that modern society had only the two alternatives for organizing its affairs, the bureaucratic way or the way of charismatic leaders, including chiefs and their cronies. Obviously, this doesn't leave much room for choice. To the contemporary mind, one option carries a distinct odor of death and the other suggests the nightmare of a lawless, freebooting society run by willful patrons and their bootlickers. Even when we recall that Weber was only describing highly idealized types of social arrangements, it still leaves us with a menu of social choices for organizing our affairs that incorporates only unsatisfactory features, as all the real options are but impure mixtures of the two types.

Yet Weber's "bureaucracy" is much too sweeping a concept, in part because he wrongly assumed characteristics to be natural and necessary to any and every large-scale social institution. Modern discussions, as I've earlier indicated, start at the point of noticing that bureaucracies take on a momentum and life of their own. But, having already dealt with Sloan and Taylor, we are in a position to see that this is not just an open-and-shut proposition. Sloan in particular devoted the best part of his creative life to attacking that problem by trying to devise organizational and other measures to keep the routine and necessary elements of GM's giant organization responsive to the thoughtful, deliberate directions of its top leaders. If the "problem of bureaucracy" is its tendency to take on a life of its own, then Sloan's innovations constitute a noteworthy and successful counterstroke against the bureaucratic colossus. In fact, Sloan's efforts appear to have borne fruit in practice and to be capable of further refinement.

Corporate form is, historically speaking, the response best calculated to "solve" the problems posed by "bureaucracy." But we must add a critical proviso: It is the response from the top. I'm introducing a distinction here that—unhappily but unsurprisingly—is not normally introduced in these discussions. Sloan does not appear to have known of Weber's work, but he certainly saw a similar problem, namely, that GM's bureaucracy wasn't sufficiently responsive to top management. On the other hand, Sloan— with Taylor—wanted to make it *less* responsive to the workers' desire for more congenial working conditions. The modern bureaucratic colossus poses different problems at the top than at the bottom, and very often the solutions at the top end worsen the situation at the bottom end. Taylor and his associates constituted a "bureaucracy" for the purposes of top management but directed against Schmidt and his comrades. "Bureaucracy" is much too clumsy a concept to take up this discrepancy and give it the practical and (therefore) theoretical importance it deserves.

Sloan's solution from the top to the unresponsiveness built into bureaucratically organized structures like GM was to superimpose on it a class structure of production. As already seen, he placed top management in a much different relationship to the middle group than to the bottom. The middle managerial, professional, and technical echelon was given a special place, a special treatment, a special functional role, and a special reward system that were only slightly watered-down copies of the place, treatment, role, and rewards accorded to the top managers. The whole thrust of Sloanism is in the direction of establishing a balanced, collegial relationship between the top and middle of corporate management, a relationship built upon a careful delineation of role, responsibility, and privilege. He created a situation in which middle-level employees were neither his satraps nor his bureaucratic clerks but instead his junior colleagues. Because this relationship is founded on real considerations of mutual advantage and of actual power between the two groups—is a "political" relationship—it has proven a successful and long-lived one. GM, like any modern corporation or, for that matter, any large organization, endemically suffers from bureaucratic problems, but the story doesn't stop there. The immense social and technical success of the corporations stems in good part from their having, if not "solved" the problem of bureaucracy, surely developed a series of effective antidotes to its worst manifestations as viewed from the top.

This leads us to see the chief difference between Weber's analysis and the one I am proposing under the term "corporate form." Weber's concept emphasizes the formal elements characterizing modern bureaucracy, for example, hierarchy, plan, specialists, salaried functionaries, and so forth. But all these things were present in the South Vietnamese "bureaucracy" twenty-odd years ago, as they are present today in the Romanian "bureaucracy" or that of Chad or of Guatemala. And yet not one of them exhibits the *results* that Weber and his followers imagine to come from such modern arrangements. South Vietnam I knew in person and the others only by report, but I think it broadly accepted that all four of the countries cited suffer(ed) from padronism, cronyism, rampant corruption, and administrative ineptitude to a degree recalling the way things were done before they copied Western models of "bureaucracy." The difference between their inept and corrupt "bureaucracies" and the very able, businesslike "bureaucracies" of the modern corporation is that the latter, unlike the former, are animated by real relations of cooperation and advantage between classes, in this case top management and the middle element. Because of the presence of the two classes, there is an ethos and a structure of sanctions that persuades "bureaucrats" that even their narrowest personal and family interests are served by acting in a businesslike and professional way. Absent that animating class structure, as in, say, modern Haiti or El Salvador, each "bureaucrat" sees quite correctly that the formal aims of the organization—be it army, government department, police, or company— promise much less advantage than can be had by becoming a *padrón* or attaching to one, giving and taking favors, selling official responsibilities for the best price, and so on.

Thus we see in what sense "bureaucracy" is too global a concept. Ancient China, medieval Islam, and modern Italy have all had "bureaucracies." Some have performed brilliantly, and some not at all. I would suggest that how they perform is really a function of the class relationships that gave rise to them, that they express, and whose interests they do or do not serve. "Bureaucracy" is only a *genus*, that is, a type of types, not, as Weber clearly believed, a *species* (his "ideal type") of which there were more or less faithful instances. If I am right in this, the term "bureaucracy" cannot be used willy-nilly to explain why Gorbachev is having trouble in the Soviet Union *and* why the New York Housing Office allows slum lords to prosper *and* why the AFL-CIO is unresponsive to younger workers. One must instead look to understand which social classes are involved in the bureaucracy, how they are involved, how the bureaucracy does or doesn't serve their interests, whether it conflicts with or advances the interests of other social structures in which the dominant classes have interests, and so forth.

That's all the view from the top. What of the view from the bottom? One of the values of corporate form is that it permits an unusually powerful and discriminating control over the work of workers. In this sense, corporate "bureaucracy," that is to say, the middle-element class, dominates over the workers. This emerges not from broad trends in society as a whole toward more rational, calculating ways of doing things but from the concrete needs of the other two corporate classes. It is guided by a Taylorite rationality, not a Weberian one. And although it results in more functional industrial arrangements, it also creates the dreadful reality of Schmidt as the archetypical modern worker. In short, as applied to industrial matters per se,

Weber's notion of a socially neutral "bureaucracy" is in fact a disguising and distorting conception for the administrative-technological dictatorship exercised on the job by one class over another. This should serve as a warning that we must always look at so-called bureaucracies to see whether and, if so, how they are forms for the domination of one class by another.

This subject is largely absent from Weber's analysis, mostly because he sees the several classes as purely and very narrowly economic in nature. In his view, the various classes always have sharply opposed interests "in the marketplace," but less so in other parts of society. His view even appears to carry the broad implication that these class oppositions will be bridged by the development of modern "bureaucracies" like cartels and trade unions, which will see the bigger picture that eludes the grasping individual businessperson or anarchically inclined individual worker. The analysis of corporate form directly confronts and confutes the Weberian concept. It says, in effect, class antagonisms are not muted within modern "bureaucratic" institutions; rather, those institutions are shaped by class antagonisms and those antagonisms continue to play themselves out within the institutions. Consequently, if we want to know why Western corporations usually function well whereas non-Western governments often don't, we must look to see why certain industrial classes find a common, compelling interest in the corporate "bureaucracies" yet pre-industrial and nonindustrial classes merely pursue their personal and family interests—even though their "bureaucracies" are, from the purely formal point of view, excellent instances of a Weberian "bureaucracy."

Social and Political Taylorism

In the industrial setting, Taylorism represents an historical development within corporate form in which the mental, control, and creative aspects of work are steadily stripped from the workers and relocated within a new class of middle managerial, professional, and technical specialists. As I have already suggested, something like Taylorism has also developed in the wider society, specifically within the main social institutions, and in politics as well. We may take the schools as an instance of the first. What emerges from this investigation underlines striking parallels between middle-element-worker *class* relationships in both industry and the schools.

Schooling and the public education movement generally preceded the development of the modern corporation, but the latter has caused mighty changes in them. At the beginning of the corporate era, the bulk of the U.S. population had characteristically completed grade school and was, as a result, largely literate in English. Since that time the number of years of schooling boys and girls receive has steadily risen. By the 1930s a high school education had become the norm, just as today a few years of college are becoming the norm. Parallel with this development, there have been changes in both the organization of the schools and in the teaching and educational professions. These changes are quite similar and are related to the changes we have been observing in the business world. That is, the developing corporations began to demand candidates for their burgeoning middle-echelon ranks, who had been trained in socially neutral or controllable schools and not in the world of the skilled-crafts unions. Moreover, just as the producing companies underwent a burst of amalgamation of smaller units at the turn of the century, so, too, did the schools, although somewhat later. The union school movement of the 1920s amalgamated hosts of tiny, independent public schools into larger administrative units and at the same time brought them under closer regulation and control by state departments of education. The one-room schoolhouse of Lincoln's day or even later is now quite a large enterprise headed by a team of senior educators who spend their time doing pretty much the same job in the same way as do the leaders of a large corporation. This is somewhat true in the local school district and even more true in a big-city school system or in the big-city and state university systems. We are correct to see in this an instance of corporate form.

Beneath these top education managers there is, as we would expect under corporate form, a largely separate echelon of educational specialists. The schools' middle element consists of teachers, of course, but also of large numbers of advisers, budget analysts, technical people concerned with plant and equipment, computer wizards, experts in getting money from foundations and the state legislature, personnel managers, insurance and benefit plans specialists, and numerous other modern professionals. Even the teachers are different than they used to be. For a start, they are better educated, which is perhaps to say only that they have spent more years in the education system as students than did the teachers of yesteryear. Like professionals in the private corporate world, they are becoming ever more specialized. In the high schools the teachers of different subjects have long since been trained differently and see themselves as part of separate professions, like history or science. In the universities this professional specialization is even finer. But it has now reached the primary schools as well. Some teachers specialize in the education of the handicapped, and these instructors, naturally, are divided along lines corresponding to the several physical handicaps the children may suffer. In addition, there are now special teachers for those whose native language is not English, others for students with emotional problems, and so forth. Each of these various specialties has its professional association to "negotiate" with top management, Congress and the business world, the university establishment, the foundations, and the other professional associations to codify the rights, privileges, deference, and rewards that should go to its particular kind of professionals. Again, all this is to be expected in a system organized by corporate form.

There are also the "invisible" school employees, that is, secretaries, electricians and plumbers, groundskeepers, janitors, people who prepare and serve food, and others. These are the workers whose presence and importance in the schools, even more than in private industry, is so underrated and undermentioned. Sometimes teachers themselves are barely, if at all, ranked and treated as middle-element professionals. Often in the big-city elementary schools, teachers are treated as a low form of help who require the kind of supervision that Taylor himself would be proud to claim as his own. Younger, often part-time high school and even university teachers are commonly treated in the same way, although this is often only a temporary stage in an otherwise full-fledged, middle-element career.

This now vast institutional complex plays a number of important and usually familiar roles in shaping corporate society. From the standpoint certainly of business and government, the school system is a complex for training, judging, and channeling students into adult life, particularly into the work force. Much, perhaps the predominant part, of professional discussion in educational circles focuses on the efficiency of this system of putting students into their appropriate places in the work force. That is particularly true during what are perceived to be educational crises—as now—when it is feared that the educational system is failing the economy. As always, such discussions tend to overemphasize the training function of the schools. But it is widely recognized that the educational system also has an important role in acculturating students to the dominant national values, the legitimacy of its various authorities, and the essential fairness of its major institutions.

At some point in a student's life, a judgment must be made to determine how far he or she can go in the system. This is obviously a fairly tricky affair because the schools must motivate every student to believe it is supremely important to get ahead in school, but, at the same time, those who fall behind must blame their failure on their own shortcomings rather than on the unjust action of the system. It is in this aspect of education that conventional discussions are so inadequate. Educators are fond of emphasizing the "common values" they strive to inculcate, but a moment's thought makes it quite clear that the future M.B.A. from Harvard and the future dropout who goes into the auto plant must acquire quite different values and attitudes on a host of questions if each is to fit into his or her station in life. It is in that sense that the schools are a great channeling institution, separating students (ostensibly) by performance, fitting them with different attitudes and values, and then, accordingly, steering them along to the appropriate point at which they should leave the system.

If one steps back from these essentially familiar matters, looking instead at the whole process through eyes now used to Taylorite predilections, two points emerge. First, although educators speak blithely of acculturating their students as if each boy and girl came to them with an absolutely blank cultural slate, that is hardly the case. Just as Taylor found a developed group ethos among the workers, which had to be intercepted, broken up, and then replaced, so, too, the modern schools have historically seen it as among their primary duties to intercept, break up, and replace the values and attitudes that working-class and other lower-class students bring into the educational experience. To take an extreme example, when Henry Ford introduced his now legendary five-dollar-a-day wage in the early part of this century, workers could qualify for it only by going to "Americanism" schools set up by the company. The graduation ceremony made its point in perhaps the most blatant possible way: Candidates for graduation came on stage in ethnic costume and carrying the flags of their native countries. The procession then passed through a huge cauldron marked "American Melting Pot" and emerged with everyone dressed in "American" ways, carrying U.S. flags, and singing the national anthem. I have been told by older immigrants that the public schools sometimes staged similar graduation ceremonies.

The illustration about Ford's "Americanism" schools stresses that the cultures they intercepted and attempted to replace were foreign and foreign-language based. The pioneer work of Edward Thompson, however, should make us more sensitive to the distinctiveness of the cultures of the different classes. That is, Thompson and his followers have shown that persisting lower-class cultures coexist alongside the cultures of the higher, more dominant classes and play an important moral, intellectual, social, and— clearly—political role in helping people at the bottom of society to orient their lives and efforts. But Thompson and the others have also shown that these lower-class cultures are also oppositional cultures; that is, frequently they put forward values, ideals, myths, and so forth that are at variance with those of the dominant cultures, portray the latter in an unfavorable light, and, not incidentally, tend to fuel political and other kinds of opposition to them. In our day it appears that the schools and media accord some greater tolerance, especially toward "minority" cultures as they have become ritualized and toned down by the authorities. But it is clear, I think, that no such tolerance is extended to those cultural strains that are associated with the rise of the social democratic and related movements of the historic working class. These, clearly, the schools still normally and quite straight-forwardly see as attitudes to be transformed into "more mainstream" ideas and values.

The second point I would make about social Taylorism in the schools is related to this last. Nowadays the schools, abetted by the media, by those who target the "youth market," by both professional and amateur sports institutions, by the various counseling systems, by the health system, and so forth, tend to place much of the social reproduction of the working class under the direct administrative guidance of various middle-element professionals. This is now so common that we accept it as "normal," but it must be recalled that even two or three generations ago, the working-class boy or girl had only a fleeting relationship with authorities and mentors outside his or her own class. Certainly in the early days of the corporate system, such a child might acquire from a few years in a public elementary school the rudiments of literacy and some health and deportment pointers, but little more. Now it is difficult to find any integral area of working-class life in which middle-element professionals do not have an important, usually dominant role. In that sense, the social reproduction of the working class that used to go on at some social and cultural distance from the authorities is subject to their influence at every point.

If we take the school situation as a model for wider changes in the reproduction of individual workers, of the working class as a class, and of their and its relationships to the other classes, a fairly distinct hypothesis can be formulated. It argues that the individual worker is now partially shaped, as he or she was not—or less so—before, by his or her participation in an educational system structured much like the industrial corporation and to much the same end.

The existing literature on this subject too often points at the Schmidt-like student and says, in effect, "Look, they've really made him into a Schmidt!" For reasons we'll subsequently explore, that interpretation won't hold water. But that a Schmidt as a member of a particular class is put into certain subordinate relationships with his or her teachers, which prefigure and acculturate the student to future relationships with middle-element supervisors, technicians, and professionals—that's a different story. Here we are talking about class relationships being created and then maintained by the power of one class over another. If Schmidt the student avoids back talk, it may have nothing to do with being brainwashed and standardized but with having become so smart about power that the student knows it's wiser not to talk back—at least for the moment. Class relationships are not simply about pressing people's brains flat with a hot ideological iron; they are about the power of different groups to act and the way in which this, subsequently, comes to alter people's ideas about themselves and about social reality.

My hypothesis that there is a social Taylorism may seem well founded, but the parallel with the work experience isn't exact enough for us to draw conclusions from it wholesale. A number of differences between school and work would have to be unraveled before we could even contemplate doing that. Then, too, public schools contain not only working-class students but also students from higher classes. There are other problems and objections numerous enough and complicated enough that they can't be dealt with here. But the substantive point is clear: Today's working class, more than yesterday's, is at least partially reproduced in the schools, and this reproduction subjects that class to the tutelage of an institution that structurally replicates much of what we found in the producer corporations. The student or, at any rate, the working-class student is in at least some ways put in Schmidt's position and, as can be said with somewhat greater confidence, is expected culturally no less than behaviorally to do what he or she is told.

If anything, the hypothesis seems to be further supported by analysis of other social institutions. For example, the mass media have clearly helped to transmit the social and cultural attitudes of the higher corporate classes into the working class. Sometimes I think this is for good and sometimes for ill. But that's not my point; my point is about the direction of causality. Thus the medical profession has changed enormously the way workers think about birth control, abortion, even the duties of parents; the direction of these changes is toward the same attitudes that are and have been held by middle-element professionals. Without going further into this monumentally complicated subject, we can see that in modern society there is arguably some degree of social Taylorism, that is, systematic social and cultural subordination of the worker, the working class, and its social reproduction to the various professions and professionals of the middle element. Accordingly, working-class life and culture is socially reproduced in a setting in which it is importantly shaped by the values and ideas, hence the social interests of the middle element. This is one of the striking ways in which the modern working class does not answer to the name "proletariat." The very point, almost the very definition, of the latter is of a class of workers so excluded from the economic, social, political, cultural, and even moral life of the wider society that they are truly—as the old Marxists believed—"alien in their own countries" or, as Marx said in *The Communist Manifesto*, that they "have no country." Social Taylorism, in its intent and effect, has changed proletarians into modern workers.

The phenomenon of political Taylorism is even more complex. Here the hypothesis is that in the pre-corporate era, the working classes of the industrial countries tended in political matters to operate independently and in open opposition to the then capitalist class and its allies. This was, of course, the significance of the overtly revolutionary socialist parties resting upon a self-consciously proletarian base. Now, large parts of working-class political activity are carried out under either the actual direction of members of the middle element or at least under the tutelage of their views. Whether political Taylorism is ultimately an important phenomenon in its own right or merely an adjunct to social Taylorism will have to be explored elsewhere.

Recalling Weber, it is now often argued that modern trade unions, unlike their smaller and shakier forebears, have become "bureaucratized." What is being pointed to in this characterization is that the administrative staff of the earlier unions might have consisted of a handful of supporters of the leader, all workers with no special training for their jobs, in short, that the unions then represented strongholds of Weber's ideal "charismatic leader." For the record, it should be added that they surely differed in at least one particular from the governments, armies, and other higher-class institutions they had to combat in that early period. The older generations of trade unionist functionaries were legendary Jimmy-Higgins types. "Jimmy Higgins" is trade union shorthand for the worker still often found in union locals who views the union as his or her religion, does everything possible to help it, and (to the point here) treats "the workers' money" as a sacred trust.

As against this, the modern trade union administration is filled with middle-element professionals, and there are some who argue with, I think, fairly good warrant, that all those middle-class lawyers, accountants, pension fund advisers, financial analysts, and the rest exercise a degree of inordinate influence. More important, this influence tends to modify or even block that of the rank and file. We can see this in many areas; let one suffice to provide an illustration of the scope and meaning of the problem. Trade unions now customarily pay for the advice of economists who are little different in their views from the economists who advise the capitalists. This is true from the tiniest local able to hire an economist-consultant all the way up to the AFL-CIO. It is one of the contributing factors, though not necessarily the most basic or the most important, that has gradually led unions to discard economic ideas, programs, demands, and even people who appear hostile to capitalism in favor of what the critics call an accommodationist attitude on economic subjects. In fact, at least since the early 1940s, there have been a number of vivid instances in which workers and local unions critical of this trend have been subjected to harsh discipline for their "back talk."

The broader hypothesis suggested by the phenomena of social and political Taylorism is that productive arrangements between individuals and classes initially formed within the producer corporation have spilled over to create analogues in society and politics. This fits well with the rest of my analysis. Thus the collective style of work of top management plays a part in forming a collectively rather than a family-organized ruling class. Or the sort of independence and deference to individual performance the middle element enjoys on the job comes to identify its life-style and values in society at large. Or, as here, the Taylorite subordination of workers to the middle element on the job also to a degree characterizes their relations in society and politics. If true, this would serve to confirm the broadest and most important thesis of this study, namely, that corporate form is not only a productive relationship and a property form but also the unique germ of general social and political class relationships.

Socially Compulsory Consumption

One of the further ways in which the modern working class is modified is through the compulsory consumption of goods and services. This socially enforced form of consumption is aimed at improving the productive capacity and social malleability of the collective worker. The phenomenon itself is fairly simple and straightforward, but its existence and importance have heretofore been badly obscured by certain reigning economic ideas.

In the economic theory taught at the most prestigious universities and supported by most professional economists, the purchase and consumption of goods and services is viewed as a fundamentally free and individual act. Basically, the idea is that a person goes into a free market with a sum of money that he or she may spend as desired; in theory the consumer will "maximize the marginal utility" of his or her income. That is, the money will be spent in such a way that no alternate spending pattern would yield as much advantage and satisfaction as the one the individual actually chose. For example, the person will spend money on, say, a car only up to the point at which that same money yields as much satisfaction as the money spent on, say, food. Any further switch of income from car to food or from food to car will yield less overall advantage and satisfaction than that one. When the consumer has found that pattern of spending in which all expenditures together yield maximum satisfaction, that consumer is said to have "maximized the marginal utility" of his or her income. In economic theory all consumers always maximize the marginal utility of their incomes. This is one of the principles upon which modern economic analysis is founded.

But the principle assumes that the consumer spends income on goods or services that he or she *freely* chooses. Thus it seems to assume that all income is really discretionary income, in other words, that nobody is ever compelled to spend money on one thing over another. A common-sense objection can be raised here, although, quite naturally, it will be dismissed by the well-trained economist. Suppose a person only has enough money for absolute necessities—a minimal amount of the poorest food, rags to keep warm in, a crude shelter to keep off the winter wind; what then? Can that person truly be said to choose freely how he or she spends that bare minimum of money? The economist will reply: The principle of maximizing marginal utility still holds because in theory the person *could* choose to spend all the money on drink or gambling or even food, ignoring what you or I might feel is the need for at least some clothing and perhaps shelter for the hardest winter months. As can plainly be seen, there is no logical possibility in this theory that anyone can ever be under compulsion to spend his or her income save as the person freely and individually chooses. The point of a free-market economy is that one is *always* free.

Unfortunately for the adequacy of this theory, it appears to ignore about half the actual expenditures made by corporate workers in the United States and in the other industrial countries at this time, and a considerable amount of the consumption of all workers. And the catch-22 to the principle of maximizing marginal utility can't explain away that this sort of worker consumption is essentially social in nature, not individual, and compulsory in nature, not free. There are in fact two distinct kinds of socially compulsory consumption, comprising so-called benefits on the one hand and government social welfare expenditures on the other.

For workers generally, and especially for corporate workers, some good part of their wages are paid in the form of benefits. In 1980, for example, approximately one-third of an average GM worker's hourly income came in the form of benefits such as pension, medical, supplementary unemployment, vacation, and other plans. GM workers have won excellent benefits, but virtually all unionized workers get extensive benefits, and recent years have seen their spread to non-unionized workers as well. Moreover, we shouldn't suppose that these benefits systems are a fairly recent affair that economics has not yet taken account of in its theories. Modern benefits plans are simply the successors to the sort of "welfare capitalism" so widely touted by U.S. Steel and other paternalistic companies at the turn of the century.

The consumption of these benefits cannot be treated as voluntary or as a form of individual consumption. To work for the company is to accept the benefits; there is no choice, especially if there is a union. The benefit is imposed upon the collective worker; the individual worker rarely has the option to take cash in lieu of the benefit. Moreover, the consumption of the benefit takes collective rather than individual form in that the individual is subject to the rules, limitations, and administrative decisions of the managers of the particular plan. In short, the form of consumption is both involuntary and collective.

Second, there are government social welfare expenditures, that is, schooling, public health, subsidies for scientific and cultural activities, and so forth. These, too, are very old; the modern system for all the industrial countries probably traces to the pioneering efforts of Bismarck's Germany, in other words, to a period 100 years ago. From the standpoint of the worker-citizen who eventually consumes these things, they, too, come in an involuntary and collective form. One *must* pay for Social Security and public education. Of course, one could rely on private savings and private schools, forgoing the actual consumption of the benefit, but the option is not a real one for the normal worker whose relatively limited income is already strained by other expenditures; it is well known, for example, that the large Catholic school system in the United States is increasingly in financial and other distress. For the working class, then, Social Security and public schools are effectively compulsory and collective. This tax-imposed consumption is no small matter; in 1979 for example, roughly 29 percent of the average worker's consumption came in that form.

The figures for company benefits and social welfare are not additive, of course. But they do suggest that something like half the average corporate worker's consumption is essentially involuntary and collective. The phenomenon is worldwide: It would appear that at least a third—perhaps more—of all worker's consumption throughout the industrial world has this character. Even in the absence of a reliable percentage, such a massive phenomenon cannot be dismissed in political economic analysis.

None of the familiar concepts of the working class enables us to make much sense of these numbers. The economist's contribution to this discussion, the concept of maximizing marginal utility, is simply bizarre—perhaps worse than bizarre because, recalling Galileo's opponents, it argues in effect that there can't be anything like this phenomenon, as all consumption must (theory proves it!) be fully free, not compelled. The proletarian concept of the working class is not of much help either, for we are talking here not of the deprivation of consumption but of a form of forced consumption.

Curiously enough, a comment by Marx, whose name is closely associated with the theory of a proletariat, seems to provide the germ of an explanation for this socially compulsory consumption. In the first volume of *Capital*, Marx writes (though in support of the proletarian theory):

> The maintenance and reproduction of the working class is, and must ever be, a necessary condition to the reproduction of capital. But the capitalist may safely leave its fulfillment to the laborer's instincts of self-preservation and of propagation. All the capitalist cares for, is to reduce the laborer's individual consumption as far as possible to what is strictly necessary, and he is far away from imitating those brutal South Americans, who force their laborers to take the more substantial, rather than the less substantial, kind of food. (Chapter 33, *Capital*, Volume 1)

What appears to be the case is that under corporate capitalism, the exception has become the rule. That is, under the older market or entrepreneurial capitalism "the maintenance and reproduction of the working class" could be left to the principle of maximizing marginal utility; each worker and working-class family could be relied upon to spend their meager income in the way calculated to stretch it as far as possible. Neither the capitalists themselves nor capitalist society had to worry about such things.

On the other hand, I would argue that Marx's remark about employers "who force their laborers to take the more substantial, rather than the less substantial, kind of food" points the way to the fundamental economic relationship between present-day capital and labor. In modern capitalist society, the productive powers of the working class are explicitly viewed as a form of capital, and like all capital assets they can be improved by selective *investments* aimed in that way.

Certainly, investments aimed at improving broad worker cultural and health levels would tend to expand the productive capacity of the collective worker and to increase the employable portion of the working class. Here, again, the figure of Schmidt provides a useful clue to the central point of the corporation's wage policy. The premium wage he was offered—about half again over the prevailing rate—was conditional upon his obeying Taylorite orders that, in Taylor's expectation, were tantamount to improving productivity fourfold. In the example, the wages offered to Schmidt are given the explicit form of an investment to boost his daily labor output in the interests of creating a greater surplus. In other words, Taylor wasn't interested in paying the lowest wage possible so as to lower the costs for a relatively static output. He was concerned with the dynamic relationship between the costs of paying Schmidt and the likely returns of varying that pay. This was a radical departure from the wage practices of the time. In a later era, the common corporate practice of paying higher-than-average wages, of spending monies on benefit systems, good personnel relations, in-house training and orientation of workers, schooling and retraining schemes, dealing with the union (even when, as now, it lacks effective bargaining power) all can plausibly be seen as investments in greater worker productivity, that is, improving the collective worker as worker. Moreover, it is not left up to the workers themselves to spend all or even most of this premium wage. Some good part of it is withheld in the form of taxes and benefits so that the workers' consumption patterns can be socially guided in ways the dominant classes think useful and necessary.

As if in confirmation of this, the generalized attacks on the welfare state now being made by the major capitalist parties in Britain and the United States aim not at removing benefits from the entire working class but only from that part of it that isn't working or cannot work. Both the Reagan and Thatcher governments have been willing to expend some money on improving worker skills and on forcing workers to enter training programs; increasingly, they exclude only those parts of the working class that are not productive ("the underclass") or cannot be (the elderly, the chronically ill, those with particularly obsolete skills). We have already seen that there now appears to be a middle-class demand to "privatize" many of these same social benefits so as to provide a higher quality of service that needn't be shared with the class or classes lower on the scale. In light of this, it would appear that the phenomenon of compulsory consumption of government benefits will be increasingly limited to workers.

This idea of socially compulsory consumption is not only consistent with but is really required to make sense of the generalized proprietary claim accorded workers in the corporate sector through the de facto and de jure acceptance of collective bargaining. The ability of the worker to produce—what Marx called "labor power"—may be treated statically as a factor cost of today's process of production, thus to be minimized, or dynamically as something that can be invested in, with a view to gaining greater ratios of returns to cost over time. Much in actual corporate practice suggests that the big companies have in fact achieved the latter standpoint. Corporate form makes such a position possible precisely in that it subjects the utilization of labor power to the dynamic action of the middle element, not only in the physical equipment used by the workers but also in their organization, discipline, and motivation. Taylorism does this on the job; social Taylorism extends it off the job.

Not all but certainly much of this socially compulsory consumption is such as would tend to improve the social productive powers of the working class. Public health and education expenditures as well as private medical and dental plan expenditures would normally have this character. In general, arguments linking consumption of these goods and services to the improvement of the productivity of the working population are too well known to repeat here.

As we have already seen in social Taylorism, the relationships characterizing corporate form within the corporation's productive activities are replicated in those institutions that administer the consumption of much if not most benefits and social welfare services. In the benefits systems as in the school systems, small groups of upper managers control through financial and policy mechanisms a middle element of professionals, managers, and technologists who administer the consumption processes of large classes of goods and services for workers, the forms of that consumption being both collective and involuntary to a significant degree. These are *generalized class relationships* that originate within corporate form, inside the corporation, but then spill over into society itself.

I am arguing that Marx's point is quite apt for corporate economic and social policy. Modern capital does imitate those South Americans who forced their laborers "to take the more substantial, rather than the less substantial, kind of food" because the production and expropriation of a greater surplus (i.e., profits and growth) demand continuously greater physical and even cultural exertion on the part of the working population. Hence the modern corporation deals with the collective labor power on and off the job not statically as an unavoidable and irksome cost but dynamically as a form of capital. The processes of maintaining and reproducing the working class can no more be left to the working class than can any other element of capitalist production because to do so is inconsistent with the capitalist imperative to expand the size of the surplus as rapidly as possible. As a result the broad class organization of society and of the key social institutions comes more and more to replicate the class relationships that originate within the immediate capitalist production process: corporate form.

Whose Trade Unions?

It is, I believe, generally accepted that trade unions are the chief, often the only, major institutions in a modern industrial society that are predominantly under the influence and control of workers. In addition, it is widely understood that the trade unions furnish not only a defense of the immediate industrial and economic interests of workers but also provide important political, social, and even moral benefits to individual workers and to the class as a whole. Accordingly, it has long been the fashion in the Western countries, particularly in the United States, to stress the difference between our ostensibly legitimate, worker-controlled unions and those of the communist world, which are (or largely have been) mere arms of the state. In fact, there are even two international confederations of trade unions, one of which, the International Confederation of Free Trade Unions, marks that East-West difference in its very name.

It is undoubtedly a comforting thought that we in the West have "free trade unions" as opposed to the "company unions" of the Eastern countries, but the distinction is vastly overdrawn and perhaps even entirely false. To a remarkable degree in all of the Western capitalist democracies, the trade unions are sufficiently under the immediate administrative control of government so as to force us to consider whether there is any such thing as a "free trade union" in the self-congratulatory sense in which the expression is used. Because of the earlier development of corporate society in the United States, it should come as no surprise that government control of the unions is further advanced and more one-sided here than in any other capitalist democracy except Great Britain—which has copied the U.S. system.

Given the vexed history of this topic, its importance for working people generally, its worldwide scope, and its intrinsic complexities, we must radically simplify the subject. Accordingly, I merely want to show that three propositions—propositions at the very core of the belief that U.S. unions are "free trade unions"—are false; that is, they are diametrically contradicted by the true state of affairs. Those propositions are (1) that U.S. unions are basically an expression of and dominated by their own members; (2) that we have a system of "free collective bargaining" in which the industrial power of the workers can, in theory, countervail against the several kinds of power enjoyed by the other classes; and (3) that the trade unions, because they are putatively independent of the state, constitute a key institution within our pluralist political system. In the course of demonstrating the falsity of these propositions, my substantive point will emerge, namely, that U.S. unions are to most effects and purposes administrative arms of the state for controlling workers and their class. In my own view they are actually quasi-governmental organizations, but there is neither the space nor the need to demonstrate that more controversial position here.

1. The conventional view treats U.S. unions as free associations of workers organized within a framework that accords them the right to industrial representation in an organization they can use to further their industrial interests. None of that is true in the decisive, national, corporate sector of the U.S. economy. Under the provisions of the controlling National Labor Relation Act, as amended, and as administered by the National Labor Board, workers have only a *procedural right* to try to be represented by a union. In Italy, for example, a worker has a constitutional right to belong to a union, period. The individual merely has to sign up. But in the United States, a worker or group of workers must engage in a lengthy legal procedure to have their would-be union "certified" in the jargon of the trade, that is, recognized by the NLRB as a legitimate collective-bargaining unit and thereby entitled to equitable treatment from both government and the employer. In Italy it is customary for several different unions to remain active at the same work site. Thus they are in constant competition in order to be able to enroll and represent individual workers. The worker may choose among them, switching loyalties as the situation demands. (A coalition of unions negotiates with the employer, the influence of each member union of the coalition more or less representing the number and influence of the workers it comprises.)

In the United States, the law requires that only a single union can represent all workers: There are only a few, relatively unimportant exceptions to this. Basically, there is no pluralism at the work site. Moreover, the process of getting that union in the United States is extremely complicated, and the employer has extensive rights to interfere with it and delay it. The government also has fairly free rein to choose which groups of workers may join in the union. That is, the NLRB—not the workers themselves— has the power to decide whether the workers in a given corporation are to be represented by a single union or permanently divided between two or more separate unions or, alternatively, to be involuntarily joined in the same union with workers at other sites. Naturally, all of these processes restrict the formation of unions and constrict the right of workers to be represented as they see fit. But that is not my substantive point.

The point is that unions are not primarily free associations of workers; the workers may form such associations only under close governmental administrative procedures. Moreover, under U.S. law and practice, how and by whom the union may be governed, the size and scope of the organization, and the powers it may exercise or are forbidden to it—all are subject to NLRB administrative controls and are so controlled by the regulators, to which the union has the responsibility to furnish certain mandatory reports. The basic principle is that a U.S. union can take only those actions positively permitted to it by law, and in all of those powers it is under the active regulation of a state agency, the NLRB. By contrast, a business organization or a free association of citizens may do anything *not* prohibited by law and may do so freely *save* where there is positive legal prohibition or regulation. Thus it is quite true to say that U.S. unions are to a startling degree extensions of the administrative arms of the state. Whether they are themselves quasi-governmental organizations then merely becomes a matter of (admittedly difficult) interpretation.

2. I think no serious observer of the political and industrial scene harbors any doubt that the direct industrial power of workers is critical to their ability to defend themselves in the social struggle. By "industrial power," of course, I refer to the strike, sit-down, "slowdown," picket line, "work to rule," and other devices workers use directly at the job site. It is widely recognized that workers, as workers, are traditionally weaker in the political arena than certain other classes, but in "free trade union" theory, their industrial power makes up for this. Yet the dominant trend in the thinking and practice of all the capitalist democracies is to sharply restrict this industrial power. Again, the United States stands in the lead. In the United States, the issues workers may strike over; the number and variety of unions that may join in a common strike; who may authorize a strike and under what circumstances; the scope, sites, kind, times, and intent of picketing; the duration of the strike; the terms of its settlement; the use of other industrial tactics, such as boycotts and other sympathetic actions, "slowdowns," "skippy," and "sick-outs"; and the assistance one union may extend to another are all regulated by the NLRB. Needless to say, in corporate society the aggregate corporate public has seen fit to administer with an eye to its own interests, "free trade union" rhetoric to the contrary notwithstanding. But, again, a milder point is enough for our purposes, namely, that the direct industrial power of workers and their unions is subject to close administrative control by a state agency that is itself subject to the political process. In short, the industrial power of workers is subordinated to the political process in which even conventional opinion recognizes that workers are hard put to defend their interests against the other classes and groups. One may further observe the ripple

effects of this industrial weakness on the trade unions' political and cultural influence over both workers and society as a whole.

3. Quite evidently, U.S. trade unions are not nearly "free" enough, even in the purely formal sense, to play the role they are supposed to play in pluralist political theory, namely, as one of those autonomous groups that force other autonomous and competing groups to deal equitably with them so as to assure that various rights and opportunities remain open to their members. In fact, the foregoing argument establishes the presumption that the reverse is true, that the trade unions—in their relations with the aggregate corporate public—are much more control mechanisms answerable to such outsiders than they are representative mechanisms for their own members.

I don't want to take this conclusion to an absurd length, and I am certainly not hostile to the existing unions, for all their faults. U.S. unions clearly play many useful and representative roles for their members. Having myself served as a shop steward defending my fellow trade unionists in grievance procedures, I can directly attest to that. Among union officers and activists one finds hosts of men and women who, even in these cynical and difficult times, labor away day after month after year with the dedication, intelligence, and militance of Jimmy Higgins at his very best. Moreover, even the limited industrial effectiveness of the unions has an incalculable moral and cultural effect on vast numbers of workers, and this in turn sharply strengthens the place of workers in corporate society. Thus even without factoring in the (limited) ability of the unions to win pay and other gains, it is clear that they play an important, positive, and often indispensable role for their members and for workers generally. But this is *not* their primary significance in corporate society.

Historically, the main significance of trade unions in U.S. corporate society was that they helped to create and then integrate the collective worker into corporate form. Subsequently and on that basis, the collective worker was integrated into his or her proper, subordinate place in corporate society. The trade unions themselves have been integral to the formation of the collective worker and, I believe, will remain so in spite of their present difficulties.

Here the crucial step is to mark the difference between the *substantive* rights that in Western law and practice are associated with the "free individual" and the sort of purely *procedural* rights available to workers under the NLRB system. An illustration will serve to underline the vital difference between the two kinds of rights. Imagine that you personally have the right to vote in an election for president, for Congress, or for some local officials, but only under certain definite conditions, as follows: First, you have to convince a majority of the people in your local area that they should want to vote in that particular election *and* who or what to vote for. Second, other powerful, wealthy groups, who may not even live in your area, have free rein to propagandize against your effort and to use economic and certain other kinds of intimidation. Third, a government board could restrict or expand, as it saw fit, the size and composition of the local group you were trying to persuade. And, fourth, that same government board could decide what questions and even candidates you could or couldn't vote on. That—detail for detail—is what it means when we say that a U.S. worker has a procedural but not substantive right to be represented by a trade union. Practically speaking, it means that the worker as worker has rights only insofar as he or she is a cog in that procedure and, if successful in it, wins a share in its rewards, for example, a union, a raise, a new benefit. Under the NLRB system, the individual worker has virtually no personal, substantive rights at all; in Europe the situation is considerably better in this respect.

Obviously, this is not an entirely invidious relationship. Corporate workers generally, led by the victories of trade unionists, enjoy scales of pay, benefits, and other perquisites appreciably greater than those available to workers in the noncorporate sectors of the economy. Not least of these are the right to contend for part of the growing social surplus under collective-bargaining procedures and the right to limited job tenure through the seniority system. Like all industrial relationships in corporate form and all class relationships in corporate society, economic, political, social, and other advantages are, to a degree at least, not the exclusive property of this or that individual or class but inclusive of all.

But we *are* dealing with corporate form when we deal with the NLRB system. The corporate public dominates the overall policymaking board in Washington whose policies are interpreted and applied in myriads of technically different cases by scores of middle-element-staffed subboards throughout the country. The collective worker meets this system and is dominated by it in his or her national trade union or, in the odd case, directly in the local board. But in any case, the government-regulated trade union is one of the most important ways in which the individual flesh-and-blood worker is prevented from disrupting the industrial system and exercising demands not consonant with its needs and desires.

As I think I have already made clear, these matters do not turn on the issue of "democracy in the trade unions," an issue with seemingly infinite power to seduce and bedazzle trade union reformers. Naturally, it is better when unions are democratic than when they are not, but even the outer scope of action of an ultrademocratic trade union cannot escape this national labor control system. In fact, given the degree to which unions within the system must enforce the decisions of outsiders over their own members, the system itself is a major factor limiting and vitiating the democratic character of even the best unions. In this respect, the present U.S. labor control system may remind us of the Jim Crow system of the South of twenty-five years ago in that neither could be overturned by purely legal and democratic means. One had to violate the law in the old South in order to win effective as opposed to feckless democratic rights or even to get substantive democratic rights in the first place. Such today is the position of U.S. workers within the national labor control system.

Sociological and Historical Methods

The foregoing observations about bureaucracy, social Taylorism, compulsory consumption, and the labor control system carry profound implications about the nature of the modern working class and its place in corporate society. Two, one substantive, one methodological, are of immediate importance.

The concept of the collective worker carries the implication that the corporate working class *as a class* is shaped and controlled by corporate society. In sharp contrast, the most familiar and popular views both of Marxist and of conventional social science have tended to emphasize that the shaping and controlling of the working class is primarily a matter of shaping and controlling *individuals*. In the familiar way of looking at the question, the weaknesses and faults of the class are emergent phenomena, that is, they are thought to emerge from and to be conditioned by the qualities and inadequacies of the individual workers and their individual consciousnesses. I have been arguing for a much different position, namely, that individual workers are shaped and controlled through control *over their class* and its institutions by the other classes. In fairness, one can find important instances of both directions of causality, but it is my view that the ultimately decisive condition and result comes about through the domination of the working class as a class and not via the route in which individuals become confused and distracted and their class awareness stupefied by the blandishments of individualism, consumerism, and the other fleshpots of corporate society.

The methodological point is intimately related to this conclusion. If these things are as important as I believe they are, it is clear that the working class one actually observes is itself a social composite: It is partly constituted by those shaping and controlling mechanisms and partly constituted by the experience of the mass of workers and whatever self-conscious conceptions they may or may not develop about their place and interests. This reality sharply limits the validity of purely sociological methods of studying the working class, that is, the direct methods of observing, typing, theorizing, and quantifying events and situations in contemporaneous time or, at best, in brief time frames. In my opinion, purely sociological means—however radical, "critical," "proletarian," or even outré one's methods, outlooks, and intentions—are unlikely to get beyond discovering the effects of the control mechanisms on the class. Instead, the longer time frames of historical investigation and analysis are necessary if in principle one wishes even to raise the possibility charting the other, autonomous features of the modern working class.

Or, to put the matter in a slightly different light, our concept of corporate society is completed by this discussion about the formation and control of the collective worker. To go beyond that notion requires that our conceptual framework itself go beyond corporate society—which is to say, the very society we live in and that shapes and limits our views. History provides the essential clue for doing this in the form of answers to two questions: How does the actual body of men and women composing the collective worker today differ from the body of those who made up earlier forms of the urban laboring class, particularly the pre- and early industrial artisan class and the classic proletariat? And what can those changes tell us about the present trajectory of this class and, possibly, about the future direction of its development?

Bibliographical Essay

C. Wright Mills and Hans Gerth have provided the essential Weberian texts on "bureaucracy" in *From Max Weber: Essays in Sociology* (A Galaxy Book, Oxford University Press, New York, 1958).

There is a methodological issue in dealing with "class" analysis we should address here. In the text, I have spoken of "three distinct and nonoverlapping classes." Yet there are places in the text, for example, in the discussion of certain teachers who are workers, where it appears that I am admitting of the possibility that one person may simultaneously belong to two classes or, at the very least, that class "lines" may be blurry indeed. The evident reality is that one does find such things; the problem is to develop an analytical framework and language that clearly express this blurring of the "line" between two classes and show that real people may be located, so to speak, in the "blurriness."

The U.S. sociologist Eric Olin Wright (*Class, Crisis and the State*, New Left Books, London, 1978) deals with this problem in a way certain Marxists have unfortunately adopted to an extent. He uses a model in which there are only two fundamental classes, corresponding to the older, classical capital and labor. Other groups, most notably the various middle classes, he denies as fundamental classes, describing them as having "contradictory locations in class relations." His empirical meaning is clear enough: A middle-class person doesn't own property and must earn a living by work. Thus he or she is in part a worker. But as a privileged person who may share in the surplus, the middle-class person may think and act socially as a capitalist does. Thus the "contradiction."

I find this analysis empirically and methodologically erroneous. Given the material about worker–middle-element antagonisms I present in this book, Wright's view would appear to erase the most direct, active frontier of class conflict in modern industrial capitalist society, the struggle between the controlling middle managerial, professional, and technical class and the class directly subject to them, the corporate working class. The purely theoretical formulation is also faulty and seems open to the jibe once directed at an unfortunate soul in a Columbia University philosophy seminar. This worthy presented an intricate analysis of some old controversy that, he announced, apparently under the spell of some undigested Hegel, was conceptually "self-contradictory." "What do all you rationalists think of that?" he demanded. "I entirely agree with you," some wit retorted as he prepared to flee the room, "and wholeheartedly disagree as well." I confess to thinking the same retort is not unfairly directed at Wright's formulation, and I remain puzzled as to what *theoretical* advantages such a bizarre logic can possibly bestow on his analysis.

There are always knotty empirical problems in identifying individuals and groups that, as it were, appear to straddle class "boundaries." But the analytical problem, to my mind, is not a substantial one. It comes from a too literal transliteration of the Aristotelian logical "class" or modern mathematical "set" into social analysis. For example, in a conventional map of a coastal area, as in the mapping of logical classes in spatial terms in Boolean algebra, the "line" separating the sea from the land is understood to be a Euclidean one, that is, it has no width and therefore can contain neither of the two kinds of things being mapped; thus the sea is blue, the land white, and there is a black line between them, but we understand that line to be merely an aid to our (and the printer's) eyes.

I would tender the view that the boundary between two classes should be "seen" as we actually see a shoreline, not a map of one: There is a zone of indifference or transition between land and sea; on a freshwater shore it is less prominent because of the absence of tides, but it is no less identifiable. That there is an intertidal zone bears not at all on our ability to make an effective and clear distinction between land and sea, to characterize each, to speak of their relationship, and so forth. Moreover, the physical and biological features of the intertidal zone are decisively conditioned by both the land and sea; no third explanatory entity is required to deal with it. We should apply that metaphor—and its formal features—to the "boundaries" between classes. As at the seashore, the zone of transition between classes has "sea" creatures and "land" creatures, as well as "coastal zone" creatures. There is a constant shift in this boundary, both in social space, so to speak, and in social and historical time. Individual creatures pass in and out of it, even through it. But none of these *formal* issues has any bearing on our ability to identify and characterize different classes. Because such zones exist, certain individuals and groups can be difficult to locate in class terms. But there is, I submit, no formidable or even very interesting formal, "theoretical" problem here.

Any reasonably thorough and respectable introductory economics text-book will present the full argument that consumers maximize the marginal utility of their incomes, as well as their salable skills, in the marketplace. The ahistorical and tautological nature of the argument is most clearly revealed by its apparent inventor in the economics profession, W. Stanley Jevons, in his *Theory of Political Economy* (originally published in 1874, Pelican edition, London, 1970). The substance and manner of Jevons's argument, however, show quite unmistakably the real origin of this for-mulation of the "welfare" issue in modern marginal analysis. In truth, this part of modern economics is simply Jeremy Bentham's old "felicific calculus" finally worked out in the mathematical form that Bentham so fervently desired. David Baumgardt, a mentor whom I recall with both affection and respect, has tried to argue that Bentham's felicific calculus was *not* the elaborate tautology I believe it is; see his *Bentham and the Ethics of Today* (Princeton University Press, Princeton, 1952). Curiously, Baumgardt would appear to have been unaware of Bentham's enormous influence on the development of modern economics.

"Americanism" schools are often cited by authors writing about Ford, as, for example, Robert Lacey in his *Ford: The Men and the Machines* (Little, Brown, Boston and Toronto, 1986). Edward Thompson's seminal study of working-class culture is contained in his *Making of the English Working Class* (Vintage, New York, 1966).

The management-union relationship is too often viewed solely as an antagonistic one. For a counterview, see William Serrin's excellent *The Company and the Union: The "Civilized Relationship" of the General Motors Corporation and the United Automobile Workers* (Vintage Books, New York, 1974). William Junius Wilson, *The Truly Disadvantaged: The Inner City, the Underclass and Public Policy* (University of Chicago Press, Chicago, 1987), provides a particularly useful discussion of the issues surrounding "the underclass." Henry Phelps Brown, *The Origins of Trade Union Power* (Oxford University Press, Oxford and New York, 1986), is a fine summary of British developments as well as arguments in behalf of state regulation of labor unions. Unlike so many U.S. authors with a relatively similar position, Phelps Brown is broadly sympathetic and respectful of trade unions and their members, liberal in his social values, and judicious and fair-minded in his remedies. Note that this 1986 issue is slightly revised and improved over the original 1983 version. Bruce Feldaker, *Labor Guide to*

Labor Law (Reston Publishing Company, Reston, Va., 1983) is a very effective and useful summary of his subject. For a more encyclopedic treatment, as well as the texts of the most important legislation, see Benjamin J. Taylor and Fred Witney, *Labor Relations Law* (5th edition, Prentice-Hall, Englewood Cliffs, N.J., 1987).

7

Neither Artisans nor Proletarians

The development of corporate society raises in a particularly acute way two fundamental questions about the modern working class. I have previously alluded to both but left them hanging in favor of analyzing corporate society. First, to a great extent the modern working class is shaped and controlled by the action of the other two corporate classes. I have already suggested, however, that there is another, autonomous dimension to the class. How is this to be characterized and what have been its effects on the class itself and on the wider society? Here, I am not only concerned to mark its static "sociological" differences but also to gain some insight into its role as a dynamic and a continuing factor in the history of the corporate era. Second, how does the modern corporate working class differ from earlier forms of that class? The two questions are closely related, so much so that they are best pursued more or less simultaneously.

Proletarians and After

Today's working class represents a far more potentially powerful social antagonist than did the classic proletariat. Moreover, a plausible case can be made that it has been in many ways the most dynamic and influential of the modern classes in the evolution of a more humane society. In saying these things I am more than aware that both conventional and Marxist social scientists almost universally view the history of workers in this century as a history of decline from a revolutionary political force to passive consumers or, perhaps, the depoliticized "masses."

Yet this derogatory conclusion is less rooted, it seems to me, in any objective review of that 100 years' history than it is in the outdated conceptions such social scientists impose upon the workers themselves. We have already observed this phenomenon in another context, namely, in the way in which certain writers have romanticized skilled workers or artisans, contrasting their sense of community, achievement, self-conscious pride, and so forth with a modern working class that, they say, has lost all of these values.

The concept of "the proletariat" introduces an even greater distortion into these discussions. Marx's descriptions of the proletariat in the *Manifesto*, in *Capital*, in his histories, and in various other works are so telling, so comprehensive, and so profound that the notion has almost become a synonym for workers under capitalism. Among Marxists, the proletarian idea lurks in the background of almost every discussion and concept of the working class, where it plays a double role. Polemically, it is a means of minimizing or even denying the very possibility of improvement in the situation of urban industrial workers. Analytically, it stresses their impoverishment by underlining the ways in which workers are denied access to the social surplus they produce. Quite ironically, even non-Marxists tend to accept the *logic* though not the *truth* of this idea. That is, if—in their view—workers were a distinct force in society, they would behave like classic proletarians; but the workers don't behave in this way; ergo, they have become fully integrated into a society that no longer "exploits" them.

At bottom, what is so distorting about the proletarian concept is that it obscures the forced social development of the working class that has been one of the primary features of the corporate era. As earlier indicated, it has been characteristic of the corporate era, almost from its beginning, to treat the working class as a productive asset per se and to subject it to selected expenditures with a view to improving its productive powers. Social investments are imposed on the working class so that, in respect to the individual worker, more often than not his or her consumption has a compulsory character. In my view these socially compulsory forms of consumption have helped to create the more powerful working class I alluded to above.

This conclusion should come as no surprise, especially in light of my earlier analysis. Insofar as the modern corporation was, in part, a response to the social democratic movement, it represented both an accommodation to that movement and an opposition to it. In that sense it would have to yield to some of the demands of social democracy. Because many of those demands would, if met, create a more productive working class, there clearly existed a mutual basis for the new sort of capital-labor relationship that subsequently developed. By the same token, however, because of the intrinsically social nature of modern production, a more productive working class must by that very fact grow in its broad social and even political capacities. As earlier suggested, a mass of deracinated, impoverished, sullen workers existing at best on the margins of civil society—for that indeed is what "proletariat" means—is hardly suited to the productive activities of the modern corporation. It is socially imperative for modern capitalism that the working class' cultural, educational, technical, and health levels be raised; the conditions of its social existence must be stabilized, and it must be brought into society and made an integral part of it. The attempt by modern capital to shape and control workers must also of necessity lead to a strengthening of that class as a potential social antagonist. Thus the paradox that the transition from proletariat to modern working class, a transition from a relatively autonomous class to a class subject to stifling social controls, represents a net strengthening of the latter.

Corporation and Worker: A Symbiotic History

As I have already implied, the evolution of the modern worker and of the modern working class is not something that occurs outside the rise and development of the corporation. Yet this is precisely the way the subject is too often handled. In the conventional treatment, there is the history of business and the history of labor, and those two histories, it is acceded, occasionally touch each other in the form of a strike or some other conflict, but little more.

Put in those bald terms, it is easy to see that the conventional treatment is very unlikely to be true. Yet no other history of these matters exists; a history of the symbiotic relationship between the modern corporation and its working class remains to be written, even though in its absence one simply cannot understand the capital-labor relationship today, nor corporate society, nor the dynamic factors that, acting in the present, also shape the future. It is, of course, impossible to make good that absence in these present pages. But it is possible to characterize, however briefly, a few of the main dimensions of worker-corporate interaction, especially as it has helped to shape the cardinal features of today's working class. The following *observations* are offered to that end.

Wages, Hours, Job Security. We have already analyzed the higher-than-average wage paid to "Schmidt," observing that that higher wage was seen as an investment leading to greater productivity and profitability. But from Schmidt's standpoint the higher wage was a step up from the bare subsistence pay characteristic of the time. In modern terms, we would think of it as a "family wage," as such it was. As it spread within the corporate world and beyond, it led to the gradual demise of child labor within big industry and to a general improvement in family health, housing, and educational conditions.

There had been a broad movement among workers for the eight-hour day (i.e., forty-four- or forty-eight-hour week) in the mid-1880s, but that had been put down in bloody fashion by the authorities (in the Haymarket affair of May 1886). As a result, the ten-hour day for five and a half days was about normal, though in the steel industry as late as 1919 nearly half the work force was on a six-day, seventy-two-hour work week. U.S. Steel, the industry pacesetter, had large numbers of its workers on a seven-day, eighty-four-hour work week until 1924.

In a related vein, in the pre-corporate era and even in the earliest days of the corporations there was virtually no job security. Almost all workers were constantly being fired, not laid off. They were fired to fit them to the seasonal or business cycle, for trying to organize unions, for mild protest of conditions, for refusal to sign pledges (the "yellow dog" contracts) that they would never join a union, for illness, for age, in fact, for any reason supervisors found convenient. In business the governing doctrine at the time was "employment at will," that is, a worker could be terminated at any time by the employer. The corrosive social impact on workers and their families of recurrent bouts of unemployment was one of the most oft repeated themes of the early social work professions. But as the Taylorite idea took hold that a more or less permanent, trained, and loyal work force was to the companies' advantage, seniority, benefits, pensions, vacation plans, and the like began slowly to emerge as well. Similarly, companies adopted a shorter work week once they learned that it led to better utilization of equipment, lowered accident rates, helped to retain key workers, and, recalling Ford, quickened "Americanization." With the other steps cited above, however, it was also an important factor in freeing workers for at least a degree of social, cultural, and physical improvement.

Unions. The development of unions in the United States has been intimately related to and helped by the growth of the corporations. As a rule, unions find that large companies in growing industries, with high and steady profitability, uniform management practices, and a well-defined production work force are necessary for their own existence and stability. By and large, these conditions have only obtained in the private sector of the United States among the largest corporations or among industries such as interstate trucking, whose prosperity and stability are closely linked to the big corporations.

Nowadays most business leaders see that their firms win complementary benefits from the presence of a union, but they learned that only after many years and much travail. In the early part of the corporate era, company and union stood—at best—at arm's length from each other. Unions, of course, were virtually absent from the scene in the very earliest years of the corporations. By 1890 the American Federation of Labor had become the most important labor organization in the United States, but its main strength was in the skilled trades. Where it existed in the new corporate world, as in the steel industry, on the railroads, and in coal mining, it represented only the skilled minority of craftsworkers, neglecting the unskilled as unorganizable. In fact, during the period we are talking of, the AFL and its affiliates worked actively to *prevent* the organization of unskilled workers. As a result, AFL affiliates existed more or less on the sufferance of industry and where that failed, as in steel in 1892 (Homestead), the unions were rather easily destroyed.

Efforts to organize unions among the unskilled, already the vast majority of workers in corporate industry, continued in spite of the AFL. Some success was met by the Brewers, the United Mine Workers (coal), the Western Federation of Miners (gold, zinc, silver, other metals), Debs's American Railway Union, and even by the Industrial Workers of the World, especially in textiles. But often the success was short-lived or merely local. Nonetheless, from the 1890s there was an ever-renewed effort on the part of workers to organize unions of the unskilled, called industrial unions. After bloody failures in the first decade of the nineteenth century, again during the 1920s and even early 1930s, Debs's conception of an industrial union finally won through in the brilliant Flint, Michigan, sit-down strike against GM in 1937. Workers in other mass-production industries exploited that breakthrough to establish the unions we now have. In this period (1936–1941), with few exceptions, business leaders still bitterly opposed unions, as evidenced once more, for example, in the Memorial Day massacre of steel workers and their families in South Chicago in 1937.

World War II brought a sea change in the union-company relationship. Under the stress of war mobilization, company and union finally discovered that their shared interests were every bit as important as their evident differences. Because of the war, roughly a quarter of the labor force was taken into the armed forces and had to be replaced by an even larger number of new workers who, for the most part, were utterly without industrial experience. Union-company cooperation was vital in recruiting, moving and housing, training, acculturating, and disciplining this new mass of workers. Ultimately, it led most of big industry to the view that unions, provided they were not too militant, gave a net advantage to the companies. Even today this is the case; there has been no industry-wide movement— as there was in the 1920s—to create a "union-free" environment. For the most part, the big companies still see unions as a factor supporting higher morale, higher productivity, lower absenteeism, work-force stability, and so forth. In their eyes (and in fact) the union's real and proper role is that of intermediary between worker and employer, and not the worker's representative per se. As if in confirmation of this, the give-backs industry has enjoyed in recent years would have been impossible without union assistance; in the pre-union era similar attempts to roll back wages were normally met by strikes, riots, arson, and other violence.

In my own view, the relationship between union and employer has become too close, and unions, with notable exceptions, have become too much the intermediary between worker and employer and too little the representative of the working man or woman. Nevertheless, the fifty-year presence of unions in the mass-production industries has undoubtedly been the single most important factor in winning for the average worker, union member or no, a tolerable place in corporate society. Even if, as many believe, present-day unions are an outmoded industrial form, they represent a constructive phase of working-class history and the necessary prologue to any better future.

Immigration. We can also see this complementarity of interests between worker and corporation in the great immigration wave of 1890–1924. I think it is now generally accepted that the big companies deliberately and carefully fostered mass immigration as part of the program of newly expanding corporate capital. That is, the immigrants came here as much because they were recruited to work in this or that industry as from any general impulse to flee conditions in their homelands. In this early period, immigration served several crucial corporate purposes. Obviously, it expanded and cheapened the labor force. By providing numerous and obedient "Schmidts," it enabled corporate form to develop more rapidly in the United States than in Europe. In this way, the limited industrial power of native-born workers, based on skill monopolies, was rather quickly and easily broken, as it was not, for example, in Britain and Germany. Moreover, because each wave of immigrants was ethnically different than its predecessors, it vastly slowed the development of a unified industrial working class.

Yet, although the short-run effects of immigration on the U.S. working class were undoubtedly harmful, in the longer run the immigration very rapidly increased the size of that class from a small fraction to a major factor in the overall U.S. work force. It also brought to an excessively provincial and often "nativist" working class the powerful and fruitful influence of social democracy and other modern, reforming ideologies.

This time lag in the effects of immigration is a decisive factor in the history of the corporate working class. Moreover, it is a factor with multiple dimensions. For example, in the period in which U.S. industry went from pre-corporate to corporate forms of organization, just over 25 million immigrants came to the United States, with the vast majority entering an industrial labor force that in 1880 stood at 3.3 million people. Certainly, by the turn of the century, the industrial laboring population was largely foreign-born, often not even English-speaking, and this would continue right up into the 1920s. As already indicated, these largely unskilled newcomers were met with hostility from the AFL and from skilled workers generally; characteristically this combined a contempt for their lack of a craft with fear of their foreignness. As important, though less commented upon, the vast majority of these immigrants were nominally Catholics, thus doubly feared and despised by the native-born, usually Protestant workers and nonworkers. In time, of course, the foreign-born and, especially, their children would come to dominate the working class.

Corporate-induced immigration also had a delayed political dimension. In theory all adult, white, male U.S. citizens could vote. But the immense number of the foreign-born and their children among the working class in the early period limited its ability to act in the political arena. Thus immigration had much the same electoral effect as did the restricted, adult male franchise in Great Britain and, later, in France or the antidemocratic systems of Germany, Russia, and several other European countries.

Because of these political restrictions, until about a half century ago worker organizations, worker efforts, and worker leaders had little protection against the political authorities, who in almost all cases were hostile to strikes and other industrial protests, suppressing them by frequent and generous use of the police power or, if necessary, the military. It is little appreciated that physical conflict of this sort between bodies of workers and the state's police power was more common and more bloody in the United States than in any of the other industrial nations. Predictably, in this area the "commercial model" of the government-corporation relationship predominated. In fact, the earliest competent investigative police agencies in the United States were the private, corporate-financed ones such as the Pennsylvania Coal and Iron Police, the Baldwin-Felts Detective Agency, and, of course, the Pinkertons. As a rule, these agencies were endowed by the industrial states with full public police powers—to arrest, question, charge, and hold "agitators"; to gather intelligence; to disperse gatherings; to employ firearms and explosives; and so forth.

The widespread use of these and other private industrial police was not checked until the famous hearings of the La Follette Committee of the U.S. Senate, when, following the rise of the CIO (Congress of Industrial Organizations), "public opinion" came to agree with the unions that peaceful methods were required to settle industrial disputes. In their turn, both the committee and that altered public opinion reflected the changed political climate created in large part through the New Deal of President Franklin Roosevelt which was, in truth, the first organized, national electoral expression of the children of the immigrants. Shortly thereafter, the new unions and the corporations joined in the effort to mobilize the economy for war, thus bringing to a final end the era of open strife between capital and labor.

From Servant to Employee. These changes in the industrial relationships among workers, unions, and companies were paralleled by fundamental alterations in the way they came to view their own roles in the productive process. Undoubtedly the most important development on this front was the emergence of the concept of an "employee" in place of the idea that workers were merely a sort of servant. As this change is still little understood, some explanation is necessary.

The modern concept of an "employee" represents a shift toward a distinctly functional conception of our roles at work and in society. Well into the mid-nineteenth century, the relationships of employers and their employees were framed with social eyes that still saw things in terms of master and servant; in fact, even in early corporate practice it was not uncommon for workers to be physically chastised by their supervisors. Worse yet, the master-servant relationship in the harder, dirtier, more dangerous, unskilled, and poorer-paid employments had traditionally included elements of outright compulsion: In 1880, for example, chattel slavery was still a recent memory, debt-slavery (through sharecropping contracts) was still growing in the U.S. South, and indenturing was still very common, as was the renting of convict labor for particularly disagreeable jobs— including factory work. The phenomenon of the company town, particularly important in the textile industry, is undoubtedly part of the effort to retain the worker in—quite literally—a servile position. Even the seizing of men for involuntary service at sea (the shanghai) was to remain legal until World War I. Moreover, the free use of the police power to compel workers to work, to defeat strikes and dissolve unions, to maintain inferior social conditions, and to hold down wages must be viewed in this light. Surely, well into this century the attitude remained that workers had a moral and juridical obligation, not solely a contractual and functional one, to obey the employer whatever the circumstances. Thus the commonly voiced worker fear of "wage slavery" in the early period of this century clearly reflected more than rhetorical excess.

Both abstractly and in practice the employer-employee relationship to this day contains quite definite implications about the superior right and (among certain conservative ideologues) ability and character of the employer. But precisely because both social democratic preference and corporate need call for purely functional and not honorific distinctions in industrial life, the latter continue to erode. Thus, even though the employer-employee relationship remains a lopsided one in terms of power, status, reward, and responsibility, it represents a considerable cultural and social advance over its predecessors.

Cultural Changes. As I think must be readily appreciated, the shift in the workers' industrial status from "servant" to "employee" contained within it the seeds of wider social and cultural changes as well. This is one of the concrete ways in which an emerging corporate society has acted to undercut and destroy traditional private-property society, and it confirms my view that workers have both a different and better position in society at least in part because of their place within the modern corporation. The rise of social Darwinism and other forms of racialist thought at the end of the last century may be offered to illustrate this point.

As invidious distinctions about work and workers began to erode in the workplace, there arose an attempt among the then educated classes to restore them through social theories and social ideologies that elevated the nonlaboring population at the expense, naturally, of the lower classes. In the United States, the influence of Herbert Spencer was of dramatic importance. Spencer's social Darwinism crudely applied Charles Darwin's biological theories to social life. In this view a person's superior social position and wealth were seen as marks of biological superiority. Thus owners were intelligent; workers were congenitally stupid. Middle-class people had high morals whereas those of the workers showed uncorrectable depravity. Aristocrats had profound aesthetic sensibilities; workers, of course, had the sensibilities of animals, much given to drinking and oversized families.

These contemptuous theories about the intellectual and moral capacity of the working class were given a semblance of plausibility by the widespread illiteracy among workers and the primitive ideas of sanitation and health care among a population only recently removed from the countryside. Workers were also seen as using excessive amounts of alcohol and other drugs, so much so that an underlying theme of the prohibition movement, throughout its entire early history, was that banning alcohol would protect the other classes against worker depravity. In addition, although it is true that many workers were not only literate but often highly cultivated, particularly the printers and the cigar makers, the general level of worker culture was extremely low.

The outcome of all this was that in the earlier part of the corporate era workers were commonly seen by the "respectable" classes to stand more or less outside the national, civilized community. If, as so often both here and in Europe, the workers had socialist sympathies, this was evidence of their disloyalty, their positive hostility to "real Americanism," "real Britishness," and so on. And if the workers couldn't be accused of socialism, then they could be readily thought of as ignorant, disease-ridden brutes, jealous of the "better classes of people," given to drink and riot, in short, as a species of subhumans, outside society though necessary to it, but hostile and threatening on every point. It would be difficult to exaggerate the universality and intensity with which such ideas were held. But the evidence is there in the historical record, not only in the speeches, letters, and diaries left by educated people but also in the enthusiasm with which they encouraged the repression of worker protest; the shooting, beating, and sabering of demonstrators; the summary "justice" handed out so freely to worker leaders or merely those necessary to "set an example" to the others.

The evolution of corporate society has clearly brought about a remarkable shift not only in the position of workers in the United States but also in the way in which they are viewed by educated opinion. The crude racialist ideologies so characteristic of the 1890s, many parading about in scientific trappings, have been replaced by dominant cultural and social scientific attitudes that are at least dubious about attributing superiority to this or that group. Part of this change has been forced by the political and social power of organized workers, particularly by the combination of the New Deal and the CIO, as I argued above.

Interestingly enough, in spite of the ever-deepening need and preference of corporate society for functional social ideologies, there still exists important opposition to it. The shift from cultural and social scientific theories emphasizing the ultimate inequality of the different classes and orders to those of a more democratic and egalitarian cast has been so marked that conservative theorists and spokespeople now, once again, appear to be searching around for scientific, theological, ideological, and other barriers against what they see as the excessive egalitarianism of the era.

Social and Cultural Integration. The growing social and cultural attainments of workers have surely helped them toward ever greater social and cultural integration. In politics they must now at least be formally placated and the state's repressive arms used much, much more carefully and restrictively than before. Socially and culturally, the inclusion of the working class into corporate society is also extremely important. The working class as a whole has attained basic literacy and has become thoroughly acclimated to the peculiar necessities of living in great urban conglomerations. In certain of the arts, most notably in music and perhaps in dance, film, and the graphic arts, the influence of workers is now dominant. Here one must remind oneself not to substitute "proletarian" for "worker." Modern films, for example, do not celebrate proletarians, but they do increasingly reflect the contributions, outlook, problems, values, and such, of so-called ordinary people of ordinary means. It is not even rare to find the morals, values, and accomplishments of these ordinary people being touted as superior to those of the higher classes. This would have been unthinkable in the "high culture" of a century ago.

The presence of increasing numbers of working-class students and teachers of working-class origin in high schools, colleges, and universities has arguably resulted in important intellectual changes in, for example, the fields of history and literature, leading to some "democratization" of these once exclusive, higher-class precincts. Conservative scholars and publicists have, predictably, decried this development, too.

Thus, in some respects, the modern working class appears to have even gone beyond social Taylorism, taking off, so to speak, on its own trajectory by embracing or engendering ideas and values that exceed those called for by its restricted place in corporate society. The cultural level of the working class as a whole seems now to be rapidly growing, not remaining static or even declining, as was perhaps the case in the 1880s and 1890s. The general question whether the gap between the social-cultural levels of workers and the other classes is closing or widening is difficult to estimate. But in a number of specific areas the workers come off quite well in the comparison. As the recent presidential campaign of Jesse Jackson indicated once again, workers are far less susceptible to the social superstitions of race than are, certainly, the middle classes. They are in general more socially tolerant, more skeptical of the rectitude of government and big business, and appear to be becoming less inclined to national chauvinism and calls to martial adventure. The electoral base for a more libertarian, racially and socially tolerant society, as well as for internationalist—not imperial—foreign policies rests, and has rested for many years, primarily on the U.S. working class. This point is not well understood, although it is shown in virtually every survey relating political and other attitudes to social class. In this sense, if we believe that the electoral process has been a source of democratic and egalitarian tendencies in U.S. life, we must attribute those changes primarily to the power and the social action of the working class.

A **National Class.** All of the "observations" so far cited are intimately associated with the rise of corporate industry and its subsequent growth at the expense of purely local or regional firms. Corporate industry brings with it not only its more cosmopolitan and functionalist outlook but also a working class that has won and now enjoys rights in both the workplace and society far beyond those of workers in the pre-corporate era. Here, too, we meet the paradox earlier discussed: The spread of corporate industry is among the main factors that have expanded and strengthened the social power and the political influence of the working class.

There is in fact one quite startling dimension to this strengthening. In no country during the last century were workers widely scattered through the population. In every country, workers were concentrated in a few cities or regions, often, as in Germany, Italy, Britain, and the United States, far from the centers of political power. Only in czarist Russia and, of course, in France were the workers present in vast numbers in capital cities, where by sheer strength of numbers they might occasionally cow or at least frighten the government. In the United States this geographical dispersion was particularly important, especially given our Madisonian system of representation.

Now, the spread of corporate activity away from the older cities and industrial regions has also made for a national class of workers. This is particularly striking in the United States. Even as late as the 1950s, industrial workers composed at best a regional (or several regional) working class(es). If we take the widest definition of industrial workers, including miners and railroad and maritime workers, the industrial working class was numerous and potentially influential only in the states on the eastern seaboard from

Massachusetts to Maryland, along the shores of the Great Lakes, along the Ohio River, and in the states on the upper West Coast. Perhaps Nevada and Colorado should be added as well. But that's all: The industrial working class was present in significant numbers in fewer than half of the lower forty-eight states and territories. Currently, even the South, formerly a bastion of regionalist classes and groups, is increasingly becoming integrated into a national corporate society and culture, as have been the Southwest, the Plains states, the upper Midwest, and southern California.

The language historically used to talk about workers and their movements belies their—until recently—minority status. This is particularly true of the proletarian concept, which speaks so freely of "the masses," by implication a majority. But in the 1890s, in no country save Great Britain were workers even a large minority. In fact, urban workers in industry, mining, and transportation were not at the time the main laboring population in the United States. Here, property-owning or property-leasing entrepreneurial farmers, their laborers, and their satellite artisans (harness makers, blacksmiths, well-diggers, carpenters, and so on) in the smaller towns and rural areas vastly outnumbered the workers of the great cities and great new industries until fairly recently.

Thus we meet one of the most striking ways in which modern workers differ from the classic proletariat. In the United States (as in each of the European industrial countries), the urban, corporate-based working class has become the main national laboring class both in numbers and in importance. This once minority grouping will even become, in the calculable future, an absolute majority not only of the national laboring population but of the population per se. Until almost the present time, "the masses," "the democracy," "the people" were only honorific titles for modern workers. We can already foresee the time when they will become simple descriptives.

In summarizing this series of observations, it is tempting to say that the urban workers of the 1890s, as of the surrounding decades, were, purely and simply, proletarians. But in the interests of accuracy we should say instead that, first, in the early corporate era there were very powerful tendencies at work to proletarianize these workers. More specifically, workers at that time—here certainly, and for the most part in Europe—were permitted only the most minimal standard of living, and this in economies in which a plentitude of new industrial products and conveniences was beginning to emerge. In that precise sense, workers were placed outside of—one might say beneath—the various national economies, contributing mightily to them but receiving little or nothing in return. That expression "outside of" also describes their political, social, and cultural position. They were excluded, sometimes by force, sometimes by circumstance, from participating in the various political systems.

The same can be said of their position in the societies they were ostensibly part of. Workers got by on their own and through the cooperative efforts of family, neighborhood, ethnic society, and union; the modern idea that the public authorities should provide social services of one sort or another, even clean water and effective sewage systems, was only just getting started. Of wider social services there were virtually none. And, as we have seen, workers were viewed as deeply alien to the various national cultures.

Second, workers almost everywhere had extremely low cultural levels; illiteracy, superstition, crude health and sanitation habits of clear and recent rural origin were low enough, as we saw, to make plausible their exclusion from society. If we view them, as Marx so often does, as peasants who have been stripped of their qualities, their rights, and their differences, they had only recently been stripped, and they surely retained at least some of the worst characteristics of their low origin, "worst" meaning traits that severely weakened the workers' ability to improve their individual and collective situation.

Third, workers were only a regional phenomena and, save in Britain, not only a minority of the population but a minority of the national laboring population as well.

Perhaps the account just given contains only a few surprises; historians sympathetic to workers, as well as workers themselves and their spokespersons, are much given to reminding us of the subordinate and deprived position workers have occupied and still occupy in our capitalist civilization. But that workers still occupy a lower position in society should not hide from us the stupendous changes that have occurred in their situation. The summary changes here are extremely significant: Workers who once stood outside their national cultural, social, economic, and political communities are now within them where, though they still have only a lesser voice, they nonetheless have a substantial and, as I will subsequently argue, growing voice and influence. Second, where once they had a low, perhaps declining cultural and social level—and therefore political and social capacity—they now appear to enjoy a rapid cultural and social development and, therefore, presumably, a growing capacity to act in and on society. And, of obvious relevance to the foregoing, a once minority laboring population now moves steadily on the path to becoming an absolute majority of the population as a whole. Finally, it is evident that these changes are not the result of one or a few abrupt, irrepeatable events but represent a fairly gradual, although uneven accumulation of changes, many directly brought about by the development of corporate form, which have been building over the past 100 years.

What Is Class Consciousness?

This raises perhaps the most acute question in modern social analysis and historical theory: Why these changes? And, in particular, what has been the causal influence, if any, of the workers themselves? There are a number of popular answers. On the one hand, there is a virtual cottage industry, especially in the United States, that holds that the gradual amelioration of worker life over the past century proves that "the system works," that Marx has had his comeuppance at the hands of "democratic capitalism," and that we are witnessing the end of the class struggle or, as Daniel Bell once put it, the "end of ideology." Whole herds of thinkers, again most notably in the United States, celebrate what they see as historic proof that the "American way of life" has managed to short-circuit the chronic social conflict that once so beset Europe. If fact, with the decline of the European parties of the far left, people who take this view now argue that Europe has seen the light and is learning to emulate U.S. success. What's more, in this view of things the workers played no really essential role in bringing about these changes. "The system" gets the credit.

On the other or left side of the aisle, the real changes in the lives of workers are often minimized, or it is emphasized that capital has permitted such changes only to "co-opt" the workers. These are common arguments among those who are partial to a theory of a proletariat. Social theorists who emphasize the artisan theory we mentioned earlier in this chapter often deny that there has been any overall improvement, weighing against each of the changes I have already cited the harmful effects of the end of craftsmanship and of the independent worker communities associated with them. The French writer André Gorz is perhaps best known in this regard.

Given the facts as we have reviewed them, particularly the long accumulation of changes that have improved the lives and influence of workers in modern capitalist society, the more straightforward, less contentious position is simply to accept that the changes have been mutually advantageous to both capital and labor and, in some sense, have come about and been accepted as more or less permanent because of that mutual advantage. Any other position, I would submit, simply doesn't do justice to the historical record and, in fact, requires theoretical commitments that would cleanse it of facts and developments that fit uncomfortably to that record.

This is not an argument that "the system works": far from it. It would be a rather simple and straightforward task to show that each of the improvements cited, both in detail and in tendency, was opposed by the representatives of "the system" during the times when it was being fought for and won by the workers. Limitation of hours; trade union recognition; expansion of public education for workers' children; a ban on child labor; freedom of assembly; limitations on the police in dealing with industrial conflict; egalitarian theories of social science, of culture, and of history; protection of the civil liberties of dissidents—all of these were resolutely and often bloodily combated by the most reputable and authoritative representatives of "the system" in the past. To say that "the system works" and therefore that social conflict and even a bit of illegal and disorderly behavior "outside the system" is unnecessary is simply false. The present "system" we have is not "the system" we've had at various times in the past, and it is not even a system built smoothly upon the foundations provided by the past; in almost every case the changes we have cited are the outcome of bitter, often protracted conflict between workers and the so-called better classes. In virtually every case, worker blood was shed in behalf of the changes.

That's an important point. But a related point matches it and brings us closer to an all-important principle of modern social development. When we look back over 100 years with today's eyes—with today's social ideas— we are struck that these social and industrial improvements in worker life, and in general social life, were prefigured only by workers and by writers and spokespeople active in their behalf. That is, if we look to the social and industrial future as envisioned by representatives of "the system" in the early corporate era, we find that a majority (and the most influential) liked things just the way they were. The remark of railroad president George Baer during a coal strike in 1902 accurately conveys the nature of that vision: "The rights and interests of the laboring man will be protected and cared for, not by the labor agitators, but by the Christian men to whom God in His infinite wisdom has given control of the property interests of the country." (This oft-cited quotation appears, among other places, in Samuel Yellen's *American Labor Struggles*.) Included in this trusteeship from the kindly deity were ten- to twelve-hour days, child labor, cheating workers of their wages, widespread bullying by the Coal and Iron Police, and the usual dangers to life and limb from coal operators who skimped on safety. Baer and many of his ilk can, of course, serve as straw men in these arguments. They were, after all, out-and-out reactionaries. But even when we turn to the most enlightened representatives of "the system" at the time, for example, progressive employers like Carnegie, or the emerging social work professions, the best social vision they have is only, in the words of the contemporary observer Charles Gulick, "paternalistic and autocratic."

On the other hand, turning to the workers and their supporters, we find in their palpable aims and aspirations a pretty good reading of what we now actually have and are further striving for. For example, the eight-hour movement of the mid-1880s consciously sought more leisure so that the workers could, among other things, raise their level of culture. In fact, in a period in which representatives of "the system" thought that fifty-five- to eighty-four-hour work weeks were a kindness to the workers, keeping them from drink and other depravity, the intense debate within labor, socialist, and worker circles eventuated in our modern concept of the right to leisure time or, as described in Paul Lafargue's famous pamphlet, *The Right to Be Lazy*. Similarly prefigured is the idea that workers had a right not just to a living income but to a rising income, that is, to a share of the new riches being generated by industrialization. Marx's stress on "surplus value" in his economic analysis singles out this aspect; he was not interested in wealth per se—a static thing—but in economic growth and in the distribution of its rewards. The ideas of a more democratic culture, of equality between men and women, of equal rights for minorities, of new kinds of family planning and child rearing, of expanded civil rights and civil liberties, all are found being debated among workers and their supporters at the time. Margaret Sanger, after all, was a socialist, as was Helen Keller. Her remarkable teacher, Annie Sullivan, was even a member of the IWW. The civil liberties movement was originally rooted in the defense of worker, socialist, and anarchist martyrs such as Joe Hill, Big Bill Haywood, and, of course, Sacco and Vanzetti. These progressive and liberating ideas were rarely found in circles far removed from the social democratic and workers' movement, certainly not in "the system." In short, "the system" didn't work. It was replaced by a new system and that new system was prefigured to a remarkable degree in the ideas of the working class, not in those of their foes.

Thus we return once more to the great paradox of corporate society. Corporate form represents a more purely capitalist phenomenon than its predecessors and places the working class under the industrial dictatorship of the middle element, to which it is also socially subordinated. Yet the historical evolution of the modern working class, in its longer time frames, is considerably more than a history of social and political Taylorism. Other elements enter into the story, many of which appear to originate within the working class itself.

There is a way to make sense of these phenomena. It means accepting that our present-day society is purely and simply a position of equilibrium in the class struggle; that is, it represents an historic though changing balance in the deep social competition between capital and labor. This in turn implies that within corporate form and at least to the present time, capital and labor are classes with both deeply competing and deeply complementary interests, so that their conflict can be brought into equilibrium—not into static equilibrium: The historic record surely argues against that. But history also shows that neither can dispense with the other and so must acquiesce to a degree in the other's interests.

Very crudely speaking, the formula for that ever-changing equilibrium in the corporate era has been that the workers are not blocked in their pursuit of greater social, cultural, economic, and political rights *provided that* those rights are consistent with the desire of the capital–middle-element alliance for higher and higher productivity and for the steady expansion of the corporate system. In fact, because these improvements in worker life create a more productive, more useful working class for capitalism, they often come to be supported by the capitalist–middle-element alliance. This ostensible parity between the two antagonists should not dim our recognition, however, that the creative, pioneering element in this historic struggle—often its *conscious* element—is more often than not to be found on the workers' side of the lines.

The action and vision of the worker side of the social struggle are integral to the evolution of corporate form in the modern capitalist enterprise and to corporate society. One of the historical components in the development of the modern corporation was fear of and attempts to deal effectively with the growing urban, industrial laboring force. I think the record shows that the initial impulse of the Baers, Vanderbilts, Scotts, and Fricks, that is, the earlier generation of big capitalists in the United States, was simply to create a proletariat. The workers resisted that process of proletarianization; paradoxically, Marx's greatest contribution to the process may have been in *preventing* the formation of a proletariat by forewarning workers what was in store for them. That warning seems to have played a central role in worker resistance to the worst excesses of capitalism. At any event, the early workers succeeded in demanding and enforcing a degree—but only a degree—of accommodation to their interests, for the working class then had neither the size, the political capacity, nor the experience to create a different system.

Meanwhile, more far-sighted individuals such as Morgan, Taylor, Gary, and, especially, Theodore Roosevelt and Mark Hanna, saw the threat of socialism and trade unionism and tried to devise ways to defuse worker discontent while at the same time increasing productivity and profits. That double process has shaped and is still shaping the modern working class: On the one hand, the working class is forced by circumstance, social inertia, and its own social and cultural incapacity, to exist in a subordinate position in capitalist industry and society; on the other, it makes increasing demands on its masters. In acceding to these ever-changing worker demands, capital has been forced to shed features and residues of the past, forced to devise new responses to old (and often new) problems. Like two great powers locked in an arms race, capital and labor develop and perfect their powers of both offense and defense in the social struggle.

The development of the system of productive relations called corporate form is shaped by this process of conflict and accommodation between hostile but complementary classes. Basically, the laboring population successfully resisted being proletarianized, that is, being placed fully outside civil society, as before. Capital meanwhile successfully broke the artisan class, artisan elements, and what we might call the artisan principle among workers, primarily by replacing a crafts-based technology with a new university-based one. Thus workers forced a place for themselves within civil society but on industrial-technological terms enforced by capital. Those are the recognizable terms of the historical accommodation between capital and labor as crystallized in the modern corporation and the society built upon it. Workers must submit to the technical-productive discipline of capitalist enterprise where profit-making, efficiency, and purely quantitative growth are gods. At the same time and in historic exchange, workers have limited rights in the enterprise and extensive rights in the society.

There is no contradiction in that formulation. By extending rights and even privileges to workers in society the workers themselves become further inured, acculturated, and trained for their very subordinate place in the industrial scheme. Moreover, and at least to date, the remarkable productivity and riches of modern capitalist industry have depended on a draconian industrial discipline in which workers labor under an absolute technological and administrative ("management") dictatorship of another class, the middle element. Thus modern capitalism rests on a sharp and irresolvable contradiction but one that has heretofore proved temporarily manageable: A more and more democratic and humanitarian society, the product, I would argue, of the efforts and social vision of its workers, requires as its necessary condition a severe form of technological and administrative bondage. Workers are offered, in a sense, full equality in the wider society, but only if they accept a subordinate and, in many ways, increasingly restricted role in the productive mechanism. As part of the same processes, the working class continues to grow in both its quantitative and qualitative dimensions.

In his influential *The Making of the English Working Class*, Edward Thompson argues that there is a sense in which a laboring class both forms part of and historically transcends its own society. Thompson purports to find among British laboring people an underclass culture that preceded British capitalism and helped these laborers to make the difficult transition into what he identifies as a specifically modern working class. Such a view is consistent with and, I believe, confirmed by the argument I have made here. Even in the United States, parts of the historical culture of craftsworkers and of artisans played an important part in the growth of the modern working class. Surely, it, like Marxism, was a major factor in helping a would-be proletariat to prevent its own proletarianization.

In saying this I don't accept the current tendency to paint an idyllic picture of artisan culture. Resting as it does on a sharp division of attainments, rights, and rewards between skilled and unskilled workers that backward culture is far better replaced by a much more modern, working-class idea. In this idea, the skill, a craft, even a solid income have nothing to do with social worth. Instead, the mere willingness to work, to contribute to the common pool of goods, services, and cooperation we call an economy, is enough to confer all social rights and privileges on all workers. This idea comes from the unskilled workers or, at the least, was socially established by their efforts. It clearly exceeds in its democratic and humanist potential even the most far-sighted of the artisan class.

My analysis implies that one must attribute to the modern working class as an historical class an existence that partly transcends what we have earlier described as the limits of sociological reality. With Thompson, it implies that the class contains within itself cultural and organizational seeds that, unchecked by the actions of the other classes, reach beyond the present and beyond the mental, moral, and cultural limits of contemporary capitalism. We could call this a form of "class consciousness," but that term is so immured in ancient controversies that it may be better simply to avoid it. Moreover, "class consciousness" is traditionally used as a synonym for the conscious espousal of a full-fledged political program at some specific point in history by workers or on the part of those who purport to speak for them. I would prefer to speak of the *class intelligence* of the working class. Essentially a term of historical analysis, it is a way of saying merely that in its historical tendency the working class of the corporate era has demonstrated a powerful adaptive, innovative, and autonomous intelligence. It is "adaptive" in that the class exerts steady, intelligent pressure on that society to expand its own place, rights, and opportunities. "Innovative" connotes a social intelligence that reaches beyond the class' present social position, seeking new social forms and values for its own advantage; "autonomous" suggests that it never fully succumbs to the cultural hegemony of the dominant classes.

It is, of course, impossible to read the future and dangerous to believe that it will be something like the past. Nevertheless, it is important to record that to the extent that we have witnessed broad social amelioration within the capitalist world through this century, we find much to support the view that it has come largely through the efforts and the social vision of the modern working class. In fact, the more we concentrate on the moral and cultural elements of the changes and the less on the technological and material elements, the more pronounced do the beneficial effects of this class intelligence appear. Even our modern humanist ideal seems to me to be drawn directly from the vision and gains of the modern working class. This ideal is of a multisided, even cosmopolitan person, knowledgeable about and tolerant of many different kinds of people and values, functioning within society with rights and powers stemming from universal, unlimited rights based on the individual's social contribution through work. This class intelligence is arguably the dominant, creative social force in modern capitalist society. Its existence and importance are obscured by its very constancy, its longevity, its seeming naturalness, and, of course, by the ideological dominance of other classes.

This conception of class intelligence, I hasten to add, does not imply that modern workers are milk-and-water socialists in their collective hearts, content to await the long pull for their betterment. Movements in the CIO in 1937, Paris in 1968, Korea in 1988, Italy's "Hot Autumn" of 1969, and South Africa for some years now testify to the capacity and willingness of today's workers to act like revolutionary proletarians should conditions demand it or the occasion present itself. But unlike the unique burst of explosive behavior called for in the proletarian theory, the characteristic mode of action of modern workers has been to exert constant pressure at almost every point in society for changes in their situation. Although they sometimes flood capitalist society with their demands, their normal mode of operation is to transform society rather than merely to reform this or that worst excess.

A final observation on this subject: I earlier noted that in pre-corporate and even in the early phases of corporate society, some significant fraction of the middle classes made common cause with the workers. In fact, the historical social democratic movement, the dominant movement of the modern working class to date, is probably best seen as one in which a significant fragment of the middle classes assumed a leadership role for a young working class that, if it was able to project its own values for society, was by itself culturally and politically incapable of securing their adoption. Corporate society is in many ways a strategic countermove to that historic phenomenon; that is, it represents a form of society in which the link between middle class and upper class is so cohesive, so founded in mutual advantage as to preclude any substantial portion of the middle group from passing to the other side of the social struggle. Schematic though this historical observation may be, it poses perhaps the fundamental questions for the future of the modern working class and for corporate society itself: Will the working class, in spite of the weight of social and political Taylorism, prove capable of assuming its own cultural and political leadership? Is the class sufficiently developed to act alone—without a middle-class alliance—in the social struggle? Are its class capacity and intelligence now sufficiently developed that it may comprehend, as Marx puts it in *The Eighteenth Brumaire*, "the general interests of society" and thus contend for cultural and political hegemony in its own name and right? Is it capable, in short, of pushing society beyond corporate society? These, it seems to me, have become timely questions.

Highly Cultivated Donkeys

Unlike artisan and proletarian classes, the modern corporate working class is shaped and altered deep within capitalist society. Young artisans learned their views of economy and society in their apprenticeship, a corner of economic life from which the higher classes were excluded. In legend and in fact, the young proletarian learned his or her view of these things in the tenements where no employer, and only the most foolhardy policeman, would dare to venture. But the young worker of today goes to school, watches television, sees films, and hears music that are not products of a specifically working-class culture. Instead, he or she is the product of a society and culture whose overt and explicit motifs, especially in the short run, are unabashedly mainstream, committed to "respectable" modes of thought and behavior and strongly supportive of capitalism. This is, to use an earlier expression, the phenomenon of social Taylorism.

The modern working class is shaped and reproduced by both the modern corporation and the society that parallels it. As the corporations expand, so does the class. As the corporations move into the South and the West, into small-town and semirural areas, so the working class expands accordingly. If the corporations come to employ, directly and indirectly, more and more people, the working class grows in exact proportion. When corporations employ millions of women, the working class loses its heretofore predominantly male character and outlook. Black people get new job opportunities, as do Hispanics, and Asians; accordingly, the working class once so heavily white and European becomes a rainbow of different colors, languages, and cultures. Thus as the labor force of the modern corporate system becomes more reflective of the racial, gender, and ethnic diversity of our people, the working class itself becomes, in sociological terms, more representative of the U.S. population as a whole. In a worldwide setting, the progressive addition of new faces and cultures into the corporate working class reminds one of the refrain from the revolutionary hymn "The Internationale": "The international working class will become the human race."

These changes in work life are paralleled in the evolution of our social and cultural institutions. Like the producer corporations, the nationally oriented school system replaces the local firm. National corporate tastes in music, film, food, clothing, vacation styles, home decoration, and architecture come to replace the local products. Each of these developments, like the spread of the producer corporations, adds new regions and new people to the national working class and further unifies its life-style and interests. These are striking and important developments, for they create an abstract possibility that workers will come to contain within their class ranks people sufficient to mirror and possibly represent the interests of the broad national population. But the sociological, geographical, and quantitative expansion of the working class within corporate form, important enough in its own right, is not, I think, the most interesting part of the story.

What kind of workers are being produced? What kind of a working class is being reproduced and with what sort of social outlook? Clearly, the kind the corporations need. They don't need artisans and they don't need proletarians; consequently, they take steps not to produce and reproduce them. Unfortunately, once again the ideological strictures that insist on portraying workers through artisan and proletarian concepts blind us to the positive side of what has been occurring.

The productive system of a modern corporation is a deeply social process, in part because of its technological character, in part because of its scale, in part because so much of our social and material civilization arises within its producing activities. For the workers, who lack nearly all control over the work process, this requires special strengths. Workers must be able to fit themselves to the requirements of numerous jobs. Each worker, it is true, is often forced to do one repetitive job, like installing a car seat or entering data into a computer or sewing a cuff. But industry doesn't want and won't hire people who can *only* install car seats or enter numerical data or sew cuffs. For modern capital, the technical side of these jobs is dominated by the middle-element technician, manager, or professional. From the worker it is required only that he or she be adaptable to any of these jobs. Again, technically speaking, this imposes no strain on the worker's training, as it merely calls for literacy, a degree of dexterity, high stamina, and so forth.

Such a worker is not a craftsperson who can take pride in the thing produced; what he or she produces is only a small step in a complex process. Instead, the modern worker must be able to take pride in and feel responsible to something wider, must display intelligent social behavior on the job. The great requirement of modern, high-speed, technically complex productive systems is that every person must do the job right or the whole system will fail. Management thus seeks to develop a high worker morality based on each worker's sense of contribution to important tasks. Basically, the ideal production worker must understand and appreciate that he or she is part of an intensely social work process in which not technical proficiency but intelligent, responsible behavior—often in the face of a mind-numbing task—is absolutely required. He or she must be psychologically able to fit into any phase of the productive process and behave effectively, to work hard, avoid absence, and concentrate on a narrow task. To do this well requires that the worker see that the social group, not this star or that craftsperson or that technical specialist, creates the product. And he or she must be able to become and remain motivated primarily by loyalty to and pride in the group, not the craft or the individual accomplishment. Thus we see one of the deepest contradictions of corporate form and of corporate society: Modern capitalism must strive to deepen among its workers many of the elements we correctly associate with legendary working-class consciousness.

My sense is that this truism of industrial life is well understood as a point of, say, worker behavior on the job. But I think social investigators have generally failed to appreciate the importance of the broader worker morality and consciousness this leads to. On the job it often makes the individual feel particularly loyal to his or her co-workers or department or perhaps even company. But unlike an artisan consciousness, this newer sort of worker consciousness has no necessary natural boundaries within the working class and in fact can flow (and historically has flowed) into feelings of identity with and loyalty to others like situated, in short, into feelings of class solidarity. In this respect, it is on the surface much like a proletarian class consciousness—but with a more profound difference.

The class consciousness associated with the proletarian was a political consciousness developing out of a total rejection of one's place. For this reason, classic proletarian thought demands a total change of circumstance, a revolution—in short, an abstract, universal remedy as a logical response to the wholesale rejection of the present system. By contrast, modern working-class social attitudes are not per se political in content. When and to the extent that such feelings have become political, as in the Italian "Hot Autumn" of 1969, they have demanded detailed concrete changes in their work and social lives and demanded them now, and not as a result of some future revolution. From the nature of the case these changes directly challenge the mental, technical, and controlling role of the middle managerial, technical, and professional class.

This is not, by any means, the only contradiction intrinsic to the further development of corporate society. By and large, workers in corporate society, especially the younger workers, are offered an impossible choice in life. The individual worker must either "advance" out of his or her class or be condemned to life in the most constricted, least rewarding, and least esteemed class in society. Within our socially mobile society, with its much-heralded "equality of opportunity," the working class is, by definition, the class of those who didn't make it. Yet this is the class upon whose passive cooperation corporate society ultimately rests.

A donkey who worked on a modern assembly line would pose no problem. As argued, the technical task imposed on the assembly-line worker is a donkey's task, but the social task requires a man or a woman able to perform hard, repetitive work because he or she is a socially responsible person, that is, consciously responsible to some mates, union, company, industry, country, or class. The point is not which group but that it is a group responsibility the worker must embrace and internalize. This requires that capital raise the social and cultural levels of the workers, make workers more unlike donkeys so that, being human, they can act with the discipline of donkeys. In a sense, the ideal modern worker would be a highly cultivated donkey with a deeply split personality. The tragedy, from the standpoint of the higher corporate classes, is that they're not donkeys and they don't have split personalities. The higher and higher social and cultural levels imposed on workers by a corporate society that they themselves have helped to bring about makes them more and more socially and culturally demanding—that's the history we've been reading—and, I think, is increasingly making them socially and industrially restive. That, I believe, is the history we *will* be reading.

Bibliographical Essay

Both Charles Gulick's *Labor Policy of the United States Steel Corporation* (1924; AMS Press, New York, 1968) and Samuel Yellen's *American Labor Struggles* (Pathfinder Press, New York, 1977) have the virtue of giving a plentitude of concrete details on the social conditions of the early twentieth-century working class in the United States. Though Yellen's book was first published half a century ago, his sense of what was central, and why it was central, remains so acute that the book is as fresh and germane as if written yesterday.

Paul Lafargue was Marx's son-in-law. His *Droit de la Paresse* has been published in English under the title *The Right to Be Lazy* (Charles Kerr, Chicago, 1975). Selig Perlman (*Theory of the Labor Movement*, Augustus M. Kelly, New York, 1928) in many ways the official philosopher of sober, socially responsible "Wisconsin school" trade unionism in the United States, is my source for the claim that the AFL policy under Gompers and Green was aimed at preventing the organization of the unskilled and foreign-born. He claims in his book that it was the "main, though *invisible* function" of the federation (his emphasis). Accounts of the CIO are often cast as impersonal, institutional labor history; for a more personal account, which also brings out the political and historical dimensions, there is the fine autobiography of the great strategist of the Flint sit-down strikes, Wyndham Mortimer. Unfortunately, though not unexpectedly, the Mortimer autobiography neglects to mention his own Communist-party affiliation, as well as that of Bob Travis, the actual leader of the sit-down. See Mortimer's *Organize: My Life as a Union Man* (Beacon Press, Boston, 1972). For a vivid, first-person account of the epochal Flint strike and of Travis's brilliant tactics in winning it, see Henry Kraus, *The Many and the Few* (Plantin Press, Los Angeles, 1947).

The membership of Margaret Sanger and Helen Keller in the Socialist party is well known; Annie Sullivan's association with the IWW was pointed out to me by the labor and women's historian Rosalyn Baxandall. André Gorz's *Farewell to the Working Class: An Essay in Post-Industrial Socialism* (Pluto Press, London, 1982) argues for the social superiority of a laboring class based on artisans, their technology, and the social structures (and, indeed, society) resting upon them.

Epilogue:
Alberich and Prometheus—
the Modern Corporation
as a Social Institution

The modern corporation is a social institution in the extended sense. It really cannot be viewed just as a commercial organization or a technology user, a legal entity or an instance of bureaucratization, an economic departure or a phase of financial-industrial history. Nor can it be viewed as a social institution in the narrower sense in which popular books often view it, that is, as a sort of playground for rich people, connected people, dishonest people, or even rich, connected, and dishonest people.

I mentioned earlier that we might compare it to other organizations of world-historical significance, such as the Jesuit order, the mandarinate of old China or the Roman army, but even this analogy is flawed. The Jesuit order of Loyola's time was extremely influential, but it had little to do, for example, with the banking changes then occurring in Genoa or the important changes in commercial practice then arising in Amsterdam. The mandarinate dominated ancient China, but its influence on the evolution of Chinese tools was surely minor. Similarly, the Roman army did not influence the shape, content, or audience for Horace's poetry. The modern corporation, however, has much to do with each of these areas of life and more besides. It would be hard, in fact, to recall or even discover any organization in world history so centrally involved in so many social, cultural, economical, technological, military, legal, political, and even moral changes as the modern corporation.

I do not mean to assert that the corporation is somehow the *cause* of all or most of these changes. For our purposes it is enough simply to observe the obvious. All of the immense swirl of changes that have developed in the past 100 or so years have flowed in and around the corporation.

We need not say they were caused by the corporation, merely that the corporation as an institution is always present in the equation. Whether as cause, effect, factor, dimension, symbol, vehicle, embodiment, expression, "occasion" is immaterial at this point. But even this modest observation provides the foundation for a "deep" hypothesis about the most general relationship between modern society and the corporation.

Still, the modern corporation *has* had an enormous formative effect on twentieth-century social evolution. The alliance of the two higher corporate classes should be seen as a major causal factor in what I earlier described as the remaking of our physical-social world of tools, buildings, foods, materials, physical processes, and so forth. Through that remaking of the physical-social landscape, it has been the often inadvertent author of the most significant and influential changes in social relations as well. Increasingly, as it enters "the government business," the corporation is in the business of refashioning social, health, cultural, and other services not only as commercial products but as products that reflect the corporation's own class, property, power, and value relations. All in all, then, it is appropriate to view the modern corporation as a *fabricator of social relationships*, directly, indirectly, blindly, and by design, as the case may be.

By and large, previous writing and thinking on the subject has been too narrow, tending merely to treat the corporation as something *within* society. That is not, in truth, an adequate viewpoint. Certainly the sheer scope and variety of the changes we associate with corporate activity, corporate influence, and corporate tendency do not fit comfortably into this or that corner of society. The presence of the modern corporation is reflected in every part, every aspect of modern society. In short, that presence reaches out to the very borders and even horizons of modern society, touching, it would appear, each nook and cranny.

We should finally view the modern corporation not as something that rests within society but something that creates a society, in all its dimensions, in the present and in the future. We should see it as the institution erasing the traces of earlier societies and shaping an entirely new one—from the foundation up—to put in its place.

Traditional writing about the modern corporation has mostly tended to swing between highly partisan extremes. Thus the populist tradition, especially powerful in the United States, has been wont to warn of the dangers the corporate Alberich poses to democratic society, whereas its opponents, for example, Adolph Berle or Peter Berger, have tended mostly to lavish praise on the class-blind corporate Prometheus.

In many ways Alberich and Prometheus are fitting symbols for the corporation. Alberich, the evil gnome of Richard Wagner's great operatic cycle, *The Ring of the Nibelungen*, renounces love as the price he must pay for unlimited riches and power—which he subsequently lusts for as he had never lusted for any woman. Prometheus the Titan appears in ancient Greek mythology. Man, deprived of fire by the gods, had to live without its protection from the cold and the beasts until Prometheus stole that fire, gave it to the human race, and taught them how to use it to provide light, warmth, and the means to make tools. He is thus the great symbol of the liberating effects of human knowledge and productive activity.

Each of these symbols is apt in its place, but neither alone captures the full force of the modern corporation. But together they do. They provide a cautionary symbol: The grasping spirit of Alberich has never been more powerful, and in the modern alliance of the corporate public and the middle managerial, professional, and technical class, he finds to hand a productive mechanism that, like the fabled ring of Wagner's tale, can create an entirely new world in which the mass of men and women would be enslaved . . . to Prometheus' gift. This is the ultimate enigma posed by corporate society.

About the Book and Author

The modern corporation, praised and condemned by thinkers from Weber to Bell and Dahrendorf, is *the* institution of modern society. Its enormous success has made it our premier social, as well as economic, institution, and modern society is increasingly coming to reflect the social structure, values, priorities, and hierarchies that have evolved within the corporation.

So argues John McDermott in *Corporate Society*, an original and far-reaching analysis of the impact of the modern corporation on contemporary social structure. Combining business history with political insight, McDermott offers a systematic critique of the post-industrial order and the illusions it fosters. He warns against the development of a "post-society industry" in which the corporate order replaces democratic institutions as the primary organizer of social and cultural life, and he argues that the corporation harbors a set of explosive socioeconomic contradictions. The need to confront the challenges of this new order, with its potential for a uniquely modern class conflict, makes *Corporate Society* a crucial work for teachers and students alike.

John McDermott is professor emeritus of labor studies at the State University of New York, College of Old Westbury. Previously, he served as senior editor for *Viet-Report*, and he is currently on the editorial board of the *Review of Radical Political Economy*. The author of *Crisis in the Working Class*, he has authored articles that have appeared in numerous journals, including *Dissent, The Nation,* and *The New York Review of Books.*

Index

Accounting firms, 89, 90
Aristotle, 99
Arms race, 61–64, 71
Artisans. See Working class
Averitt, Robert, 55

Baer, George, 187
Banks, 89–90, 95–96. See also Finance
capitalism
Bell, Daniel, 3, 6, 16–17, 76, 106, 186
Berle, Adolph, 10, 49, 79, 80, 87, 94, 105,
106
Braverman, Harry, 138, 142–143
Bureaucracy, 10–11, 19, 42–43, 145–149, 168
Business firm, theory of the, 10

Capitalist class. See Top management
Carnegie, Andrew, 24–25, 27, 28, 44, 65,
187
Cartel system, 50
Chandler, Alfred D., Jr., 31, 40, 41
Charismatic authority, 146–147
CIO. See Congress of Industrial
Organizations
Citizen's Industrial Association, 66–67
Class, 6–9, 149, 168–170. See also Class
conflict; Classless society; Corporate
form; specific classes
Class conflict, 5, 11–12, 19, 134–138, 188–
190
Classless society, 17, 79
Collective bargaining. See Union movement
Collective property, 22, 77–86, 88–92, 94,
108
vs. family property, 6–7, 8–9, 80, 91–92,
93, 98–99
and stockholders, 86–88
Compensation
middle element, 30, 41, 81, 82, 83–84,
127, 134–135, 136, 137
top management, 30, 40–41
working class, 37–39, 81, 83, 134–135,
136, 158, 160, 166, 175, 188
Congress of Industrial Organizations (CIO),
179, 182, 196

Coolidge, Calvin, 113
Corporate form, 4–5, 22, 41–42
and arms race, 61–64
and bureaucracy, 11, 147–149
as class structure, 4, 21, 22, 69
in education, 151–155
evolution of, 57–70
vs. finance capitalism, 48–49, 50–51
and new technology, 59–60
and public sector, 107, 112, 114–116
and social democracy, 68, 72
top management as owners of, 78–79, 81,
84, 87, 88–89, 92, 95
and trade unions, 165, 166
See also Collective property; Corporate
public; Corporate society; Middle
element; Top management; Working
class
Corporate public, 11–12, 89–92, 93, 97, 98–
99, 117–121
Corporate society, 118–121, 199–201
vs. liberal society, 5, 12, 13–14, 97
working class in, 16, 161, 180–183
Corporation
development of, 43–45
legal definition of, 75–76
size of, 21, 49, 109
stereotypes of, 1–3, 27

Dahrendorf, Ralf, 9, 16, 80, 105, 106
Debs, Eugene, 65, 67, 177
Diversification, 26, 27, 47–48, 97, 109
Domhoff, G. William, 9, 93, 105, 122
Du Pont Corporation, 110
Durant, William, 27, 28

Economic theory, 2, 60, 70, 138, 157–158,
159, 170
Education, Taylorism in, 150–155
Ellul, Jacques, 10, 42, 52, 53, 57, 134
Engels, Friedrich, 99
Entrepreneurial class, 22, 97, 130–131, 140,
141. See also Pre- and non-corporate
classes; Small-business workers

Europe
  corporations in, 49–50, 51
  far left in, 186
  public sector in, 109–110, 111–112
  working class in, 64–65, 137, 138, 143,
    163, 166, 184, 192, 195
Executives. *See* Middle element; Top
  management

FAA. *See* Federal Aviation Agency
Federal Aviation Agency (FAA), 94–95
Finance capitalism, 48–49, 50–51, 68, 88.
  See also Banks
Ford, Henry, 51, 88, 126, 152, 170
France. *See* Europe
Free-market ideology 1–3, 13, 71, 116, 157–
  158, 159. *See also* Private property
Frick, Henry Clay, 65
Friedman, Milton, 2, 50, 116

Galbraith, John Kenneth, 10, 54, 57, 80,
  108
General Motors Corporation (GM), 26–31,
  45. *See also* Sloan, Alfred P.
Germany. *See* Europe
GM. *See* General Motors Corporation
Gompers, Samuel, 65
Gorz, Andre, 186
Government. *See* Government regulation;
  Public sector
Government regulation, 89, 90, 94–95, 113,
  164. *See also* Public sector
Gramsci, Antonio, 106
Great Britain. *See* Europe
Gulick, Charles, 187

Hanna, Mark, 189
Harding, Warren G., 113
Harriman, E. H., 67
Hilferding, Rudolph, 48, 50, 51, 79, 88
Hoover, Herbert, 95, 113, 123
Hughes, Howard, 88
Hunt brothers, 88

Immigration, 178–179
Income. *See* Compensation
Industrial revolution, late nineteenth-
  century, 58–61, 71
Industrial Workers of the World (IWW),
  56–57, 65, 70–71
Interstate Oil Compact, 113
Italy. *See* Europe
IWW. *See* Industrial Workers of the World

Japan, 33, 51

Keller, Suzanne, 11
Kennedy, John F., 114

Labor. *See* Working class
LaFargue, Paul, 188
Law firms, 89, 90
Legal issues, 74–76, 85–86, 94
Lenin, V. I., 51
Liberal society, 3, 13–14, 72
  vs. classless society, 17
  vs. corporate society, 5, 12, 14
  and private property, 14, 18
Line-staff system, 28, 29–30

Making of the English Working Class, The
  (Thompson), 101, 190
Management, 22–39. *See also* Taylorism
Marcuse, Herbert, 14, 106
Marshall, Alfred, 10, 60
Marx, Karl, 11. *See also* Marxist tradition
Marxist tradition
  and compulsory consumption, 159
  on middle classes, 11, 19, 68, 99, 100, 129
  proletarian concept in, 155, 173, 174, 185,
    189
  on property, 79, 94
  on public sector, 12
  on ruling classes, 103, 105–106
  on social control of working class, 14
  on surplus value, 188
  on Taylorism, 138
  and union movement, 64, 65
Means, Gardiner, 10, 26, 49, 79, 80, 87, 94,
  105, 106
Media, 155
Meritocracy, 16–17, 134
Middle class, traditional, 100, 121, 192. *See
  also* Entrepreneurial class; Pre- and
  non-corporate classes
Middle element, 4, 22, 70, 122, 168–169
  career tracks, 127–128
  and class conflict, 134–138
  compensation, 30, 41, 81, 82, 83–84, 127,
    134–135, 136, 137
  as control on workers, 11–12, 15, 42–43,
    68–69, 128, 129, 149–150
  in education, 151, 153–154
  evolution of, 51–55, 57
  geographical mobility of, 139–142
  identification with technology, 31–32, 39,
    41, 51–55, 81, 82–83, 84
  importance of, 11, 125–127, 133–134
  Marxist views of, 11, 19, 68, 99, 100, 129
  myths regarding, 135–138
  political involvement of, 134, 139–140,
    142, 155
  property claims of, 81–84, 129–130
  and public sector, 114, 137
  Sloan's development of, 23–31, 39
  and technology, 10, 31–32, 39, 41
  in union movement, 156

See also Corporate form; Middle element-top management alliance; Professionalism
Middle element-top management alliance, 11, 42–43, 107, 122, 137, 148
and isolation of working class, 68, 97, 100, 128–129
mutual benefits of, 53–54, 99–100
Mills, C. Wright, 108, 121–122
Moore, Barrington, 15
Morgan, J. P., Jr., 24, 26, 44, 65, 66, 67, 88

National Civic Federation (NCF), 67
National Labor Relations Board (NLRB), 85, 163–166
NCF. *See* National Civic Federation
New Deal, 94, 99, 113, 139–140, 179, 182
NLRB. *See* National Labor Relations Board
Nonprofit organizations. *See* Public sector

O'Connor, James, 14, 106
Outside directors, 89, 90–91

Parsons, Talcott, 10, 17, 105–106
Pennsylvania Railroad, 24
Perkins, George, 67
Pluralist democracy, 3. *See also* Liberal society
Political Taylorism. *See* Taylorism
Pre- and non-corporate classes, 5, 20, 63, 100, 121, 192. *See also* Entrepreneurial class; Middle class
destruction of, 15, 16, 22
Principles of Scientific Management (Taylor), 33–35
Private property
definition of, 73–75
disappearance of, 6–7, 8–9, 11, 18, 73
as family system, 6–7, 8–9, 76–77, 80, 91, 93, 98
as ideology, 5–6, 9, 14, 18, 20, 86
middle classes under, 100, 125
private vs. public sectors under, 12, 106–107
ruling class under, 103–105, 107
See also Liberal society
Privatization. *See* Public sector
Production, class structure of, 4
Production, private ownership of. *See* Private property
Professionalism, 21–22, 41, 52, 82, 129–134, 151–152
Proletariat, 155, 173–175, 184, 189
Property. *See* Collective property; Private property
Public-private sector integration, 19–20, 102, 107–118, 122–123
conspiracy theories, 112–114

corporate public role in, 89, 90, 102, 107–108, 114–115, 117–118
Marxist analysis, 12
and middle element, 131, 132, 137
and national security field, 62–63, 110–111
and self-regulation, 94–95
and social democracy, 68
See also Public sector
Public sector
crippling of, 119–120
ethos of, 108, 115
foreign examples, 109–110
social welfare programs, 3, 118, 119, 158–159, 160–161
under private property, 12, 106–107
and union movement, 179
See also Public-private sector integration
Pullman, George, 38
Pullman strike, 65, 66, 67

Quality circles, 33

Reagan, Ronald, 112, 113–114, 116, 117, 142, 160
Right to Be Lazy, The (LaFargue), 188
Rockefeller, John D., Jr., 67, 76
Rockefeller family, 65–66, 76, 88
Roosevelt, Franklin D., 94, 99, 112, 113
Roosevelt, Theodore, 68, 189
Ruling class, 101–108, 117–118, 121–122
Ruling class. *See* Corporate public; Top management; Upper class

Schwab, Charles, 24, 25–26, 44, 49, 51
Scientific management. *See* Taylorism
Scott, Thomas A., 24, 27
Sloan, Alfred P., 23, 26–31, 39, 40, 45, 47, 126
and bureaucracy, 43, 147–148
compensation system, 30, 41, 82
and professionalism, 133
and property, 78, 80, 82, 88, 92
Small-business workers, 55–56, 68. *See also* Entrepreneurial class
Social Darwinism, 180–182
Social democracy 64–69, 72, 178. *See also* Union movement
Social Taylorism. *See* Taylorism
Social welfare programs, 3, 118, 119, 158–159, 160–161
Specialization, 51–52
Steel, importance of, 58–59
Stigler, George, 50
Stockholders, 78, 80, 81, 86–93, 95, 98

Takeovers, 87
Taxation, 119–120, 158–159, 160

Taylor, Frederick Winslow, 23, 32. See also
    Taylorism
Taylorism, 11, 31-39, 100, 128, 176, 193
    and bureaucracy, 147, 148
    and compulsory consumption, 160, 161
    in education, 150-155
    and political activity, 120, 155-156
    and property, 80
    and technology, 41, 138
Technique, 52. See also Technology
Technology, 10, 19
    apprenticeship system, 22-23
    government impact on, 63
    identity with middle element, 31-32, 39,
        41, 51-55, 81-82, 84, 125, 142-143
    late 1800's revolution, 58-61
    necessity of corporate form for, 52-53
    subordination to capital of, 48, 53
    and Taylorism, 41, 138
Thatcher, Margaret, 116, 117, 142, 160
Thompson, Edward, 101, 152, 190, 191
Thompson, J. Edgar, 24, 25, 27
Top management, 4, 22, 40
    compensation, 30, 40-41
    and corporate public, 91, 115
    in education, 151
    evolution of, 47-51, 63-64, 71-72
    property claims of, 78-79, 81, 84, 87, 88-
        89, 92, 95
    and public sector, 63, 114, 115
    and technology, 51-52, 125
    and working class, 65-67, 187
    See also Corporate form; Corporate
    public; Middle element-top
    management alliance; Upper class
Trade associations, 89, 90, 95
Trust movement, 26-27, 67, 77

Union movement, 101, 114, 139, 142, 156
    corporate relations with, 65-67, 142, 170-
        171, 176-178, 179
    government control of, 162-167
    and immigration, 178, 196
    and workers' property claims, 71, 83-84,
        161
University system, 82, 131-132
Upper class
    vs. corporate public, 92, 93
    vs. ruling class, 101-102, 117-118
    See also Top management
U.S. Steel Corporation, 25-26, 49, 66, 71,
    158, 176-177

Vietnam War, 113
Volcker, Paul, 113

Wages. See Compensation
Wealth. See Upper class

Weber, Max, 10, 11, 25, 42, 43, 145-150,
    156
Welfare capitalism, 66
Wilson, Woodrow, 70
Working class, 4, 22
    and apprenticeship system, 22-23
    class consciousness of, 195-196
    class intelligence of, 191-193
    compensation, 37-39, 81, 83, 134-135,
        136, 158, 160, 166, 175, 188
    and compulsory consumption, 157-162,
        174
    corporate investments in, 15, 37-39, 66,
        160, 174-175, 190
    and education, 152, 153-155
    employment patterns, 127, 175-176
    evolution of, 15-16, 39, 45, 55-57, 179-
        180
    in government agencies, 114
    homogeneity as ideal for, 56-57, 126, 194
    ideologies regarding, 180-182
    immigration, 178-179
    improved condition of, 186-188
    informal social groups within, 32-33
    isolation of, 68, 97, 100-101, 128-129
    Japanese management system, 33
    "middle-class status" of, 15, 136
    middle element as control on, 11-12, 15,
        42-43, 68-69, 128, 129, 149-150, 154-
        157
    as national class, 183-186, 193-194
    national labor market for, 139
    political involvement of, 155-156, 179,
        188
    pre- and non-corporate classes as
        opponents of, 15, 16, 20
    and privatization of government, 118
    vs. proletariat, 155, 173-175, 184-185,
        189, 195
    property claims of, 83-84, 161
    removal of technology from, 31-32, 39,
        41, 142-143
    romanticization of, 142-143, 173-174, 186,
        191, 197
    social control of, 14, 100, 150-155, 193,
        194-196
    strength of, 15, 16, 174-175, 178, 183,
        185-186, 189, 191
    stupidity as image of, 36-37, 120
    subordination of, 14, 128, 154-157, 167-
        168, 179-180, 190
    traditional middle class alliances with,
        100, 121, 192
    values of, 153, 182-183
    See also Corporate form; Taylorism;
    Union movement

Yellen, Samuel, 187